A Phoenix Once More

A Phoenix Once More

Phoenix = "a mythical bird that burnt itself on a funeral
pyre and rose from the ashes…"

O.E.D.

by

Gerald Urwin

Librario

Published by

Librario Publishing Ltd.

ISBN: 978-1-909328-07-7

Copies can be ordered via the Internet
www.librario.com

or from:

Brough House, Milton Brodie, Kinloss
Moray IV36 2UA
Tel/Fax No 00 44 (0)1343 850 617

Printed and bound in the UK

Typeset by 3btype.com

Contents

Introduction   7
Explanatory Notes   9

Chapter One – 1549 to 1559   11
Haddington Burgh Council – 1551 to 1559   15

Chapter Two – 1560 to 1567   56
Haddington Burgh Council – 1560 to 1567   58

Chapter Three – 1567 to 1603   68
Haddington Burgh Council – 1567 to 1602   71

Chapter Four – 1603 to 1625   156
Haddington Burgh Council – 1603 to 1625   159

Chapter Five – 1625 to 1660   218
Haddington Burgh Council – 1656 to 1660   221

Chapter Six – 1660 to 1685   238
Haddington Burgh Council – 1660 to 1685   240

Chapter Seven – 1685 to 1688   287
Haddington Burgh Council – 1686 to 1688   289

Chapter Eight – 1689 to 1702   302
Haddington Burgh Council – 1689 to 1702   304

Conclusion   331

Glossary   335
List of Names   339
List of Place Names   351

Introduction

This book is an attempt to marry the broader political and social history of Scotland, between 1549 and 1707 representing the conclusion of the Siege of Haddington and the Act of Union, with a day by day account of life in Haddington itself over the same period up to 1702. This latter account is drawn from old records of Haddington Burgh Council, carefully written out by C. Bishop, Writer to the Signet, and dated February 1880. He wrote out the text exactly as he found it in the original bundles of documents.

"The documents included in the inventory lay at the bottom of an ancient wooden chest in the Town Clerk's chambers at Haddington, without order or arrangement of any kind."

There follows a brief description of the contents of each of thirteen bundles, including a Royal licence to the burgesses of Haddington to remain at home from joining the army during August to October 1565, with the handwritten signatures of Darnley and Mary, Queen of Scots; discharge from raids at Leith (1571), Hamilton and Selkirk (1579); decrees etc., regarding the marches of Gladsmuir and trespasses by neighbouring proprietors (1583–1626); a heritable debt on the Mills of Haddington due to James Cockburn (1603); documents relating to the Convention of Royal Burghs (1574–1644); copies of the Burgh Treasurer's accounts (1554/5, 1558/9, 1565 and 1571/2).

The names given to the various courts held at Haddington include the Burgh and Sheriff Court, the Heid Burgh Court, the Court of Council, the Court of Shillinghill in the Pretorium of Haddington. It is very interesting to observe the gradual evolution of a separate, exclusive Court as it moves away from the more routine, mundane functions of the Council. It is also very interesting to read about the gradual separation of the school education system from the Church; the manner in which the Guild system arose from the old crafts; the dominance of the burgesses and markets in everyday trading; the ceaseless and unsuccessful struggle against plague; the confusing and peculiar currency which included merks, Scots pounds and English pounds, 'dollers' etc.; the very pronounced continuity of the same names throughout generation after generation.

Above all, the text provides a fascinating insight into everyday life in Haddington for over 150 years. The humdrum and trivial sit alongside the dramatic and famous; the beggar and vagrant vie for attention with the Provost and the lord. It is difficult not to feel anything but the most profound admiration for those in charge of Burgh affairs, as they played out their part in improving the lot of all who dwelt within the town walls, despite the continual intrusion of national politics, devastating plague and rapacious outsiders. Fortunately, the legacy resulting from their efforts remains in large portions for us all to enjoy.

Explanatory Notes

1 Town officials

Provost: The civic head and chairman of the Burgh Council and the chief magistrate – corresponding to the English Mayor.

Bailey: A Burgh magistrate next in rank to the Provost.

Deacon: The chief official of a craft or trade.

Sergeant: A burgh official appointed to arrest those committing crimes.

Dean of Guild: The head of a guild or Merchant Company of a Royal Burgh.

Burgess: A citizen/freeman of a Burgh.

Freeman: A full membership of a trade or guild.

2 Currency

Scots Pounds: in 1700 worth one twelfth of the corresponding English sum.

Merk: worth 2/3 of a pound.

Box Penny: A market duty levied for the benefit of a craft of the Burgh.

3 Weights and Measures

Ell: A measure of length, approximately 4/5 of the English one.

Boll: A dry measure of weight or capacity varying according to commodity and locality e.g. a boll of meal = 140 pounds.

Firlot: The fourth part of a boll.

Rood: A small plot of ground, measuring 36 square ells – a piece of ground belonging to the Burgh rented or feued for building or cultivating.

Drop: one sixteenth of an ounce.

4 **Expressions etc.**

Corn and candle: Board and lodging, with especial reference to soldiers staying in Haddington in the seventeenth century.

Poinding: To seize and sell the goods of a debtor.

Sasine: The act or procedure of giving possession of feudal property.

Feu: A landholding where the tenant has the exclusive possession and use of property in return for a feu-duty payment.

Chapter 1

1549 to 1559

Mary of Guise reined in her horse, gazed around her at the still-smoking ruins, the broken buildings, the debris strewn all about, and exclaimed "Zey av lef nozzeeng. Nozzeeng but ze plague !"

Then she pulled her horse's head around and rode off towards Edinburgh. Her retinue, of courtiers, servants and armed guard, went with her, leaving behind a group of somewhat bewildered, disconsolate civilians. This group comprised former citizens of Haddington, market town whose ruins they now surveyed. It was October 1549, and the eighteen months siege of Haddington was over. The remnants of the besieged English army had retired to Berwick, the army garrison and headquarters. It was the results of their actions which the forlorn group now contemplated, silently, each man lost in his own thoughts. This was the former market town in which they had lived and worked. Now it would have to be rebuilt as it had been on at least three previous occasions going back to 1216, each time destroyed by an English army.

The task that faced them was enormous for there was barely a house which had survived unscathed from the besiegers' bombardment over eighteen months, or from the fire which the retreating English force had started. All of the houses, which had previously faced on to the river Tyne had been destroyed in order that a wall be built allowing the English cannon a free view of the enemy on the far bank. Of the remaining buildings which formed the longstanding, elongated triangular shape of the town, those which had been incorporated into the wall had suffered badly from cannon fire. The Tolbooth was completely demolished. The church of St. Mary's, albeit it stood outwith the walls erected by the English garrison, was a ruin.

Nevertheless, it never entered the heads of the Cockburns, the

Aytons, the Forrests or the Hepburns, to abandon Haddington altogether. The way ahead would be hard but rebuilt it would be.

Meanwhile, the French and Scots armies, who had besieged Haddington for eighteen long months, firstly the Spanish mercenaries at Coldingham were all slain or captured. Nearby Fast castle was recaptured by the Scots. Broughty Castle, on the banks of the Tay, was besieged and eventually yielded. The forts at Douglas, Roxburgh and Eyemouth were surrendered.

The French commander, Andre de Montalembert, Conte d'Esse, was ordered by Mary of Guise to move to Tweeddale and get rid of the Spanish force at Jedburgh. Between seven and eight hundred Scots went with him. Unfortunately, a shortage of food and supplies caused d'Esse to halt at Peebles until his army could be provisioned. The Spanish commanders at Jedburgh, Pedro Negro and Julian Romerous, made a tactical withdrawal to England. On hearing of this, d'Esse returned to Edinburgh.

Lauder Castle, the only remaining English garrison in Scotland, was besieged and was in dire straits when finally peace was signed at Boulogne, bringing all fighting to an end.

Rebuilding began immediately in Haddington once the siege was over. It was already late autumn and the winter blasts would soon fall on the town. Clearing the rubble, especially from the main thoroughfare, was a task for the unskilled. The masons, carpenters and skilled tradesmen set to work on the houses, beginning with those which had suffered least. Once a house had been made habitable then it provided shelter for workmen. For sustenance they had to rely on deliveries by cart from Edinburgh because the ground on all sides had been laid waste for miles around by the respective armies. Until the burgh was fully functioning then tax levies would not be available and application to Edinburgh would have to be lodged to that effect.

Stone from local quarries was the basic material used in rebuilding. Houses were built to a similar design in the majority of cases, with one up and one down, or two up and two down. In either case an outside stair provided access to the upper floor. Turf and straw gave cover for the roof, at least until such time as more durable material, i.e. pantiles, could be found. Houses were built with the gable end facing the street outside. At the other end, strips of land (rigs) were marked out, ready for the planting of crops once clearing work had been completed.

Gradually the Burgh resumed its former shape. Those houses forming the base of the triangle had to be rebuilt entirely. As the houses resumed their former shape and solidity so the population began to grow as those who had fled at the outset of the siege returned. The road to Aberlady was reopened and access to the port for Haddington was restored. This meant that fish could be brought in and the possibility of trade overseas emerged.

After the rebuilding of the houses it was the turn of the Tolbooth, erected in its usual position towards the southern, i.e. river, end of the town. At long last gazes turned towards the ruin of St Mary's, the 'Lamp of Lothian,' which the English gunners had 'pierced through and through.' Clearing the rubble still left a church with no roof or windows but at least an altar was found and a service could be held. Protestantism had gained a foothold in East Lothian ever since the days of George Wishart, who had been arrested near Haddington. However it was still a Catholic mass which was held. John Knox was yet to put in an appearance.

Communications between the capital, Edinburgh, and the rest of Scotland were slow moving. Haddington was more favoured than most in that, as a Royal Burgh, it sent a representative to the Convention of Royal Burghs held in Edinburgh. Since Haddington was only a day's ride away, news from the capital was also received more frequently from travellers and tradesmen than was the case for other burghs. Communication for the Haddington populace usually meant listening to the loud voice of a town crier, his arrival announced by the 'swasch', a drummer bearing the Burgh colours of blue and white.

Following her success in seeing off the English, Mary of Guise moved quickly to consolidate her position. The rising Protestant movement was never going to be allowed to establish itself – not by a staunchly Catholic Queen from France itself. Burnings at the stake and a scorched earth policy in Fife which had been a Protestant stronghold, were indicative of her determination to stamp out the 'viper' in the midst. Such tactics made her increasingly unpopular and, even though she achieved her aim of becoming Regent, it did not prevent an overwhelming outcry of relief and satisfaction at her demise, from dropsy, in 1559.

In all this time work had not stopped at Haddington. Now all the buildings had been rebuilt, crops had been sown and normal life restored. On 7th March 1551 the Council Court was again in session.

Haddington Burgh Council Records
1551 to 1559

1551

17th March

Council Court – Thomas Wauss, Provost. John Thomson, bailey.

Which day the provost, baileys and Council ordered tenant farmers to pay Robert Maitland the sum of 8 merks for keeping safe the documents of the Burgh of Haddington, and to hand them over to the Provost and his party who are travelling to the Convention of Burghs at Edinburgh.

Upon the 30th April 1552 – received from Robert Maitland the new registration document of the 'freedoms' of the Burgh of Haddington.

Item – One gift of King Robert the Bruce of the freedom of the Burgh of Haddington. A bequest for St. James' Altar. A bequest from John Brown to St. Crispin's Altar. A document showing the grant of King Robert the Bruce of the freedom of Haddington and passage to Aberlady. A Pardon granted to the whole Burgh of Haddington. A decree of the Lords of Council about the harbour at Aberlady. An instrument and letter of assignation of the price of grain for a year of 6 merks in Haddington from Ralph Eglin's acreage. A decree given against Robert Crummy about Ralph Eglin's holding. Another decree from the same. A renunciation of Aberlady harbour by Mungo Hepburn. An agreement between the Burgh of Haddington and the prioress of the Abbey. A charter of John Samuels' lands to St. Crispin's Altar. An agreement between the Burgh of Haddington and the Laird of Wauchtoun about the haven at Aberlady. A charter of farm rent given to John Burrell for land held in tenure lying in the Sidegate of Haddington given by the deacons of the Craft of Shoemakers to the said John Burrell. An agreement that Bartholomew Kello would act on behalf of Harry Cockburn, Bartholomew Cockburn, William Cockburn, James Cockburn, Harry Cockburn, all burgesses of

Haddington, and William Campbell, to give to Henry Campbell and Beatrice Kello, his daughter. An instrument of John Burrell's lands. An executorship granted to the Burgh of Haddington and baileys, covering John Burrell's lands in the Sidegate. An instrument of seizure of 8/3d to the High Altar, and ornaments of the Choir of Haddington belonging to the late Patrick Brownlee. A gift of fleeces, farm buildings, scythes etc. A guarantee of £30 to the Laird of Clerkington for the Friars' Wall. A decree, given by the Sheriff of Edinburgh, within the precincts of Haddington, regarding Ralph Eglin's acreage. The gift of the Friars' Wall given to the Laird of Clerkington. A donation from the late David Forrest given to the Altar of the Kings of Cullen under one instrument; notary John Fleming. An instrument of the Friars' Wall. One instrument of a tour of Gladsmuir made by Sir Robert Lawder. A transcript of a charter of King Robert requiring all customs men to confirm any goods from the said Burgh, plus confirmation of other documents. One document between the Lairds of Haddington and Ledington. Another tour of Gladsmuir by Thomas Somerville of Cornwacht. A charter of the granting of the freedom of the Burgh of Haddington, with mills, walls, meadows and haystacks listed. The deeds of the Altar of Trinity. A book of the old register of Haddington with a red cover. A decree of Ralph Eglin's acreage, giving a gift of non-entry of the acres called Ralph Eglin's acreage, given under the Signet (the failure of an heir to a deceased vassal to obtain entry I.e. to prove himself.) The documents between the Prior of St. Andrews and the Burgh of Haddington.

1552

6th May

Council Court of the Burgh of Haddington – Thomas Wauss, Provost, Thomas Dickson, John Thomson, baileys.

Which day the Provost, baileys and Council ordered, with the unanimous approval of the whole community, that no freeman or inhabitant of the Burgh of Haddington should take an acre of land from anyone who may be forced to agree, unless it is taken as a pledge in security, or else buys it outright. Under penalty of a £10 fine, to be paid to whoever it was taken from.

Which day John Forrest, burgess of Haddington, acting as guarantor for the worthy and mighty Lord Seton, declared that he would bring the silver bell that his horse won on 10th May 1552, to the said Burgh of Haddington, with the proviso that the said bell be run for on the same day, so that the winner thereof may be given it. John Forrest entered his own name in the Common Book of Haddington to ensure that this promise was kept on the 10th of May.

13th May

Council Court.

Which day John Thomson, bailey, confirmed that he had received tax for the Burgh, to the sum of £46, to be used for the deputation going to Flanders, and agreed to deliver the sum, which he has done.

Which day the Council was alerted to the fact that some of the townsfolk wanted their money back from the tax levy to Flanders, namely John Douglas, baker, 21s., John Douglas, mason, 21s., John Haddow, 9/4d, Alexander Barnes, 23s., and asked the Provost and Baileys to go among housedwellers and seize and fine those who still owe the tax to those who have already paid I.e Thomas Ponton, 11s., Thomas Wauss, 25s., John Allen, 2s., Mungo Thomson, 2s., Henry Cockburn of Clerkington, 13/4d., John Clavie 6/8d., Christian Dickson 2s., John Blain 16d., George Brownhill, 2s., Robert Straughan 2s., Thomas Vache, 2s., James Guthrie, 2s,.

8th June

Janet Sheil has sworn an oath before the baileys of Haddington, that, if she is ever arrested in Haddington, either with or without a child, she should be condemned to death.

17th June

William Dunn, of Saltoun, agreed that if he was arrested for speaking disrespectfully of the Provost, baileys and other officials of the Burgh of Haddington, he would be banished from the Burgh after being scourged throughout. He entered the same in the Common Book of the said Burgh.

8th July

Catherine Harrot swore, on oath, before the baileys of the Burgh of Haddington at the Market Cross, that if she was ever arrested within the same Burgh, either openly or secretly, she would be condemned to death.

29th July

Council Court of Haddington.

Which day the Provost, Council and Baileys ordered the millers from the west and east mills, I.e. George Campbell and James Tweed to remain on the following WhitSunday, 1553, to give 10 merks as feu to their tenant farmers of Haddington, otherwise they would be instantly removed. They were instructed to perform all the services that millers normally do or ought to do. They were to acknowledge no master but the Provost and baileys of the said Burgh. They were to present themselves before the provost and baileys of the said Burgh, 20 days before the 'terms' of WhitSunday and Martinmas, to see if the town would let them continue for another year. The said George and James made a promise to observe their duties.

Which day the whole Council and townsfolk of the said burgh, acting on the advice of the Provost and Baileys, performed a deed for the general good and profit of the said Burgh of Haddington, I.e. the present community or their successors would never lease, or give lease to any person or persons whatever, to break up the common moor of Gladsmuir, or dig for coal therein, unless it was the burgesses, merchants or craftsmen of the said Burgh. For the observation whereof the said Council, townsfolk, Provost and baileys of the said Burgh have 'acted' themselves I.e. entered themselves as being under a bond or obligation, and sworn to observe the same.

11th October

Burgh Head Court of Haddington.

Thomas Wauss, Provost, Thomas Dickson and John Thomson, baileys.

Which day the old Council chose a new one viz: Thomas Wauss, John Forrest, William Gibson, Adam Wilson, William Brown, Thomas Ponton, John Ayton, Henry Campbell, John Douglas, Henry Thomson and John Young.

Which day the old and new Councils, together with the deacons of the crafts of the Burgh, chose James Oliphant as Provost for the year. Thomas Dickson and John Thomson would continue to serve as Baileys for the year.

13th October

Council Court.

Which day the baileys and Council of the said Burgh, convened in the Tolbooth for the benefit of all, ordered that malt be sold at prices at prices which conform to the Acts of Parliament, i.e. 4s. for a boll of malt, less than the usual price for beer, since beer was priced at 20s. Therefore malt might and should be sold for 24s. per boll, and ale was to be sold at 20d per gallon henceforward.

The said baileys and Council, as convened, decreed that all types of baker within the said Burgh, might and should bake good, sufficient Court bread at 24 ounces for 4d. Bread that came from outside on market day, would be sold at 30 ounces for 4d. Every baker was to have a distinguishing stamp to put on the bread. Every baker was to bake a third of his batch as 2d. Bread. All bread from the bakehouse was held to be the responsibility of the baileys of the said Burgh. If maltsmen broke these agreements, they would be liable for a fine of 20s. For a first offence, 21s. The next time, and, for a third offence, forbidden to make malt for a year. Similarly, if bakers and brewers broke the law, they would be liable for a fine of 8s. for a first offence, 16s. the next time, and, for a third offence, would be forbidden to bake or brew for a year, and their bakery chimneys destroyed for their disobedience.

Ordered: all types of good, sufficient candles, mad of rags or fine cloth, must be sold for 8d. a pound. Those with a hard wick would be sold for 7d. a pound; under a penalty of 8s. for a first offence, 16s. for a second, and for a third, ordered to stop selling for a year. If anyone tried to sell grease candles, covered with a fine tallow, they will be confiscated by the Provost and baileys of the said Burgh.

John Blane was to be the overseer of the Fleshmarket. Robert Straughan was to be the keeper of the Fishmarket. Assessors of ale would be Robert Straughan and Robert Brownhill.

No scoundrels, ragamuffins or vagabonds would be allowed to buy any type of corn until 12 noon. No one would be allowed to buy wheat or beans until 11 a.m., nor any meal before 10 a.m.; the penalty for breaking this law would be a fine of 8s. No corn was to be sold inside houses, under a penalty of confiscation.

Robert Redpath was to be Keeper of the mealmarket.

Robert Hoip was to be Keeper of the beanmarket.

Patrick Martin was to be Keeper of the wheat market.

No one was allowed to buy wool, skins or hides within the Burgh, unless they were Freemen: under penalty of confiscation.

Which day Martin Wilson, by his own confession, agreed that if he were ever to condemn the Provost and baileys of the Burgh in the performance of their duties, or in any other way blasphemed against them, he would be fined £5 in the currency of the Realm, plus a further £5 to go towards the common good of the Burgh.

8th November

Burgh Court of Haddington.

James Oliphant, Provost, Thomas Dickson and John Thomson, Baileys, Dempster, William Haig.

Which day the Assize found that Alexander Thomson swore at officials, and ordered him to appear before the Provost for sentencing. The

Provost and baileys ordered officials to break down his door and leave it in that condition unless and until he was made a Freeman. If he were to re-offend he would be punished with the full rigour of the law.

The Assize found that George Brownhill disobeyed officials by acting in an ignorant manner. He was told to appear before the Provost and baileys to be punished as they thought fit.

15th November

Which day John Sydserf, James Raeburn, James Begbie, James Cook, Patrick Cook, Thomas Henderson, John Douglas, James Spottiswood, William Quentin, William Burrell, Harry Burrell, William Congilton, John Clare, John Shaw, Patrick Lyall and Andrew Brown all had their names called thrice from the Tolbooth window in the Burgh of Haddington, for breaking the bye-laws of the said Burgh. They were designated as 'Unfreemen' and 'Strangers' and told to conform to the laws of the Realm, especially of the said Burgh thereof. None of them had offered a lawful, reasonable defence as to why they should not be deprived of the Freedom of the Burgh; therefore the Provost and baileys, acting on the advice of the full Council, decreed that the aforesaid had forfeited their 'Freedom' and were deemed to be 'Unfreemen' and 'Strangers' thereof. Sentence to this effect was pronounced by the Dempster of the said Burgh.

December

Burgh Court of Haddington.

James Oliphant, Provost, Thomas Dickson and John Thomson, Baileys.

Which day John Saddler was summoned at the request of Squire Thomas Mauchline, Chaplain, to pay an annual fee of 4s, owed to him by the said John, for a landholding lying on the east side of the Tyne. He denied that he owed anything, claiming that his mother and he had paid the feu to the said Squire Thomas Mauchline at Our Lady's Altar, in the parish kirk of Haddington, which is bounded by the land belonging to Our Lady's Altar in Edrom to the east, the land of Knox to the south, the Common Gate to the west, and the land of Bothanskirk to the north.

23rd December

Council Court of Haddington.

James Oliphant, Provost, Thomas Dickson, John Thomson, Baileys.

Which day the Provost, baileys and Council decided that no burgesses would be created, and that whoever is heir to a burgess, or a second son, or an outsider, would have to present himself to the Tolbooth before the Provost and baileys for consideration; failing which he would have to pay 10 merks to the Common Good.

Which day the Council, on the advice of the provost and baileys, disposed of the position of the Abbot of Unreason.

Which day the Council ordered that no position of burgess would be assumed unless it had the permission of the Treasurer. No burgess office would be given to anyone who required alms; it was to be paid for in money which would go to the Treasurer.

Which day the Council decided that the Provost should have no more than 6 merks.

Which day the Provost, James Oliphant, argued that no increase should be given to any future Provost, and that every honest man to be made Provost would do so year in and year about.

1553

27th January

Lepers, petty thieves, scoundrels and footpads – none found in the Burgh.

3rd February

Suits called. Court affirmed. Dempster Laurence Getgood.

Which day the Assize acquitted David Glen of drawing blood from John Johnson, but found that God's peace and the Queen's had been disturbed, so both were put at the mercy of the Provost and Baileys for causing trouble.

Which day John Hausthaw has taken the East Mill haugh in hand for one year, his entry date being 1st March.

Which day John Forrest has taken the West Mill haugh for 4 merks, cash in hand, for one year, his entry date being 1st March.

Which day the Provost and Baileys of the Burgh, on the advice of most of the Council, ordered that, whoever in the Burgh lets his beast loose on his neighbour's grass, and it is proven beyond doubt, would pay 12d. to the person to whom the damage was done.

20th April

Which day the Provost, Baileys and Council of the Burgh, ordered that malt should be sold for 20s. per boll, and ale be sold for 16d. Per gallon, and ordered that the 4d. loaf should weigh 32 ounces of good quality ingredients.

Which day the case of the theft of an apron by Isobel Dickson and Margaret Tweed was heard. Both parties agreed that the Provost should sit in judgement. The said Isobel Dickson and Margaret Tweed, by their own confession, agreed to be banished from the Burgh if they were found guilty of the crime of petty theft or receiving.

24th April

Burgh Court of Haddington.

James Oliphant, Provost. Thomas Dickson, Bailey.

Which day Walter Anderson was indicted for the crime of stealing a pair of shoes on 22nd April from David Jamieson, and for the theft of a purse full of money from Alexander Rantoun in Highfield in March 1553.

Which day the whole Assize found Walter Anderson and John Glendinnon guilty of stealing one pair of shoes, confirmed as being the same shoes. The judges ordered that Walter Anderson's ear be nailed to the pillory post. John Glendinnon was to be scourged through the Burgh and then banished. If he were ever to return then he would be hanged. All this was by their own confession.

29th April

Burgh Court of Haddington.

James Oliphant, Provost. Thomas Dickson, bailey. Dempster Robert Straughan.

Assize – John Forrest, Archibald Kyle, Bernard Thomson, George Brownhill, George Richardson, John Thyne, William Langlands, James Lewis, William Brown, James Benning, William Horsbrugh, George Boag. Chancellor – Alexander Youll of Garmilton.

Which day the aforesaid Alexander Youll, with the approval of the Assize, found Matthew Creyton guilty of theft by putting his hand in the pouch of Gawain Charters, and to have taken his purse out of the same, in which act he was not stopped. He knew what he was doing. He was also found guilty of stealing a purse, containing 10s., from William Scraven. The judges gave sentence that Matthew Creyton be scourged through the Burgh and his ear nailed to the pillory post.

18th May

Council Court.

James Oliphant, Provost. John Thomson, bailey.

Which day the Council of the said Burgh, acting on the advice of the Provost and Baileys, ordered all sheds and houses built in the streets of Haddington outwith the eisdrop (the space liable to receive the dripping of water from the eaves of a house) of the main houses, are to be taken down apart from those which stand where the main houses come to an end. No more were to be built from this day forward. Anyone who built such a house or shed would be told to pull them down within 15 days. Failure to do so would result in the Provost Council and Baileys doing so themselves as well as administering punishment to those who disobeyed the laws.

Which day the Council, acting on the advice of the Provost and Baileys, instructed the Treasurer to pursue John Ayton for non-payment of rent due from the Hangman's Acres.

30th May

Burgh Court of Haddington.

Which day James Benning was cited by Christine Lamb for ripping and tearing her clothes and for the shedding of her blood, which charge was proven by Sergeant Thomas Hope. The said James did not appear but was made outlaw in his absence and sentence on him pronounced. He was ordered to appear before the judges on 6th June.

Which day the Assize acquitted Stene Richardson of causing trouble between himself and Alexander Howieson.

13th June

Burgh Court of Haddington.

Which day George Simpson was cited for causing trouble in the Burgh and shedding the blood of David Douglas, which charge was denied. Likewise David Douglas was cited for causing trouble in the said Burgh and shedding blood, which charge was also denied. The judges referred the case to the Assize.

Which day George Simpson was found guilty of bloodshed and causing an affray and was so informed.

Which day John Allen confessed that he struck the first blow against James Horn (the younger).

Which day James Horn sought the mercy of the Provost and Baileys for causing an affray and shedding blood. Similarly John Allen.

Which day the Assize acquitted Ellen Paterson of fighting Margaret Barns on grounds of not proven.

Which day Robert Straughan and Alexander Aitken were summoned before the judges for causing trouble.

Which day the majority of the Assize, as announced by the Chancellor, John Ayton, found both parties guilty and sentence was given.

Which day the Assize found Martin Wilson guilty of a felony by striking Ellen Cockburn. Sentence was pronounced.

28th July

The Court of Shillinghill of the Burgh of Haddington.

Provost James Oliphanr. Thomas Dickson, Bailey. Dempster Laurence Getgood.

Absent: James Cockburn, John Douglas, Thomas Ponton, John Quentin, Robert Lister, John Hausthaw, Thomas Spottiswood, Thomas Wauss, James Gall, Adam Cockburn, mealmaker.

Which day the above were called to appear in the case of John Forrest and John Ayton, mill tenants, to answer charges of grinding corn from the common mills of the Burgh. They failed to appear and were made outlaw, sentence pronounced on them and ordered to appear on Thursday, 3rd August.

John Romananco's wife was granted 4 bolls of ground corn.

22nd August

Burgh Court of Haddington.

James Oliphant, Provost. Thomas Dickson, John Thomson, Baileys. Dempster William Haig.

Convened to hear cases of affray and bloodletting.

Which day Alexander Barns brought John Bailey before the judges, accused of drawing blood from William Bickerton. Likewise William Wemyss accused William Martin, David Cockburn accused William Bickerton. John Bailey and William Martin appointed Alexander Youll of Garmilton to be their advocate in all actions concerning them before the specified judges on the day.

Which day Alexander Youll of Garmilton, advocate for the said John Bailey and William Martin, reminded William Bickerton that he was on oath, and asked, if in all conscience, whether he threw a stone at the said John Bailey or not, and did he not swear that he did not know that John Bailey was waiting for him at the West Gate and that he did not throw a stone at him and that William Martin chased him as well as John Bailey.

Which day William Bickerton called William Burrows as witness of the assault by John Bailey and William Martin. Burrows swore on oath that he saw John Bailey and William Martin waiting at the West Gate as William Bickerton approached, and that he saw him strike William Bickerton who was injured.

The Assize unanimously announced, through William Gibson, Chancellor, that they found John Bailey and William Martin guilty of assault on William Bickerton, who was acquitted of all charges laid against him.

Which day David Cockburn stood surety for William Bickerton so that he would not suffer in any way from John Bailey of Samuelston. William Martin of Panston was ordered to redress any loss suffered by David Cockburn

Which day John Forrest stood surety before James Oliphant, Provost of Haddington, in the sum of £5 for the illegal bloodletting committed by William Martin. The same day legal security was given for William Bickerton, so that John Bailey should have no claim on him.

27th August

Thomas Halbertson, skipper, entered his ship in the account books of Haddington, wishing that she might be sold, including 800 fir wood spars, 500 large nails and 800 hoop poles.

13th September

Burgh Council of Haddington.

James Oliphant, Provost. John Thomson, Bailey.

Which day Thomas Spottiswood was summoned before the above judges accused of fighting and assault in the said Burgh upon Mungo Alan, who was cited for the same charge against Thomas Spottiswood. Both parties denied the charges. Provost and Bailey referred the case to the Assize, who were duly admitted and sworn in under Chancellor Bernard Thomson

Which day the Provost and Bailey had Thomas Kerington and Maurice Innes arrested because they were present at the alleged incident, and were required to swear before the Assize what they heard and saw. Thomas Kerington swore that he had seen the said Thomas Spottiswood's horse in Mungo Alan's cornfield. The latter went to seize it. He saw Thomas Spottiswood emerge from behind a stack, take a fork from a man and tell Mungo Alan to leave the horse alone. When Mungo Alan did not let the horse go, Thomas Spottiswood hit him on the head with the fork. The said Mungo Alan drew his dagger. They both fell on the ground wrestling. Thomas Spottiswood got hold of the dagger and threw it into the cornfield, then took the fork and hid it in a bush. Maurice Innes swore that Thomas Spottiswood approached Mungo Alan with a fork in his hand and tried to wrest his horse from Mungo Alan's grasp, but he would not let go. He saw Thomas Spottiswood strike Mungo Alan and hit him on the neck, as he thought. Mungo Alan lunged at him with a dagger. Thomas Spottiswood got the dagger from him and hit him on the head with it. If he had not got the dagger from him he would have been slain. The whole Assize, with no divergence of opinion, unanimously, as announced by Bernard Thomson, Chancellor, and after hearing the sworn statements of Thomas Kerington and Maurice Innes, found Thomas Spottiswood guilty and acquitted Mungo Alan.

7th October

Burgh Court of Haddington.

James Oliphant, Provost. Thomas Dickson and John Thomson, baileys. Dempster William Haig.

Assize; William Braund, James Horn, John Forrest, Henry Thomson, Thomas Ponton, John Douglas, Thomas Wauss, Robert Brown, John Ayton, John Blackburn, William Gibson, Crystal Galloway, George Richardson, John Young, Adam Cockburn.

Which day Robert Simpson, advocate for Cuthbert Simpson, disagreed with those named above for ordering the destruction of Cuthbert Simpson's house on 6th October, and robbing him of his goods which were there at the time. He raised an action of theft against them. As far as the bad language which it was alleged that he used against Thomas Hope, official, he placed himself at the discretion of the Council and requested a legal remedy.

Which day the said Provost answered that he would proceed to administer justice, notwithstanding the claimed allegations, and follow legal procedure.

The Assize ruled, unanimously, as announced by Chancellor William Brown, that Cuthbert Simpson had shown contempt by disobeying the Provost, Baileys and Council in building a house and shed. They were destroyed by the Provost, Baileys and Council, because they knew that he had been previously forbidden to build. He promised them that he would take it down in one day, but he did not. He used bad language and showed contempt to them, and would have struck them with a weapon had not John Mayne stopped him, in the presence of the Provost, baileys and Council, who filed a formal accusation against him.

10th October

Head Burgh Court of Haddington.

James Oliphant, Provost. Thomas Dickson and John Thomson, Baileys.

Which day John Mayne argued that if the Provost, Baileys and Council of the said Burgh did not choose a craftsman as well as a merchant to be Provost, that the position, (the gift of the late King James I, whom God absolve) should be made void.

Which day Adam Wilson was elected Provost, Thomas Ponton and Bernard Thomson, Baileys for one year.

Which day Cuthbert Simpson placed himself at the mercy and discretion of the Provost and baileys for the many offences down to him. If he were to offend either Provost or Baileys in the future he was prepared to forfeit his freedom. The Provost, Baileys and Council ordered the remainder of his lean-to shed to be taken down.

12th October

Burgh Court of Haddington.

Which day George Simpson submitted his accounts for the two acres known as 'Hangman's Acres', valued at £10 in the currency of the Realm, for the last ten years, and he gave up his claim to the 11s. which was awarded to the old hangman when Monsieur Lorge was in the Burgh, as well as £3 when the English were in occupation, when it was lying waste. He gave 10s. To the Treasurer. The said George had remained out of town while he prepared his accounts which totalled £4/10s. He made himself responsible for the payment thereof at whatever time the said baileys and Council decided. Failing which he would offer the tax received from the said two acres in settlement of that which was assigned to him. On the next purification of Our Lady, which is called Candlemas, he would pay 30s.; on the following Whit Sunday, 1554, he would pay 30s. and at the Latterday of Our Lady he would pay 30s. in settlement of the total sum of £4/10s.

Findings of the Head Court – of layabouts, ruffians, lepers and petty thieves within the Burgh – none found.

To inspectors of the Fleshmarket and Fishmarket and assessors of ale – they were to visit the markets to check flesh and fish and standard weights and measures. If they failed to find any faults which later turn out to be present they were to forfeit their offices.

Council and Baileys set the price of fine 'Court' bread at 4d. for 11 ounces, with one third baked as 'plack' bread, one third 2d bread and one third 1d. Bread, with 5 loaves of 3d. bread in each batch. Malt was set at 13s. per gallon; ale at 2d. per pint.

The penalty for a first offence, in avoiding these prices, would be 8s. for a first offence, 16s. for a second, and 11s. for a third plus banishment from the Burgh. No ale was to be sold on a Sunday, under penalty of a 11s. fine given to the Common Good.

The council ordered that no swine should be found inside the gates, even though they were merely grazing or on the point of departure. If any were found, the owner would be fined 11s. which would go to the Common Good.

2nd November

Burgh Court of Haddington.

Which day John Forrest spoke on behalf of William Wauchop of Houston, in order that he might enter for the Silver Bell race which would be run the day after St. Helen's day, called Beltane. (1st or 3rd May, a Scottish quarter-day.)

Which day John Hunter was summoned to appear before the judges, because of a disturbance between him and James and William Hathaway, who both failed to appear. They were made outlaws and sentence was pronounced on them.

Which day the Assize heard George Simpson, Chancellor, accuse John Hunter of starting the fight with William Hathaway, and acquitted William Hathaway. With regard to the flight of Ellen Paterson, the Assize could not acquit either her or James Hathaway, so sentence was pronounced on them.

1554

1st March

Burgh Court and Court of the Council of Haddington.

Adam Wilson, Provost. Thomas Ponton and Bernard Thomson, Baileys. Dempster John Johnson.

Which day the Provost, Baileys and Council decreed that all land within the Burgh, except Ralph Eglin's land and the meadow, should pay 5d. per rood (a small plot of ground measuring 36 square ells.) as a levy. If the levy was not paid, then it would be liable to be paid at the rate of 5d. per yard. If it was still not paid a fine would be levied on the estate. All the roods of 'dwarfs street', Dogcanflat and the Heuch Head should pay 5d. per rood. If any land within the 'freedom' of Haddington was not paying a levy, the Treasurer would enter them into the list of Burgh expenses.

Council: William Brown, John Thomson, James Oliphant, William Gibson, Thomas Dickson, John Ayton, John Douglas, Philip Gibson, James Horn.

With the consent and agreement of Adam Wilson, Provost, and Bernard Thomson, Bailey, it was decreed that the above Act was now in effect and would be used in future.

Which day Adam Wilson, Provost, Thomas Ponton and Bernard Thomson, Baileys, acting on the advice of the Council of the said Burgh, made George Boag a burgess, in recognition of the safekeeping and returning three of the Common Books of the Queen to the said Burgh.

Which day Martin Wilson was summoned for libel by Archibald Kyle, for half of the sum of 13/4d. which was the amount named, under oath, by the said Archibald, who swore that the said Martin owed him 6/8d. As for the remainder of money owed in the libel case, which amounted to £3 due for providing pasties, pies, buns and household bread, the said Martin denied the charge. The said Archibald reminded him of his oath and his conscience, and how little he must value them, after making a deposition, under oath, on that same day.

Which day Martin Wilson was made outlaw, and sentence pronounced on him for the wrongdoing he committed against Archibald Kyle for the sum of one half-merk.

6th March

Council Court of Haddington.

Adam Wilson, Provost, Bernard Thomson and John Thomson, baileys.

Which day there appeared, at the command of the provost and baileys, in the Council Chamber of the said Burgh, the full Council, including the following members of the community:

William Brown, John Kemp, John Ayton, Thomas Dickson, Harry Cockburn, George Richardson, William Gibson, John Douglas, George Boag, Archibald Kyle, Nichol Dunlop, Thomas Spottiswood, John Thyne, William Wemyss, George Brownhill, David Lawson, Stene Burke,

Philip Gibson, Henry Campbell, Alexander Barns, Robert Brown, Adam Cockburn, John Alan, John Blain, John Main, John Johnson, John Douglas, Henry Thomson, John Romananco, Thomas Hoip, Martin Wilson, John Blackburn, James Lewis, John Hathaway, Cuthbert Simpson, William Hogg, Robert Thomson, Adam Bago, John Young, Robert Straughan, John Ayton, William Campbell, James Horn, William Lister, Adam Cockburn, John Thomson, John Forrest, Thomas Wauss, William Langlands, Patrick Redpath, George Simpson, Patrick Martin, John Alan.

Absent: George Campbell, John Sibbotson, James Cockburn, John Hausthaw, John Alan (tailor), Mungo Thomson, James Millar, Henry Lawson, John Gilzean, John Quentin, Crystal Galloway, Harry Cockburn (sheriff), Patrick Lawton, James Oliphant, James Mow, John Allen, John Mason.

The whole Council and community, with the said Provost and Baileys, gave instruction that they would not give the common land (moor) to anyone, not even those of high status, or any inhabitants of Haddington, even if they were a burgess, craftsman or merchant of the Burgh, and sworn to the teaching of the Holy Evangelist. Nor if they switched allegiance would it be of any profit to them or their successors.

7th April

Burgh Court of Haddington.

Which day the Assize unanimously accused Maurice Robinson of stealing two pairs of shoes, to which crime he confessed. Sentence was referred to the judges named.

The judges condemned Maurice Robinson to be scourged throughout the Burgh, his ear nailed to the pillory post, and then banished from the Burgh for life. If he was ever arrested again in the Burgh, he was to be hanged. Sentence was passed.

9th April

Martin Wilson swore on oath that all the pasties, pies, buns and bread he had received from Archibald Kyle were paid for, to the sum of 2s.

8th May

Burgh Court of Haddington.

Adam Wilson, Provost, Thomas Ponton, Bernard Thomson, Baileys.

Which day John Douglas, baker, took out a deposition that he had delivered a light coloured horse to the Sergeant of the Burgh, as a guarantee.

By the tenor of their presents, I, Adam McCulloch, pursuivant (follower) and Clerk to the Office of Arms, make patent that, in the action and case which is to be pursued against Alexander Strong, mace-bearer, by George Simpson in Haddington, for the horse allegedly stolen by the said Alexander, I, in the name of the said honourable office, make known and certify to all whom it may concern, especially the Provost and Baileys of Haddington, that the same action is now due. And especially this coming Tuesday, 8th May, before Master Ross, deputy herald to the Right Honourable Lyon, King of Arms, who is a competent judge in all matters concerning his office. Therefore, in the name of the said honourable office, this duty is discharged by whatever judge or judges in this or any other similar case which concerns their office. Because the same applies to Lyon or his deputies, that in the execution of the office, any may stand if there is available no other competent judge. This I make known at the will and command of Master Ross and the other brethren. At Edinburgh, 7th May 1554.

22nd May

Burgh Court of Haddington.

Which day John Douglas took out deposition that he had entered a black horse, belonging to Alexander Strong, mace-bearer, in the Burgh of Haddington, as a guarantee.

Which day John Douglas, baker, was ordered to submit one black horse, belonging to Alexander Strong in the Burgh of Haddington, before the judges. He failed to do so, whereupon he was outlawed, sentence pronounced upon him, and ordered to enter the said horse by 12th June.

Which day, before the judges referred to above, Our Sovereign's Lady's letters were presented by a boy who was allegedly acting in the name of Alexander Strong, as confirmed by his signature, which, in the same endorsement, stated as follows:

"Mary, (of Guise) by the Grace of God, Queen of Scots, to Our Sheriff of … And his deputies. And to our loving Alexander Strong, mace-bearer, messengers and former sheriffs, conjointly and separately, special greeting, forasmuch as it is humbly merited and shown to us by our loving Robert Skaithevy, that when George Simpson was alleged by the majority of officials within the Archdeanery of Lothian, to have paid to the said Robert the sum of £4, in the currency of Our Realm, and, similarly, George Wright in Cousland, the sum of 11s. at certain times long ago, under the pain of cursing, because you failed therein you were denounced as cursed by the said officials; letters, under process of which, you have kept for 11 days or more, disregarding with contempt God and the Holy Kirk, and in great peril of your own soul. Our will is therefore that you be charged to directly, without delay, by these our letters seen, pass in our name and authority, inform, force, fine and seize George Simpson and Wright's lands whereof and goods. If there are no moveable goods then you seize their land, following Our Act of Parliament, to the worth and quantity of the aforesaid sums, each of them for their part, respectively. And make the same Robert pay and confirm to the said letters of cursing, according to the law. As you will answer to us thereupon. In order to do so, we commit to you, conjointly and separately, our full power by our letters, delivering them duly executed by you and endorsed again by the bearer. Given under Our signature, at Edinburgh, 18th November, and of Our Reign, the eleventh year." – 5th November 1553.

"I, Alexander Strong, mace-bearer, one of the Sheriffs therein constituted, at the command of Our Sovereign's letters, searched for and sought the moveable good of George Simpson in Haddington, in order to have impounded them for the non-payment to Robert Skaithevy of the sum specified. I took possession of, in the said

George's stable in Haddington, 1 gray horse which I had taken away by Walter Hall and other honest men, I.e. Walter Hall, inhabitant of Haddington, who, after being sworn in, took possession of the aid horse in this way, i.e. £3 taken from the said person, and the horse which I offered to give back to the said George Simpson for the sum written, contained within their letters of £4, but he refused to pay. This I did before witnesses, Walter Hall, Thomas Blythman, John Wilson, John Baird with divers others. And because the said persons could not agree with the said seizure of goods, nor that the said George would pay £4, I, upon the seventh of the month, in the Year of Our Lord aforesaid, took the same horse to the Burgh of Edinburgh, and had John Brown, John Blain and John Nelson sworn in to value the goods. They valued the horse at three and a half merks. Thereafter, in my own house, I offered the horse back to George Simpson for this sum, who answered "I have no silver to afford for him." Finally I sold the horse to John Wilson, burgess of Edinburgh, for three and a half merks. I offered this sum to Robert Skaithevy, the underwritten complainant, who refused it. This I did before witnesses written above, as well as affixing my own signature."

12th June

Burgh Court of Haddington.

Which day Alexander Strong, mace-bearer, was summoned for a gray horse, taken from George Simpson, which the said Alexander Strong claimed was in order, citing Our Sovereign Lady's letters, which he produced dated 18th November, at Edinburgh, in the 11th year of her reign, endorsed under her signature on 5th December 1553, as shown, at more length. In Our Sovereign Lady's letters and the endorsement thereof. Which letters and endorsements were a true copy, as decided by the above judges, from word to word nothing being added nor anything removed: to be placed in the Common Book of Haddington as warranty and specification. The Provost and baileys placed instruments of the same into the hands of the Common Scribe of the Burgh.

With regard to the said letters, produced by the said Alexander Strong, mace-bearer, in judgement the said George Simpson requested time and space to consider and approve the said endorsement before the judges, who knew Alexander Strong, so far as he could within the law.

Which day, John Douglas, baker, appeared the above judges, and gave a black horse, belonging to Alexander Strong, mace-bearer, who had been arrested at the instance of George Simpson. The said judges absolved John Douglas from any further pledges regarding the said black horse.

5th October

Council Court of the Burgh of Haddington.

Adam Wilson, Provost, Thomas Ponton, bailey.

Which day the Council, acting on the advice of the baileys, decided that, for the forthcoming year, all Provosts of the Burgh should receive 10 merks as a fee; each Bailey 6 merks; each Sergeant 30s.

Which day the old Council, together with the new, chose leets for the Provostship and Baileys for the year. The leet for an elected Provost showed the foolowing names: Adam Wilson, James Oliphant, John Forrest.

Which day John Oliphant alleged that the Provost before him had £10 as a fee, and the one after him 10 merks. He, in his term of office, had received 6 merks exclusively. For that reason, he argued, if he refused the office it was because he was not receiving as much as the Provost who succeeded him. For he incurred no damages or injury, and, because the law that was made during his term of office was not enforced, he was removed from his position.

9th October

The council of the Burgh of Haddington, convened in the Council Chamber, decided that they should proceed to choose a Provost and baileys based on the leets drawn up.

Which day James Oliphant was chosen as Provost of the said Burgh. Bernard Thomson and Henry Thomson were chosen as baileys for one year.

Which day Alexander Forrest, Parson of Logie, Montrose, and Squire Thomas Kerington, Chaplain of the Three Kings of Culans Altar, situated in the parish kirk of Haddington, chose John Forrest, burgess of Haddington, to be their official adviser in legal matters. Witnessed by Henry Lawson and Patrick Martin.

25th October

Court of the Council of the Burgh of Haddington.

Bernard Thomson, Henry Thomson, Baileys.

Which day the baileys and Council found that wheat was commonly sold for 18s. per boll and the standard measure was fixed at 17 ounces of fine 'Court' bread of the old sort found in the Burgh of Haddington which sold for 2d.

The aforesaid Baileys and Council found that beer was sold for 15s. a gallon and malt at 19s. a boll.

As to petty thieves, ruffians, layabouts and lepers, there were none found in the Burgh.

9th November

Council Court of the Burgh of Haddington.

Which day the Council decided that one of the Baileys of the Burgh should go to Edinburgh to consult with men of law in order to ascertain what should be done regarding James Oliphant's refusal to accept the office of Provost.

17th December

Peter Campbell, acting with the consent of the Council, was made burgess by Provost James Oliphant, Bernard Thomson and Henry Thomson, Baileys, and was told to perform his service loyally and truly as Dempster in the Burgh Courts of the said Burgh for seven years hence. God forbid that any Court or Courts be frustrated by the default of a legal Dempster. In service of which the said Peter was to be the holder of the post thereof and was obliged and bound, together with his heirs, to refund any damages to the Provost, Council and community, as and when they occurred.

Which day Alison Redpath and James Ayton, her spouse, were summoned for the outrage caused by their use of strong language to the Provost and Baileys, expressed in the following words "I will sell as much ale as I want for 6d. a quart, whether you wish it or not." These are the words that the said James Ayton used to the Provost and Baileys.

1555

5th March

Burgh Court of Haddington.

James Oliphant, Provost.

Which day Martin Wilson was summoned before the judges by the deacons and remainder of the craft of bakers, to show where the chalice of St. Towbart's Altar was and whether it was repairable, and to swear in judgment to tell the truth. The judges assigned him that same day, either before noon or shortly after, to tell the truth.

Which day it was stated and ordered, by the Provost and Baileys, that whichever of the townsfolk found sheep, horses or cattle in their cornfields, 12d. per horse would be paid to the man who owned the corn, 8d. for each head of cattle, and for each sheep 2d. Swine would also be included, failing which those found would be killed, as required by the old Acts.

THE BURGESS OATH – copied from the fly leaf of the Volume 1530 to 1555.

> I shall be loyal and true to Our Sovereign Lord the King, and to his successors, and to the common good of this good town. I shall obey the officials in all legal and lawful things. I shall keep their counsel and I will give the best counsel I can. If any ask me, I shall procure no estate against the freedom of this Burgh. I shall defend the freedom and common goodwill of this Burgh with my body and goods. I shall

take and share, with weak and strong, as others do. I shall have no personal profits against the common good. I shall take no 'unfreeman's' belongings or hinder the King's Customs. So help me God.

The guarantee of £12/4s. in connection with the levying of the Customs of 12s. in silver from France.

"I, Patrick Craik, Messenger at Arms, acknowledge receipt from an honourable man, Thomas Wauss, Provost of Haddington, Thomas Dickson and John Thomson, Baileys of the same town, £12/4s. in currency of the Realm, on behalf of the said Burgh, and inhabitants of the same, for expenses raised in levying Customs of 12s. in silver from France. Of which sum of £12/4s. I, the said Patrick Craik, acknowledge the full payment made in the name of and on behalf of the Provost, Baileys and Council and community thereof. As I that have Our Sovereign's letters, directed to the collecting of the said sum, under penalty of being accused of rebellion and putting the said Provost and Baileys of the said Burgh of Haddington under threat of Our Lady's proclamation. And whatever claims and discharges the said Provost, Baileys, Council and community in what name and on behalf of for now and evermore. In witness of which I have caused Nicholas Swinton, scribe of the Burgh of Haddington, to inscribe and insert in the Common Book of Haddington, this same guarantee.

At the Burgh of Haddington, 12th November 1551 before these witnesses;

William Brown, Adam Hepburn, Patrick Martin, Thomas Hoip, Henry Mudie and divers others.

Patrick Craik, in my handwriting.

Witnessed by Nicholas Swinton, Notary Public.

14th December

Council Court of the Burgh of Haddington.

James Oliphant, Provost. Bernard Thomson, Henry Thomson, baileys.

This date the two Common corn mills were put up for public auction to see how much they would fetch. John Forrest and John Ayton made the highest bid, which, together with other good reasons, decided the Council to sell to them. It was felt that this was the most relevant way of devising a lease, as required by law, whereby, for an appropriate rent, they become millowners for the next three years. The entry into the Common Book of the assigning the mills to John Forrest and John Ayton was dated 9th December at 4 p.m. The sum paid was £15/10s. to last for three years. No more money, except for reasonable feu and Customs duties, would be payable. As tenant farmers, John Forrest and John Ayton, and their heirs and assignees, would be responsible for the building, repairs and maintenance of the West Mill Close and the Middle Close, between the West and East Mills, together with the building of a Duty house. If the said John Forrest and John Ayton failed to provide the money to the Treasurer for the building, repair and maintenance of theses when he required it they would pay for them themselves. Fees and produce of the Mills would go to the Council. The said John Forrest and John Ayton would pay 10 merks p.a. to each miller at the usual times of year i.e. Whitsunday and Martinmas, in equal portions.

7th February

Ordered by Council that no types of stalls or booths would be allowed at the High Gate with no canopies or coverings, but, instead, all booths etc. would be of one board placed on two trestles, without any covering on top, unless it rained. Goods would be covered by a flat board. None of the following types of goods would be allowed to be sold: French cloth, English cloth, Flanders cloth, dyed Scottish cloth, broadcloth, except for lining, silks worsteds, bombasine, fustian, cambrics, buckram, French bonnets, French hats, all types of foreign comforters, charmlets, Dutch cloth, serge, gold or silver thread, madder dye, iron, lint, hemp, wax, soap, steel alum, Bordeaux cloth, skins nor similar staple goods. Under a fine of 8s. for a first offence, thereafter the arrest of those concerned. No type of 'unfreeman' would be allowed to trade. By Act of the Book of Statutes, Burgh of Edinburgh.

No trader or traveller from outside the Burgh would be allowed to buy any kind of victuals on Market day, except in the Mealmarket alone, before 10 a.m. Nor would they be allowed to handle any sort of cornmeal, under threat of a fine of 8s. for a first offence, 16s. for the next, and, thereafter, forfeiture of the cornmeal.

5th March

No one in the Burgh would be allowed to keep sheep within the walls. Under threat of 11s. fine for a first offence, £5 for a second, of which half would go to the common good of the Burgh and half to the Council. For a third offence all goods would be forfeited. All middens were to be emptied outside the High Gate, under threat of a fine of 8s. for each week that they are not removed.

12th April

James Oliphant was instructed to bring back an 11 pound bell, for which he would pay the Customs duty. For each pound that the bell weighed, nine 'Nobles' would be sung at the Feast of Martinmas.

30th April

Thomas Hay, Provost of Bothans, appeared before the Council to argue that any procession which took place on any land which paid an annual duty to the Chaplains of the College Kirk of the Bothans, would be allowed to prejudice his Provostry or the Chaplains in their investment of Altars and services in the said College Kirk, by virtue of their property in it. Thomas Hay requested that a judgement be made in the case of a certain annual rent pertaining to Our Lady's Altar situated in the College Kirk of Bothans for the property known as 'the Painted House' described fully in the Common Book of Haddington; the person responsible was Alexander Barns.

2nd May

No lepers, thieves, vagabonds or ruffians were to be found in the Burgh. Ostlers and brewers were ordered to sell the ale brewed in their homes openly to all of the Queen's lieges. All the brew was to be sold, under penalty of having their chimneys broken plus a fine. Bread and ale, of reasonable quality, will be sold at a fixed price – to be set by the Provost etc. All cattle and sheep were to be brought to the Burgh common, or else to be put outside; under penalty of a fine for each time that the law is broken. The old rules relating to geese and swine would continue.

3rd June

Carston Yowson has put up a ship for sale, of which he is the stated owner in the Common Book of Haddington. Specifically included are 20 dozen fir spars, 6 dozen large nails, 203 dozen small nails, 3 dozen fir double-spars and 800 iron hoops.

10th October

John Thomson and George Craig, Baileys.

Ale, of good quality, was ordered to be sold for 3d. per pint henceforth. Malt to be sold for 28s. a boll and of good quality. Court bread (made to royal standard) sold for 4d. per 24 ounces. Bread was not be still damp when it came out of the bakehouse. One pound of candles would be sold for 9d.

Ale assessors appointed: Patrick Martin, Patrick Redpath and Thomas Hoip.

Anyone who provides lodging for suspect persons would be responsible for them, both night and day. If they felt that any such person was suspicious, they should be reported to the authorities.

Maltsters, who were found to be breaking the rules and showing a disregard for authority, would be fined 11s. for a first offence. Bakers, brewers and candlemakers would be fined 8s. for a first offence.

No 'unfreeman' would be allowed to buy any manner of merchandise within the Burgh except from a Freeman; under threat of a fine of 11s. plus confiscation of goods i.e staple goods.

12th October

Assize: Adam Cockburn, Adam Begbie, John Blackburn, George

Brownhill, William Campbell, William Langlands, Henry Lawson, John Thynne, John Sibbotson, George Boag, William Burn.

Chancellor; William Langlands.

John Hay was accused of the theft of one web of cloth to which he confessed while being acquitted of other felonies. Sentence was announced that his ear be nailed to the pillory post, thereafter he was to be scourged throughout the Burgh and told that if he was ever arrested again in the Burgh he would be hanged.

15th October

John Forrest, Provost. John Thomson and George Craig, Baileys.

Dempster – Peter Campbell.

James Hume (alias Awrass) was summoned for his part in the theft of one black cow from William Thomson's land. He was found guilty and sentence passed that he be taken to the Tyne and drowned.

Patrick Lyall, from the Nungate, was accused of buying six skins from Robert Young in Morham for 30d. each, contrary to the law, to which he confessed. He was also accused of the purchase of staple goods in the Burgh. Adam Wilson agreed to stand surety to the tune of £100 in case the said Patrick Lyall did not present himself for judgement, or stayed within the Burgh until the feast of WhitSunday, 1556.

17th December

James Chisholm, bailey of Dunblane, presented a handwritten indictment against John Robertson and swore it was true as far as he knew.

"John Robertson, you are indicted for the theft of a black nag from Powbait Moor near the White Stone. The horse was four years old and missing the lobe of one ear. It was taken from Thomas Whitehead, living in Glassinghall, on the Tuesday after Trinity Sunday, 1552 or thereabouts. It was stolen when Thomas Whitehead was negotiating the sale of the said black nag, which you overheard. The following morning you stole the said black nag, which you cannot deny. You are also indicted for the theft of one brown mare, black tailed and maned, hairy eared, six years old, from Pendrich on last Allhallowsday. If you were not present yourself, you certainly played a part in the theft, which you cannot deny, because it was found at your home in your possession. You are also indicted for taking part in the theft committed by William Robertson, your brother, which you cannot deny." John Robertson denied stealing anything or that he ever took part in any theft. He stated that William Robertson had been acquitted of theft by an Assize of 15 persons, at which he had been a witness. Therefore he placed himself at the mercy of the Court. The Assize acquitted John Robertson of all accusations laid against him by James Chisholm, from whom John Robertson sought damages, alleging that the party pursuing the allegation should refray his expenses since he had been acquitted (on the grounds that anyone could buy a horse not knowing that it had been stolen).

1556

30th January

James Burnett, entirely of his own free will, made an entry in the Common Book of Haddington, to the effect that, if he is ever arrested for operating unfair scales, or for receiving stolen goods, he would agree to be banished from the Burgh. If he were ever to be re-arrested, he would hang.

In order to escape from the various inconveniences, dangers and displeasures, arising from a disagreement between Patrick Redpath and John Hunter, they agreed to abstain from further provocation to each other, or to others, or to occasion displeasure in the future, If either did anything to the contrary they would be banished from the Burgh.

20th July

David Cay, burgess of Carraill, acting of his own free will, entered his name in the Common Book in agreeing to the adequate maintenance of a clock, which he had sold to the Council and which hung in the Tolbooth clock tower, for the remainder of his life. In cases where the clock was damaged, or would not strike correctly, either because of his own faulty workmanship or otherwise, the said David would present himself in the Burgh of Haddington, within eight days of the request being made, and mend and repair all faults at his own expense. If a bigger bell was bought, the said David would come to the Burgh within eight days and hang the said great bell in the clocktower at the Council's expense. Therefore, the Provost, Baileys, Council and townsfolk agree to pay the said David, his heirs, executors and assignees, the sum of £26 as deposit, in the usual currency of the Realm, and, in full, the sum of £46 for the said clock and services from henceforth until the feast of WhitSunday next.

31st July

Thomas Hoip, baker, was found guilty of offending John Thomson by using bad language. He forfeited his 'freedom' of the Burgh for both the present and the future and was forbidden from using the office of sergeant. This sentence was shouted out from the Market Cross by Patrick Martin, sergeant.

3rd August

After making a solemn oath, Matthew Bowe was made a burgess of the Burgh. He undertook the safekeeping and resetting of the Town Clock, and to provide oil for this purpose for life at his own expense. If the clock stopped, or failed to keep correct time, he would submit to the penalties imposed by the authorities. Therefore it was agreed that he be paid £3 p.a. at the usual times, WhitSunday and Martinmas, in equal portions.

28th August

James Ayton, assessor to the bakers' trade in the Burgh, together with John Douglas, baker, Archibald Kyle, John Mayne, Martin Wilson, and William Campbell, were all accused of persuading Thomas Hoip, unfreeman, to practice the freedom and privilege of burgess within the Burgh, by assisting in whatever was needed to bake a batch of bread on Saturday, 22nd August. They were also accused of helping Janet Barns, widow of the late John Bain, to practice the trade of baker on the

Tuesday before she was actually admitted to the bakers' trade. All denied the charge, protesting that the accusations did not take precedence over privilege and freedom granted to the trade of baker under the Common Seal. It was also alleged that, if the said Janet had any freedom to practice the baker's trade previously, she forfeited it when she married John Bain, because he was not a freeman or burgess at the time of the marriage.

11th September

The indictment brought against the bakers was pursued by David Borthwick and 22nd September was set for the hearing.

John Thomson was ordered to pay Janet Darrow, spouse of John Patterson, as retribution for offences committed by him to her, the sum of 10s. before he could be released from the Tolbooth, failing which he was to find surety for the payment.

John Thomson consented to be scourged through the Burgh, his ear nailed to the pillory post, and to be banished from the Burgh for ever, and, if ever he is arrested for theft again, to be hanged.

Thomas Hoip, late burgess of the Burgh, surrendered to the authorities for committing a crime against John Thomson, Bailey, whereby he was stripped of his 'freemanship' and made an 'unfreeman'. On further consideration, the authorities returned his freemanship to him, provided that he knelt at the Market Cross, in their presence, and asked forgiveness for his crimes, which he did. Whereupon he was cautioned never to repeat his crimes or he would lose his freemanship forever. Whereupon, by open proclamation at the Cross by Patrick Martin, official, the said Thomas was re-admitted and reconciled.

22nd September

The entire guild of bakers appeared in the Council House to allege, through Archibald Kyle, their spokesman, that Janet Barns, widow of John Bain, should not be allowed to practice the baker's trade because she had forfeited and broken all privileges granted to the trade. She had never previously donated a box of silver, or 'priest's meat,' or shared with fellow tradesmen as was the custom. Nor was John Bain ever elected as a burgess. Nor should Andrew Bain, his son, be made a burgess, as his father's heir, because to do so would show prejudice and cause great unrest. Nevertheless, Janet Barns was told she was free to bake and practice the baker's trade.

Andrew Bain was elected as a burgess in spice and wine, as his father's heir.

20th October

The Provost and Baileys were instructed to go to Edinburgh to confer with their counterparts about the deduction of tax raised on the 16th last.

29th October

All ale was to be sold at a price no dearer than 4d. a pint, and to be of good quality; under penalty of an 8s. fine.

Within eight days, each baker was told to make his own trademark on his bread. The 4d. loaf was to weigh 8 ounces and be of good quality, under the usual penalty.

No bad meat, coming from cattle with 'lowing-ill' or redpath, or home-cooked meat, should be brought to the market, under penalty of seizure. No meat was to be allowed to be swollen to increase it's appearance, or low yield meat to be sold, under penalty of an 8s. fine.

A pound of ragwort, or rag candles, should be sold for no more than 8d. The preferred price was 6d per pound. All candles were to be made in the back shed. No residue from melting tallow would be allowed to be collected, except at night time, under penalty of an 8s. fine per each offence.

All townsfolk were told to bring their ¼ bolls and pecks (measures) to the Tolbooth on the following Wednesday and Thursday for weighing and adjustment, and to be freshly calibrated and inscribed. Unless inscribed, it was forbidden to use old measures; under penalty of an 8s. fine for a first offence, the measure burnt and the user punished.

All grain crops, brought in for sale, had to be at the market by 9 a.m.

and not stored; under penalty of a fine of 8s. for the seller, plus a fine for the buyer.

If anyone was found in the act of cutting down willow or any other type of growing trees, or trees in the kitchen gardens, or alders in the Mill Haugh, or on the waterside or mill dams, the cutter would be banished from the Burgh.

All lodgers would be questioned closely each morning.

If stolen goods are found on a person, they must be returned or prosecution will follow.

All lead and other metallic merchandise was to be edged with iron within 15 days; under penalty of a fine of 8s. for a first offence.

No one was to sell horse-feed, except for two specially appointed persons, who would charge a specified price fixed by the authorities; under penalty of an 8s. fine per offence.

No one was to buy swine, hide or skins, except freemen only; under penalty of forfeit of goods.

No wanderers, servants or people in distressed circumstances, would pay anything except the annual customs duty.

No vagabonds would be allowed to buy butter, cheese, eggs or fish before 11 a.m.; under penalty of forfeit and personal punishment.

No staple goods would be sold at the Gate or the Cross except from inside booths; under penalty of an 8s. fine.

9th December

A tax of silver pennies was to be collected immediately, along with other taxes. Edinburgh would confirm receipt of £20 in taxes, collected by John Hathaway, John Douglas, Thomas Dickinson, George Craig and George Simpson.

James Oliphant, burgess, presented an invoice for a bell weighing 100 and a half 'Flemis,' costing £3/15s. In Flemish money, (£17/1/2d in Scots money).

19 pounds of iron would be needed to hang the said bell. the price of stone needed for this work would be 8s. in Flemish money, 22s. in Scots. 16 fathoms (96 ft.) of rope would be needed to hang the metal weights; the price of the folded rope would be 5/4d in Scots money. The total sum would be £18/8/11d, which is the sum owed to James Oliphant.

1557

7th January

Henry Campbell, burgess, was accused of impeding John Douglas in the performance of his duty while impounding goods from the said Henry's house. He was also accused of swearing in St. Ninian's Chapel, at the time of Mass, last Sunday in full view of a great multitude of people. John Ayton rang the town bell and accused Henry Campbell before a judge of the High Court. Henry Campbell confessed. He was found guilty and sentenced to be punished by the Provost according to the law.

26th August

James Oliphant, Adam Wilson, Thomas Ponton, Bernard Thomson, John Douglas, Alexander Barns, John Hathaway, George Richardson, Patrick Lyall, Crystal Galloway, Marion Carnie, Archibald Kyle and William Wemyss will each lend 20s. to the Burgh as expenses for performing the Eucharist, etc. This money, hopefully, was to be reimbursed by the townsfolk, if necessary by impounding.

29th April

Prebendaries of the College Kirk of Haddington were summoned to appear at the Tolbooth on 6 May for consultation re the augmentation of the Divine Service of the said Kirk.

The Burgh was divided into quarters, with each quarter to arrive, in turn, next Monday and for several days thereafter, at the sound of the handbell, to restore the old passageway of Lothburn, at the rear of St. Anne's Chapel, in order that water may drain away freely. Every householder was to come, or else send a servant, armed with spade, shovel and mattock. Whoever did not appear would be fined 8s. to be spent on ale and bread for those working.

7th May

It was agreed that the previous Act on staple goods would be applied, with the addition that no collars, front-coat panels, sleeves or hose of any coloured cloth or silks would be sold at any booth on market day; under penalties specified in the Act. Any offender who took money therefrom would be punished, their goods confiscated, with half going to the Provost and baileys, and half to the Common Purse. Those who denied the charge unsuccessfully would be deprived of their freemanship and burgessship.

Free benefits, awarded by the Burgh, were put on offer.

30th October

No vagabonds or outdwellers would be allowed to buy butter, cheese, eggs, fish or fowl before 9 a.m.; under penalty of forfeiture. No bribes would be allowed or traders approached under penalty of a personal punishment.

31st December

No pensions would be awarded to people for their common goods, or feus for their use of common land, or dues from the Mills, or any exchanges thereto, privately or openly, either in Council Chambers or elsewhere, nor would anyone be allowed to promise such in writing; under penalty of default.

1558

22nd January

Adam Cockburn was ordered to remove earth and gravel from his walls on the Smeddyrow, on the common road from St. Ninian's Chapel, from henceforth to Shrove Tuesday. If he failed to do so then anyone would be free to help themselves.

4th April

Lydgate, lying between Haddington and Aberlady, on the common road, together with the East Lane, which is called Barney Loan, are completely broken down and destroyed by the owners and servants of the adjoining properties. Adam Wilson, Thomas Ponton, George Richardson, John Blackburn, Thomas Dickson, William Gibson, William Wemyss and others have agreed to take stock of the situation pertaining to the said Gate, from henceforth up to Thursday next.

20th April

Those named above found that the Lydgate, stretching from West Loan to the broad ridge which descends to the east side of the land in Herdmanflat, presently occupied by Margaret Collielaw, was five and a half ells wide by one eighth, as indicated by the heap of stones marking the boundary.

28th April

Betty Mayne and Alison Mayne, daughters of the late Andrew Mayne, were granted conjointly the house belonging to St. James Altar, which the late Katherine Hoige, their mother, occupied previously, so long as they remained without a partner. Whoever was married first would pay 5 pounds of meal to the Treasurer, Adam Wilson, as a surety.

29th April

Sir James Mauchline, Chaplain of the Altar of St. James, in the College Kirk of Haddington, gave to the Burgh the various landholdings and appurtenances belonging to him as Chaplain, plus the produce of the tenants and mills thereof, to dispose of as they thought fit, in return for £4 payable at WhitSunday and Martinmas, commencing from next WhitSunday, with 11s. payable immediately.

30th June

By order a 4d. loaf was to weigh 26 ounces. No baker was to produce bread for sale until it was seen and weighed by the baileys. Camp bread was to have St. Andrew's Cross as a trademark to mark it as different from other bread; under penalty of an 8s. fine.

30th September

John Forrest and Alexander Barns, Treasurer, were told to go to Edinburgh to see if the Burgh was supposed to march with the Army, as per Queen's proclamation, or if they had reached agreement to the contrary with anyone, and, if so, would the Burgh of Haddington be allowed to do the same.

22nd September

Matthew Bowe was ordered to carry out a night watch on the Tolbooth Head, starting from 9.p.m. until 5 a.m. and, starting from Halloween, for six hours in the morning. He was ordered to cry out at the striking of each hour, until he was relieved. His duties commenced on the 21 September. The Treasurer was instructed to pay him 12d. per night.

1559

26th January

Burgesses complained of unfreemen posing as freemen of the Burgh.

10th February

Thomas Ponton, Treasurer, declared that, since full accounts of the common goods of the Burgh were regularly available to him, and because of complaints laid against his predecessors, he would never spend any money from these accounts without express permission.

29th April

Thomas Ponton, Treasurer, was instructed to buy five legs of beef and two swine for the Frenchmen.

19th August

Capitane Lucinyeis, soldier, requested that the Burgh of Haddington commission John Ayton, Provost, and John Forrest, burgess, to go to Edinburgh to find men willing to serve as soldiers. £325 (Scots) was made available for this purpose, with £200 payable in advance and the remainder held by the council in trust.

6th October

Robert Dormant was appointed as Schoolmaster for 24 merks p.a. paid out of the Common Purse. Each child would pay 12d. per term as a school-house fee. The assistant master would receive 4d. per term per child, paid by the parents or friends. The Council would provide a room and free meals.

13th November

William Gibson, Treasurer, was instructed to pay Friar John Congilton, Warden of Friars, £5/16s. out of the sum of £24 (Scots) made available by Thomas Ponton, the previous Treasurer, payable on WhitSunday and Martinmas. 61s. was also paid for Ralph Eglin's acres.

7th December

Miller, from each of two mills, were ordered to provide one mill dish full of a grain crop, of at least two bolls ground.

John Knox, from a popular engraving

Chapter 2

1560 to 1567

For two years Scotland struggled on without a monarch on the throne. Instead Government by the Lords of the Congregation took over, the nominal head being Arran who was more often to be found in his new Duchy of Chatelherault – a reward for his efforts in disposing of the English. In effect, Maitland of Lethington was the man who retained the coolest head along with young Mary's cousin James Stewart, Earl of Moray.

On the 19th August 1561, Mary, now about to take on her true role as Queen of Scots, being recently widowed in France, landed at Leith. The east coast was enveloped in a dense haar. Mary may have felt that this was a harbinger for what lay ahead. Certainly, she was never able to really come to grips with the situation in which she found herself. What she needed was a loyal, clear-thinking Scots nobleman to be at her side constantly. What she found instead was a divided kingdom. As a Catholic Queen she found she was head of a state which had split from Rome. John Knox was to become her thorn in the side. She could never oust him in debate, nor could she ever find a way to bring him properly to heel. Her travels throughout her kingdom, although bringing her to the notice of her people, did little or nothing to upset the grip Protestantism had. Her marriages to Darnley and Bothwell both ended disastrously, the former being strangled outside Kirk o'Fields and the latter going mad in a Danish pit-dungeon. Even in fleeing from Langside, where her forces were defeated for the final time, Mary took the wrong decision. She could, and should, have returned to France, where she was much admired and become Queen of that kingdom. Instead she opted to flee to England where Queen Elizabeth, forever suspicious of Mary's designs upon her throne, kept her imprisoned for

20 years before finally agreeing to her execution. She left a son, James, born in 1566.

Haddington, however, remained largely unmoved and unaffected by any of the dramatic occurrences at Court. The years of Mary's reign were characterised by confirming the place of the Catholic Church, controlling the complex system of market and crafts withing the burgh, conforming to the tax levy from Holyrood, and, above all, by devising strategies and practices to combat the renewed onset of the plague.

Haddington Burgh Council Records
1560 to 1567

1561

2nd January

Friar William Hepburn, Warden of Lanark, confessed that he had broken off the lock from the Chamber belonging to the Friars of Haddington, which is called the Warden's Chamber. James Oliphant sought legal remedy, whereupon Friar William Hepburn sought assurance that he would not be forbidden from entering the Chamber.

29th April

High Court.

Adam Wilson, Provost, Thomas Ponton and Bernard Thomson, Baileys.

Alexander Barns, burgess, presented a statement of accounts to be entered into the records:

Intromission of accounts prepared by Alexander Barns of the goods of the late David Dalziel and his wife and John Dalziel. David Dalziel died in October 1545.

Item – £58/14s. worth of goods in the estate.

Debts outstanding to the estate – 3/4d owed by the master mason.

    12s. owed by Patrick Redpath and paid to Alexander Barns.
    4/8d. owed by the late Alexander Reid and paid to Alexander Barns.
    6/- owed by William Thomson's wife.
    5/- owed by Margaret Kymew
    20/- owed by Alexander Barns.

Item – the rent of the bakehouse, plus two annual salaries for five years, amounting to £3/6s. for each of the five years.

Item – £7/8s. rent from houses occupied by James Robson and John Robson, which have remained unpaid for two years.

Item – the rent for all of the lodgings for 1550 to 1559, except for William Anderson's, amounting to £6/16s.

Item – Alexander Barns discharged himself from all debts owed to the late David and contained in the accounts: 19/- owed by John Sharp, 20/4d. owed by William Robson, 15/- owed by Simon Pynago, 10/- paid to Patrick Douglas and 4/- to Isobel Kemp.

Balance – £3/7/4d. still owed.

Item – discharged debt of £15 owed by the late David to sundry persons and paid by him.

29/- left as a legacy to Sir John Tait.

Burial expenses for David Dalziel and his wife, amounting to £4/11/6d.

Expenses accruing from the handling of the will – 32/4d.

Expenses accruing from an action against the will pursued by Andrew Hay, and for pursuing creditors – 11/-.

Item – 8/4d. p.a. for two years preceding the burning of the town, to the Laird of Blanss – 18/6d.

Item – 30/- p.a. for two years before the entry of the English, to Sir Hugh Bold, amounting to £3.

Item – to the said Sir Hugh for ten years since the departure of the English, at 22/4d. p.a. (except the final quarter) amounting to £6/14/10d.

Item – to the Abbey for two years, prior to the arrival of the English, at 3/2d/ p.a., amounting to 6/4d.

Item – 30d. p.a. and a term's rent of 15d., amounting to 26/4d.

Item – to John Forrest an annual rent for 13 years and a half years, from the time the English were here, at 5/- p.a., amounting to £3/7/6d.

Item – £20 paid to Andrew Hay on the 6 June 1546, for the restoring of the West Wall.

Item – for the board required by John Dalziel I.e. meat, drink and clothing, since the death of his father, amounting to 10 merks p.a. – in total 150 merks.

Item – to John Chalmers for his fee – 15/-.

Item – to Alexander Simpson for the preparation of a legal instrument and summons against Andrew Hay – 9/-

Item – 6/8d to the baileys for outstanding taxes owed by David Dalziel.

Item – 44/- given to Pierss the Frenchman for saving the rear lodging houses.

Item – for cleaning the place twice, first during the plague and secondly after the departure of the Frenchmen – 58/-.

Item – Expenses accrued in building and repairing the forehouse and fixing a lock to the backhouse – £6.

Item – for building the backhouse – £10/15/6d.

Signed by Alexander Barns, September/October 1561.

William Gibson was instructed to pay John Ayton, Provost-elect, the sum of £10 as a fee, because of sundry business and the action to be pursued against Lord Lindsay, plus other actions deferred for three years.

No one was allowed to take stones from the High Kirk; under a penalty of 11s.

1562

16th April

No sheep could be pastured in the Burgh from Candlemas until Michaelmas; under penalty of an 11s. fine for a first offence and £5 for a second.

No horses could be pastured on ridges, furrows, corn or grass; under penalty of breaking the law.

No one was allowed to sell wine or beer until the Council had set a price: under penalty of an 11s. Fine.

10th November

George Simpson presented the Queen's letter requested that he be allowed to occupy the Hangman's Acres as before. John Ayton, on behalf of the Burgh, offered the same to the said George for one year on payment of rent.

1563

12th February

James Oliphant and Bernard Thomson were instructed to go to Edinburgh to seek payment from Lord James, plus his surety for moneys outstanding for the rebuilding of the Kirk.

16th March

The Treasurer was instructed to settle John Swyton in his clerical office, find a room for M. Patrick before next WhitSunday, and pay Andrew to clear up and lock the Kirk doors, and to find a basin for the administration of baptism, and to confiscate the fruits of the Vicarage until the tenant farmers pay a fee to the guardian, which used to be paid to the Curate, and to refund Cuthbert Cockburn for the damage done to his cornfields at the conclusion of the church service.

4th June

In order to provide practice and training in archery, one pair of well-made bow butts was ordered to be built, and a dyke built at the north end for security purposes against misdirected arrows. To this end, the Treasurer was instructed to give John Forrest 10 merks to build the butts and dyke.

26th June

No corn sheaves were to be brought into the Burgh at harvest time unless proof of ownership could be provided; under penalty of a fine of 8s. If any corn was stolen at night, and found in someone's house, the master of that house would pay an 8s. fine, and hand over the thief; under penalty of being punished as a thief himself.

From the Queen "– the deacon and brethren of the craft of bakers in the Burgh of Haddington, wish Janet Sharp, widow of the late John Douglas, baker and burgess, and now spouse to James Cockburn, to be admitted to the craft of bakers, and to practice as one of them for the rest of her life. Dated 2nd September 1563. Marie R."

19th September

The Chaplaincy of Trinity was given to Patrick Cockburn, together with appurtenances.

Witnesses: George Craig, James Horn, Baileys. David Forrest, John Young (tailor), Matthew Bowe (official).

12th October

James Oliphant was elected Provost and Thomas Ponton and Henry Cockburn as baileys.

11th November

If any inhabitant of the Burgh was summoned to collect alms at the Kirk door on a Sunday and was absent, he would pay from his own pocket the same amount to the deacons as was collected on the preceding Sunday.

Anyone taking wares for sale to the market was forbidden to hide grains of corn in the bottom or mouth of their sacks; under penalty of a fine of half a boll of corn per sack.

Will of Elizabeth, Prioress of the Abbey: the underwritten orders were undertaken by John Hepburn in the Nungate, to the sum following, by command of Elizabeth, Prioress of the Abbey of Haddington.

To Patrick Hepburn of Queenscastle – £3 in gold, in part payment for certain sums of money, together with other goods and jewels placed with the said Prioress following the demise of the late John Hepburn, his father, which formerly belonged to him.

Merion Hepburn – 495 crowns, one headed belt, one gold ornament, one board of crimson velvet.

Agnes Stewart, daughter of John Stewart of Minto, knight, 100 double ducats.

William Cockburn, brother of James Cockburn of Langtown, £11 in gold.

Richard Congilton, brother of Patrick, £11 in gold.

John Bald, £21 in gold.

Robert Dickson, £20 in gold.

William Waterston, £10 in gold.

William Hepburn, brother of John Hepburn, 20 merks in gold.

John Nisbet, £6 in gold.

Witnesses: John Hepburn, Howe Bruce, Stewart of Minto.

The said Patrick received one silver piece from John Hepburn, plus 495 crowns for Marion Hepburn which he faithfully promised to deliver.

Alms were to be given to an honest lad staying at Alexander Gibson's house.

9th December

Maltsters: John Ayton, James Horn, John Gray, Adam Cockburn, John Romanes, James Richardson, James Ayton, John Cockburn, Patrick Wood, William Wemyss, John Blackburn and John Henderson convened to hear the Provost and Council fix the price of malt and beer, according to the Act of Parliament. They were allowed until 9 a.m. on the 14th December to respond.

14th December

The maltsters convened and agreed to the prices as fixed by the Provost and Council.

1564

17th February

Contract between the Provost, Baileys and Council on the one hand and Thomas Cumming on the other.

Thomas Cumming was elected to the position of Schoolmaster for life, to which he agreed. He promised to teach all the children in the Burgh in grammar, Latin and moral virtue. He agreed to teach by example. The starting date was set at Beltane, (1st May or 3rd). He was not to be absent for more than three days without special permission. His wage was set at 70 merks p.a. payable on WhitSunday and Martinmas, in equal portions. He was to charge each child 4s. p.a. at Beltane, Lammas, Candlemas and Halloween, I.e.12d. per child per term.

Witnesses: Alexander Cuby, Sir Robert Simpson. Patrick Redpath and Thomas Steven, Notary Public, with divers others.

Signed by James Oliphant, Provost. Thomas Ponton, Bailey. Thomas Cumming.

27th February

Provost, Baileys and Council, plus the deacons of all crafts in the Burgh of Haddington, I.e. Adam Wilson, Treasurer, John Forrest, Bernard Thomson, James Horn, Martin Wilson, Alexander Thomson, councillors. Cuthbert Simpson, Nichol Dunlop, John Douglas, mason, and John Stevenson, all agreed to convene in Edinburgh on 24th February to be taxed.

20th September

In remembering the desolation caused to the Burgh, and the ruin to the inhabitants in 1545, by the plague, while still looking forward to Michaelmas, the great danger of plague which had recently started in Danzig in such goods as lint, known as Danzig lint, caused the Council to order that no one cold bring any Danzig lint into the Burgh, under penalty of banishment, having the lint burnt and their goods confiscated.

No form of transport from Danzig would be allowed, under penalty of being burnt, while the owner would be punished according to Our Sovereign Lady's Proclamation.

4th October

Adam Cockburn, merchant and burgess, was accused of transgressing the above Act by harbouring in his lodgings one William Knox of Edinburgh, burgess, together with one pack of Danzig lint, and with buying from him two bundles of the same lint, and weighing it in John Ramsay's house, contrary to the aforesaid Act. He confessed that his spouse had taken in William Knox and his lint. He had bought two bundles of lint from him and had them weighed. He responded contemptuously to the charge by saying "Do what you like, but you can't banish me from the town." The two bundles were ordered to be burnt, and the said Adam detained, pending further consideration of his fate. Adam Cockburn argued that the lint was cleared by Edinburgh officials, having arrived here in John Lymm's ship. To prove it he showed a testimonial from the Provost and Baileys of Edinburgh.

2nd November

No merchant was allowed to sell any Danzig lint, or break it into bundles, until next Martinmas. No lint was to be brought from St. Colm's island without a testimonial from the Inspectors in Edinburgh.

24th November

It was agreed that, if any coal is dug out of Gladsmuir, it should be assigned to David Forrest and his colleagues, which was acceptable to the Provost, Baileys and Council.

1565

25th January

The Fleshmarket and Saltmarket were to be held on the 8th of February, on the east side of the Burgh, alongside the Friars' Wall, on both the north and south sides of the road. Each trader could set up stall there as he thought fit. No meat was to be sold in any other part of the Burgh, either on Market day or any weekday. The Plant market was to be held in the old Fleshmarket and in the street of that name.

2nd June

Thomas Ramsay, from St. Monans, confessed to bringing his ship to Aberlady haven on the 26th May last, and to have broken the timber moorings there. The Council forgave him, and Thomas Ramsay thereafter agreed to sell his ship's cargo: 30 oak joints, 60 rough oak spars, three dozen planks, two dozen wooden beams, 100 fir spars and 200 poles. The Customs duty on this cargo amounted to 14s.

26th August

James Horn, Bailey, the Council and townsfolk all convened in the Tolbooth to hear the King's proclamation. John Forrest, Provost, John Ayton and Thomas Ponton were appointed as Commissioners and errand bearers to the King and Queen in Edinburgh to give thanks on behalf of the Burgh for permission to stay out of the planned raid.

31st August

The fee for dispensation against taking part in the planned raid was £100, which was not available in the short term from the Common Purse of the Burgh, and so was borrowed from the following; James Oliphant £20, John Ayton £20, John Gray £20, Adam Wilson £10, Thomas Ponton £10, Bernard Thomson £10 and Patrick Lyall £10. A promise was made to repay the loan before the Feast of Martinmas.

1566

24th January

No 'unfreeman' was allowed to buy hide, skin or wool on Market day before 11 a.m. except from burgesses. Under penalty of forfeiture of the goods. Officials were ordered to carry out this instruction rigorously.

28th March

All victuals were to be sold in the Market place from 10 a.m. Nothing was to be kept in store, either in houses or booths, after 10 a.m. Under penalty of forfeiture and an 8s. fine.

No wool was to be bought in the Market before 11 a.m.: under penalty of forfeiture.

No butter, cheese or eggs were to be sold before 12 noon: under penalty of forfeiture.

John Stevenson, burgess, heir to Cherrytree Haugh, in the east of the Burgh, on the north side of the Tyne, and to the south of the common gate to the Abbey of Haddington, said that a small burn enters the Tyne, at the east part of this land, which has a ford. John Stevenson agreed never to build a mill or milldam or waterway on any part of his land, or attempt to divert the water, or to do anything which might prejudice the inhabitants of Haddington. He agreed that, if he did commit any of these acts, the Council would have them demolished. For which assurance, Bernard Thomson, Bailey and Treasurer, agreed to pay £224 to John Stevenson.

Sir William Wilson petitioned to be restored to the position of Parish Clerk, which he formerly held between 1535 and 1559. Since all Clerks had been restored to their former office, he requested the same. I.e. ministering at the parish Kirk, using water at baptism ceremonies, keeping the Kirk clean, closing and opening the Kirk doors as necessary, and collecting the 12d. duty owed from each house in the Burgh. He had been born in Haddington and would be happy to serve, and to sing the psalms each Sunday, and act as Chanter.

It was agreed that 11s. p.a. would be awarded to Sir William Wilson for looking after the Kirk.

Chapter 3

Reign of King James I and VI
Part I
1567 to 1603

On 29th of July 1567, King James was crowned King by the Catholic Bishop of Orkney, James Stewart at Stirling. The sermon, however, was preached by John Knox. Until James came of age in 1578, Morton acted as Regent.

James' reign brought some very-needed stability to Scotland. Nobles continued to confront each other, and the King himself, at times, but, James was not inclined to reply by a show of force unless there was no other way.

The 1570s saw a decisive upswing in trade. Unfortunately, initial food shortages brought about price inflation. The rate of exchange swung heavily against the Scots currency. The Scots £ depreciated against the English £.

Whereas in 1567 the ratio was 1 to 5.5, by 1587 it was 1 to 7.33 and by 1600 had fallen to 1 to 12.

Society saw a renewed emphasis on law and order. James wanted a stable Government which, although focussed heavily on Protestantism, could still accept features of the Catholic Church so that bishops were gradually introduced, albeit with restricted powers and function.

James was also committed to an alliance with England. He recognised from the start that the crown of both countries could be his provided that relations between the two remained cordial. From the Treaty of Berwick, 1586, he received a pension of some £5,000 from the English Crown. Morton was also promised a pension but never received it.

Finance was the abiding problem for the Scottish Crown. Keeping the various strands of Scottish nobility happy put a great strain on resources. As an act of desperation, almost, the coinage was debased i.e. strips peeled off it, so that £100,000 came into Crown coffers between 1583–1596. Trade was improving and exports brought in £4,496 in 1578 rising to £5,399 in 1582. Still this was not enough and in 1597 customs duties were increased sharply especially on salmon and coal. A duty on imports was introduced at the same time. Military, judicial expeditions e.g. to the Borders, brought in more taxes while diplomatic missions to England raised 200,000 merks in 1597 and a further 100,000 in 1601.

The period 1585–1592 saw a long-awaited harmony between James on the one hand and nobles and ministers on the other. It seemed that James was well on the way to restoring the prosperity of Scotland and the status of the Crown. People began to feel that they had a King they could trust. A more direct relationship was formed between central government and the regions – a new order was imposed on Scottish society in the latter part of the 16th century. A remarkable increase in the number of lawyers was noted. Craftsmen developed a new confidence which enabled them to take grievances to court, where previously this would be unknown. Lawyers also saw the chance to sit nicely between town councils and the King's government and be the trusted link. A burgeoning market in property, land etc., increasingly and inevitably saw more cases come to court.

But lawyers were not the only ones to witness a growth in numbers. Ministers, too, saw that religious differences, which previously had seen a lot of bloodshed, could now be largely set aside. However fragile, a life was possible that allowed Protestants and Catholics to play their part in the practice of religion in Scotland. Increasing numbers saw increasing privileges.

These changes were reflected in the Royal Burgh of Haddington.

Court cases were a regular occurrence, whether for assault or disputes over property. As a market town, prices of crops were constantly under review, while the Burgh Council were constantly on the lookout for those who were unlicensed to practice – the so-called 'unfreemen.' The decline in the Scottish economy saw an increase in beggars, vagrants, pedlars and the like. Haddington was not spared on this account, and measures taken against the like were a regular feature of Council minutes. A high proportion of Council time was given to the election of officials, not always acceptable by those chosen. Instructions to the Treasurer, mainly to instigate purchases, were an almost daily event.

As far as the world outside was concerned, sending representatives to the Convention of Scottish Burghs and complying with requests for men to serve in expeditions against those who had offended the King, was all that involved Haddington.

Other items which feature less frequently in Council records include: Gladsmuir and its land, attention to buildings within the Burgh, education, church matters and the problem of witches.

By far the most serious item was the recurrence of plague and the frantic efforts to combat its effects, most of which involved sealing off Haddington from the outside world.

House in
Poldrait Street

Haddington Burgh Council Records
1567 to 1602

1567

6th November

Alexander Millar, alias Barklaw, was accused of disobeying John Coreatill, Bailey, by saying "Come and kiss my arse. I will not put a foot forward for you. I set no more by you as you do for me." For which outburst, sentence was pronounced that, if he ever re-offended, he would be punished according to the laws of the Burgh.

7th November

The position of handbell-ringer (bellman) was awarded to Matthew Bowe for one year, including all profits, except for 13/4d payable by the Treasurer to the bellman. He had to be prepared to withstand abuse and the throwing of eggs. He had to ring the clocktower bell every night on the quarter-hour after 8.p.m; likewise in the morning after 5 a.m. He had to repair and set the clock with the help of a smith, provided at his own expense. He would be paid 1d each time he rang the bell. For digging a child's grave he would be paid 16. John Ayton would serve as inspector at each year's end.

14th November

All debtors were to be summoned for whatever amounts they owed to the Treasurer.

6th December

A pension of six merks was awarded to Alexander King for his expedition and expertise in pursuing the Burgh's business.

James Cockburn was accused of swearing at Provost Thomas Ponton and Bailey John Caskettle, throwing six fourpenny loaves at them, breaking the law, and saying

"Whoever dares to be so clever as to use my bread had better eat it or I shall have my revenge."

The Council's judgement was awaited.

1568

18th March

A boll of wheat was priced at 30s. A 4d loaf was to weigh 24 ounces.

26th March

Thomas Smyth was forbidden to keep any company with Elizabeth Seton in the future. Under penalty of banishment.

4th June

Thomas Ponton, Provost, and James Forrest were ordered to go to Edinburgh so that they could buy a licence to stay out of the coming raid on Dumfries.

15th September

In order to protect against the onset of plague, four watchmen were appointed to keep a daily watch, and traverse the Burgh, stopping to watch at six assigned spots. Every night six men would keep watch to prevent outsiders from entering the Burgh.

Three honest men were appointed as visitors, to pass daily at 6 a.m. and 6 p.m., each taking one third of the Burgh, accompanied by an official, to enquire "Who is dead or sick?" If any were found, the remainder of the household would be quarantined, and the Provost, baileys and Council informed. Full power to carry out these duties was assigned to the visitors. All inhabitants were ordered to obey them, under penalty of death. One third of the Burgh, starting at the late Thomas Dickson's house, thence passing northwards by Anderson's Wynd to the north side of the Tolbooth Gate, and going westwards from there. The second visitor would proceed eastwards from there to Strumpet Street; from the south side of the crossroads to John Forrest's house in the Tolbooth Gate.

The third visitor would cover the remainder of the Burgh.

No travelling corn dealers, mealmakers, herring buyers, fruit sellers, butter buyers or sellers, or any other inhabitants of the Burgh were allowed to travel to Edinburgh, Leith or any place where plague is suspected, without a special licence obtained from the Provost or Baileys. Under penalty of death and confiscation of goods.

No one was allowed to shelter anyone, no matter where they came from, without a licence.

All beggars and vagabonds were to be removed from the Burgh as quickly as possible; under penalty of being branded on the cheek, except for natives of the Burgh.

No fruit was to be sold, either in public or privately, under penalty of death.

No pedlars were to be allowed to enter the Burgh; under penalty of death.

No swine were to be allowed inside the Gate, or else they would be slaughtered.

No Danzig lint was to be sold by anyone; under penalty of having the goods burnt.

No type of horseware was to be sold; under penalty of confiscation.

No outsiders were allowed in, except under special licence, in which case they were to stay out of all public gatherings for 15 days; under penalty of death.

All markets and fairs were forbidden for next Michaelmas; under penalty of death and confiscation of goods.

22nd September

Henceforth no markets were allowed or booths erected on Saturdays. No wares were to be displayed for sale; under penalty of death and confiscation of goods.

1st October

All head rooms (top storeys) and yard dykes were to be so built as to prevent passage, which was to be confined exclusively through the Gates. Where property owners were too poor to build accordingly, building would be at the expense of the Burgh. All building was to start forthwith and be completed by St. Luke's Day.

2nd December

It was agreed that John Paterson could hold property within the Burgh, under promises made between himself and the Council.

Ports were ordered to be made which could close quickly.

No one was allowed to go to Edinburgh.

1569

23rd September

No fair was to be held on Michaelmas Day, and no markets allowed, until further notice.

No kind of merchandise, or pedlar's goods, fruit, herring, ropes, dishes, plates or suchlike were to be sold; under penalty of the goods being burnt.

No boots or shoes were to be sold henceforth; under penalty of forfeiture.

It was allowed that all corn and flesh coming in from places which were not yet suspected of having the plague, could be sold in the Burgh.

No inhabitant of the Burgh was allowed to go to Edinburgh transporting fruit or herring; under penalty of banishment from the Burgh.

No cattle market was allowed to be held in the Burgh, but instead kept exclusively to the adjoining smallholdings.

27th October

Previously, in similar times, The Provost, Baileys and officials were exempt from paying taxes, as being the most prominent and wealthy of the town dwellers. Henceforth they were to be taxed, according to their wealth, in order to give relief to the poor. The Provost and Baileys would see to it that the money was collected.

6th December

William Cranston swore on oath in order to become a burgess, at the urgent request of Sir Richard Maitland of Lethington.

1570

26th January

Whatever is found in a man's cornfield could be impounded by him, and, if not claimed, could be advertised for sale by ringing a bell throughout the Burgh. If not wanted by anyone, the finder was free to retain it.

30th March

John Ayton, Provost, and Bernard Thomson, Bailey, were instructed to go to Edinburgh, to search for a minister.

Tenant farmers from the Vicarage were told that they must put no livestock in the Kirkyard; under penalty of forfeiture to the Burgh.

The watch was to be maintained every night until the current situation was resolved; the penalty for not doing so was imprisonment and a fine of 8s. per absence.

The contract between the late Prior of St. Andrews and the Burgh was to be taken to Edinburgh to find any trace of the four types of surety mentioned.

13th April

The Provost and one other were to go to Edinburgh next midsummer to try to find an answer to the problem of the gift of a minister to the Burgh.

The late James, Earl of Moray's three executors i.e. Robert Winrame, John Hairt and James Wilkie, were to be asked about the third charge which had been levied on the Burgh before the fourth was imposed.

27th July

A vagabond called David was to be arrested and brought before the Provost and Baileys to be sentenced and imprisoned at their pleasure.

The watch was to be kept diligently and steadfastly. If any watchman failed in his duty, or was found to be drunk, or asleep, or absent from his beat, he was to be punished. The watchman on the Tolbooth roof was told to call out the hour at each corner of the Tolbooth, failing which he would be punished. If any watchman stole corn while on duty he was to be punished, according to the Acts already passed.

29th July

John Gray and James Cockburn were chosen to go to Lord Morton and ask about the coming raid, and see if an agreement could be reached, possibly involving the Treasurer, whereby Burgh men could stay at home from the raid to Linlithgow.

25th August

John Douglas was instructed to go to Edinburgh to fetch the Minister before the following Sunday.

12th October

Bakers were ordered to bake only good quality bread, with a 4d loaf weighing 22 ounces. A boll of wheat was to be sold for 30s. Bread was not to be left unweighed; under threat of the penalty contained in the previous Acts. The deacon and master of the bakehouse would inform the Provost and Baileys of these penalties.

Good quality ale was to be sold for 4d per pint subject to the aforesaid penalties.

All Acts passed previously re the selling of meat, corn, candles, residue of melting tallow, staple goods, wool, hide and skins, were ratified.

1571

21st September

William Thomson, servant to John Douglas, shoemaker and watchman, complained about David Forrest and Thomas Cockburn, claiming that, while on his watch, they attacked him with dagger, stones and dogs, struck him, knocked his bonnet off, and made to kill him, if he had not defended himself. Thomas Cockburn, he alleged, threw stones at him to try to kill him. The said David Forrest and Thomas Cockburn appeared before Provost and Council, accused of a premeditated felony.

28th October

The Treasurer was instructed to pay £100 in taxes as payment for being left out of the siege of Edinburgh; the same to be shown in the accounts.

29th November

All rents due from Chaplaincies and Altars were to be collected and given to the Schoolmaster or an assistant, to teach children, plus an Exortar (one appointed to give religious exhortation under a minister) in the Kirk, for which a qualified man was to be sought. Cuthbert Simpson disagreed with this, saying that it should be provided out of the Common Purse.

24th December

It was decided that money should be divided among the poor from the Common Purse. Matthew Bowe's son was to be provided with a coat and a pair of hose at the Burgh's expense.

1572

10th January

James Carmichael, Minister, was awarded ten merks to pay his room rent for a year, starting from last Martinmas, 1571.

1st February

The farmers and millers from the two Common Mills complained that Thomas Cockburn, merchant, on the 30th January last, broke the exit flowpipe from the mill dam adjacent to the said Thomas's yard. While they were standing on the dam wall, the said Thomas came and boasted and threatened them and said he would stop them in future by doing the same again. The Council found that the Burgh could benefit from having the dam cleaned on Thomas Cockburn's side. As for the breaking of the exit flowpipe, which allowed water to flow past Thomas Cockburn's yard, it had always done so in living memory and always would. Therefore, if Thomas Cockburn placed any impediment in the way, he would be imprisoned.

21st March

The Treasurer was instructed to construct the Kirk windows with stone and lime, together with the Kirkyard dyke and stiles. No livestock were to be pastured therein. The Tolbooth drawbridge was to be repaired as quickly as possible.

The burgh was to be divided into six parts, each having a nightwatchman. Each was to keep watch himself, except for Adam Wilson, elder, James Oliphant, Thomas Ponton, John Ayton, Bernard Thomson, Harry Cockburn, elder, and John Blackburn who would instead offer their sons, all well armed, to serve in their stead. Anyone without sons had to find a well-armed man to serve in their stead. All were to convene in the Tolbooth.

28th March

A document of lease was presented, whereby James Brown, John Seton, younger, John Douglas, elder, John Douglas, younger, Henry Campbell and John Stevens, together with their heirs and assignees, were granted the coalpit and coal of Gladsmuir for 19 years after WhitSunday next, to mine as they thought fit, to stop water getting in, the have sufficient pillars and stoops to prevent cave-ins, to build houses and yards for the coalminers, who would each be given two acres of land on the moor, adjacent to their houses. The said persons were to give the Treasurer £11 towards this venture, until a total of 400 merks has been invested. If any more were needed, accounts would be kept for presentation to the Treasurer. A half of the profit made from the coal was to go to the Council. If no coal was found, then the aforesaid would cultivate 20 acres of land, plus 12 acres of Yule's fields, for 19 years, at a rent of 20s. If they failed to do either of these things, they were to pay 10 merks rent, twice a year, at WhitSunday and Martinmas. Coal was to be sold to the inhabitants of the Burgh for no more than 12d per bag, failing which the complainant would receive 5s with 11s going to the Treasurer, Failure to abide by the above would result in the contract being declared void.

9th April

All Chaplaincies and annual rents pertaining to the Kirk should be handed to the Curate, or Common Prayer Reader, who would also serve as Schoolmaster.

27th June

The colliery account and the Treasurer's account for the coalfield, for the period 31st March 1572 to Sunday, 22nd June 1572, amounted to £137/5/2d.

28th June

Thomas Wauss was told that the common vennel on his property, lying to the east side of Hardgate, should be kept open between 5 a.m. and 9 p.m. leading to the water of Tyne.

Patrick Dawson was made a burgess, on oath, for 10 merks. He was told to keep watch, nightly, on the roof of the Tolbooth. Thomas Miller was to stand surety for him.

11th July

The Kirk windows, in front of the Fleshers' Altar, were to be made of glass. Rock steps were to be built in the Kirk yard to prevent livestock from entering. Four trees were to be planted.

The Schoolmaster was to be paid £11 p.a. from next Martinmas.

George Ferguson was to be made a burgess for 10 merks. He was to keep watch, week and week about, with Dawson for 7s. per week. Gates were to be locked at 9 p.m. and opened at 3 a.m.

3rd October

The houses and property, which had been promised to the Gladsmuir coalmen, were built each according to his job.

A bell was ordered from William Mayne which the Treasurer would pay for, setting aside four merks for the cost of his burgess-ship. The bell was to be hung at the west end of the Tolbooth as quickly as possible.

Three pounds ten ounces of powder, costing 32/6d, were ordered from Paul Lyle.

10th October

600 merks was borrowed from the Provost for the appointment of George Scott to do the Friars' work.

24th October

The Treasurer was instructed to rebuild the weir, using the stones swept away during the floods, at the Burgh's expense.

6th November

Each rood (a small square of ground) of the Friars' Wall, stretching from the Friars' Gate to Patrick Wood's house, thence to the water, was to yield 13/4d in feu duty. These dues were to be collected. The roods, stretching from Laird Sadler's House to the Friars' Kirk, were to pay 10s feu duty. All to be collected on the following Thursday along with the Burgh rent.

Two watchmen were to be paid 16d per night from the night following until Candlemas.

The Friar Kirk pavement was to be transferred to the High Kirk and relaid there.

13th November

No one was allowed to buy or sell any of the roods of the Friars' Wall, belonging to the Burgh, either for themselves or fellow burgesses; under penalty of forfeiture of their 'freedom'. Nor should it be lawful for any merchant to sell, dispose or transfer, his roods thereof to any manner of person but exclusively to fellow burgesses of the Burgh; under penalty of forfeit etc. Nor should the payment of feu-duty be delayed, or the Provost, Baileys and Council would lawfully dispose of the roods at their pleasure.

Awarded to John Gray – three roods of the Friars' Kirk on the north side, next to the room, hall and kitchen, paying an annual rent of 30s. Roods of the Friars' Croft were set at 10s feu-duty.

A stone dyke, built ten quarters high, was erected at the east end of the Friars' Croft. No houses were to be built at the east end of the said Croft. Building stone as to be supplied by the Burgh.

1st December

The Provost, Baileys and Council of the Burgh of Haddington on the one hand, and the tax assessors of Gladsmuir on the other, presented accounts of all expenditure incurred at Gladsmuir coalpit, from 31 March 1572 until 1 December 1572. The total amount was £422/7/3d of which the Burgh paid £211/0/7d.

Coalmining was ordered to cease until 15 March 1573, without prejudice to the livelihood of those involved.

4th December

The east gable end of the Friar Kirk, from the ground upwards, was awarded to Thomas Cockburn of Clerkington as a gift. If he declined, then the Treasurer was to pay him 20 merks for the trouble he had gone to.

James Cockburn, Provost, and James Brown, Bailey, were instructed to go to Edinburgh to consult the Burgh's advisors on the subject of Lord Yester's summons.

1573

4th February

The Provost and Bailey were to seek the Regent's view on Alexander Thomson's summons, and to advise on Dunfermline's summons.

The Treasurer was ordered to build the east stair, doors and windows of St. James Place.

27th February

A watchman was to be paid to keep watch nightly on the Tolbooth roof; starting at 9.p.m. until 3 a.m., accompanied by two neighbours. The penalty for absence would be 2s per night.

Mr Walter McConquell was appointed to read Common Prayer in the Kirk at 7 a.m. in the summer and 8 a.m. in the winter. He was to act as Clerk of Sessions on Sundays, Wednesdays and Fridays, and to teach in the School for a year. His pay was set at 50 merks p.a. payable at the two terms in equal portions.

Thomas Spottiswood was appointed to serve as a Reader to the Vicar or his Factor for 10 merks, as paid previously to the Curate.

The Saltmarket and Shoemarket were to be set out along the Friars' Wall, from Patrick Wood's house, and were to be erected between henceforth and Easter.

9th March

Archibald Kyle, Treasurer, was instructed to purchase one drum for the Burgh.

The townsmen were instructed to accompany the Provost, Baileys and Council, when summoned by the handbell, to the Court of Preambulation at Gladsmuir, ready equipped for fighting.

Young men of the Burgh were given 10 merks each to lay out a playing field, ensuring that the money was spent for this purpose. Under penalty of a 20 merks fine.

3rd April

One third of the annual rent from the Kirk was to be set at default, while the Collector was to impound goods to the value of the other two thirds next term.

8th April

No inheritor of any landholding on the east side of Sidegate from St. John's Port, was allowed to build any further.

20th May

The Collector and Chaplains of the Kirk were ordered to pas through the streets of the Burgh and impound for annual rents due as necessary. Sir William Cockburn consented to the will of the Council re the annual rent due for St. John's Altar. Sir Alexander Henderson sought agreement on rent due.

29th May

The Treasurer was told to loan Henry Campbell £20 towards the mining of coal, on condition that it would be repaid.

12th June

Suitable men were sought to be coalminers at Gladsmuir.

24th June

James Tweedy consented to the Council's wishes re the land and occupation of Poldrate.

John Busby's oath was heard and he was made a burgess, to work as a blacksmith, shoeing horses making iron ploughshares, bands, crooks, bushes etc., at 20d per measure. Horse shoes were to cost 2d per shoe; 12 lengths of iron rod to cost 6d.

An overseer was appointed for the coalpit, to supervise the miners between 6 a.m. and 6 p.m., at the Burgh's expense.

26th June

Henry Campbell was instructed to pay David Orkney 30s per week for four weeks for working in the coalpit, which he is owed.

15th July

The Treasurer was instructed to buy bread and wine for the communion, plus satin, boards and table linen, as necessary.

16th August

The Treasurer was instructed to pay £100 compensation for the raid on Liddesdale, scheduled for 20 August.

15th October

James Brown, James Seton, John Douglas (baker), John Douglas (shoemaker), and John Stevenson (also representing Henry Campbell), all tax assessors at the Galdsmuir coalpit, unanimously renounced their claims, rights and titles to the Gladsmuir coalpit and land, and ended their contract with the Burgh, together with all property and tools, in return for 240 merks in settlement; to be paid between this date and next Christmas.

23rd October

Bakers were ordered to bake good bread in the old style. A 4d loaf was to weigh 11 ounces since a boll of wheat was commonly sold for £3. All bread had to be checked for weight by the Provost and baileys. The Master of the Bakehouse had to ensure that all bread was weighed; under penalty of an 8s fine. Deacons of the bakers craft and the Provost and Baileys would test the bread for quality.

Malt was to be sold for no more than £3 per boll; under penalty of an 11s fine

A pint of ale was to be sold for 6d.

One pound of ragwort candles was to be sold for 15d. Cotton wool bundles to be sold for 16d; under penalty of forfeit of goods.

The Laird of Cockpen and the Council agreed a deal on Gladsmuir coal-pit whereby he provided to cover half the expense of whatever was needed.

18th November

Thomas Cockburn of Clerkington was ordered to demolish the east gable end of the Friar Kirk between this day and St. Mungo's; under provision that, if he failed to do so, the Burgh would.

26th November

Adam Wilson was instructed to buy and bring home a large cask, or puncheon, of claret wine, which was to be offered as a gift to the Regent, together with one dozen torches and some spice. £22 was provided for the purchase of the claret.

Merchants' weights were to be collected and measured against Thomas Ponton's and the late Adam Wilson's. The Stone of Lanark was to be brought to the Burgh, and all stone measures would be assessed against it.

A pint measure made of sterling was to be purchased which was to be the standard measure for all pints of the Burgh.

27th November

The Treasurer was instructed to pay Friar Patrick Allen six merks for alms; to be written in the Burgh Charter. The Treasurer was also instructed to deliver to the Regent's guardhouse a load of coal every night, plus 12d worth of candles.

Archibald Kyle, Treasurer, submitted his accounts of the Common Goods of the Burgh for the term between Martinmas 1572 and WhitSunday 1573, amounting to £1079/16/8d. The day book showed £851/5/8d. He was relieved of the responsibility of collecting the rent due from the Master of Hailes, amounting to 7 merks and 6s, and of £8/12/8d from Thomas Paterson outstanding from the final year of his burgess-ship. Also the rent due from the Friars owed to George Scott amounting to £5/13/4d. Total £20/19/4d. The Treasurer was told to ignore the rent due for the WhitSunday term from the Friars' lands and property. It was removed from the accounts, and he was also relieved of the duty of collecting 10 merks from John Stevenson for three roods of the Friars' Croft, and two merks from William Thomson for two roods of the Friars' Croft.

Also relieved – the tenant farmers of the two Common Mills – 124 merks.

Thomas Millar of the Customs Service	7 merks
Patrick Wood	10s
Andrew Smyth	16/8d
John Blair	35s
David Forrest	10s
Cuthbert Simpson	12d
George Cockburn	8/4d
David Howieson	7 merks
Thomas Thomson	5 merks
George Spottiswood	5 merks
David Allen	5 merks
Richard Tod	5 merks
James Tait	5 merks
John Cockburn – maltster	10 merks
William Brown – dealer	£10
John Stevenson	10 merks
TOTAL	£1048/3/2d
Debts owing	£180/16/6d.

16th December

Instant Justice Court.

One pint of ale was to sell for 7d; a 4d loaf was to weigh ten ounces; a boll of malt was to sell for £3/10s; previous penalties to apply.

Corn sellers were required to use accurate measures; under penalty of having them destroyed.

Skinners were to be separated from tailors because the latter failed to produce examples of their craft for examination by the Provost and Council.

24th December

Prices set by wine sellers, as required by the Sovereign's law, were to be fixed at 30s per meal, and, if the diner was not a registered guest, he was to pay 2s for his meal.

Ale was to be sold as before; one peck of oats was sold for 28d, one threave (24 sheaves) of beer straw for 4s, one threave of oats straw for 5s. Ostlers were to provide straw and stabling for each horse at 18d per day.

1574

6th January

Thomas Ponton was to be protected and kept free from harm at the hands of George Preston of Cameron, for the sum of £16 taken from the Common Purse and set aside for the baptism of Our Sovereign Lord the King. This sum was to be paid to him for his relief between this date and Easter.

The Treasurer has received no more than £44 to date to pay the Burgh's taxes.

27th January

Because the transporting of mutton carcasses and beef carcasses to the market for sale, with no trace of skin or hide, is very suspicious, an order was issued that no flesh or mutton carcasses could be sold; under penalty of confiscation and imprisonment of the seller – according to the Acts of Parliament and Acts of the Burgh.

7th April

Friar Fleck was to be paid 10 merks for titles pertaining to the Kirk. Interest was to be collected from the estate of the late Alexander Simpson at the expense of the Burgh.

21st April

The Treasurer was instructed to pay Henry White 11s for collecting the aforesaid interest.

John Auchinleck delivered all the sasines, documents and contracts pertaining to the Friars' place, plus the interest thereof, which lay within the Burgh, declaring that he would never seek any more interest, feu etc.

28th April

The Provost ordered a pair of butts to be built as previously, between this date and Midsummer's Day for £10.

12th May

The Treasurer was instructed to provide bread and wine for the Communion. He was also instructed to give £10 to the Schoolmaster for clothes etc., required for the Play, provided that the playclothes are surrendered afterwards.

28th May

The Kirkmaster would no longer serve as Schoolmaster.

16th June

Thomas Ponton and the Provost were told to attend the Convention of Burghs to be held on the 20th of June.

The Laird of Balwearie's action against his kinsman was to be heard at the expense of the Burgh

Alexander King was to be given £3 as a reward.

30th August

£64 was received from James Cockburn, Provost, repayable by St. Andrew's Day, to pay towards the furnishing of a warship to pursue pirates.

12th October

John Buchanan, Messenger, produced an order, in the Regent's hand, charging the Provost, council and Deacons to elect John Douglas (younger) Provost for the following year. The Provost, James Cockburn, Baileys, Council and Deacons all protested that their previous positions, going back as far as anyone could remember, entitled them to elect their own man.

Alexander Thomson discharged himself from any office in the town in the future.

14th October

James Cockburn asked that if he was elected Treasurer, would he be allowed to refuse?

No Councillor of the Burgh would be required to serve on any type of Assize, except those dealing with the serving of briefs.

15th October

John Douglas was elected as Provost and John Seton as Bailey and Commissioner to Stirling.

All beer, wine, ale and vinegar etc., was to be sold henceforth using an oil measure until the Commissioners bring a true pint measure from Stirling.

The Burgh's firlots (¼ boll) and pecks were to be confirmed by measuring against the iron measures because of doubts expressed recently. All other firlots and pecks would likewise be checked.

No merchant was to transport staple goods to Duns or Dunbar in future, or to those fairs which were always held outwith the Burgh. Nor were 'unfreemen' allowed to set up stalls in the market place; under penalty of a fine of £20.

3rd November

George Spottiswood confirmed that he would set up a home within 11 days of his return from Flanders; under penalty of a fine of £100 payable to the Common Purse.

The Treasurer was instructed to pay James Carmichael £5/10/2d for his expenses incurred in furnishing the Play.

1st December

A feu charter was granted to Alexander Simpson and his spouse, Marjory Ayton, conjointly, and their heirs, for two acres of land called 'Hangman's Acres', under common seal with sasine to follow, for an annual payment of £3/3/4d feu rent to the Treasurer.

A charter of feu duty, made under the Common Seal of the Burgh, with sasine to follow, was granted to John Seton, bailey, for the landholding formerly belonging to Crispin and Crispin's Altar, for an annual rent of 13/4d payable to the Treasurer.

1575

6th March

The Treasurer was granted £4/0/10d to replace a deficit of copper coin and 'Lord Heid' (a copper coin of Mary and James VI) received by him before the proclamation which removed such coinage from use.

23rd March

The Provost, Baileys and Council considered the great poverty of Friar Patrick Allen, a native of the Burgh, who had stayed in the Burgh for many years, with great infirmity of body, and decided to award him £12 p.a. for the rest of his life, payable at WhitSunday and Martinmas in equal portions, starting the following WhitSunday. He was also to receive £4 with which to pay his creditors, provided he forgot the £22 not paid to him over the last two years. The Friar's house, yards, dykes, dovecots, croft, pertinances and annual rents were to be passed over to the Council.

13th April

Matthew Bowe agreed that, for the rest of his life, he would repair the Burgh Clock when necessary, with the Burgh supplying materials and a smith. Matthew Bowe would be granted the first burgess-ship that became available for the sum of 10 merks, provided that he maintained the clock in full working order.

3rd June

The Treasurer was instructed to buy timber for new seats and stairs in the Kirk, as well as a new pulpit.

21st July

The Treasurer was instructed to find someone to make a stool for the Kirk Mill, and millstones when needed, and scaffolding for the Play. He was also instructed to clean the burn from Thomas Miller's house to the Port.

12th October

Councillors were warned to appear at 10 a.m. on the appointed day as required, unless leave of absence had been requested; under penalty of a fine of 18d.

It was agreed that the names of the Councillors, who were present, be written, following the Acts made each day; that nothing be decreed unless a majority be present, and that no Acts passed be put into execution before the next Convention.

15th November

John Carkettle, Moderator, was told to collect penalties for absence from Councillors.

1st December

Those housed in the Tolbooth were required to pay 6d jailer fee to officials on leaving.

The Treasurer was instructed to pay the Collector of Taxes £40, of which £20 represented the Burgh's portion; to be shown in the accounts.

14th December

The windows above the table at the north side of the Kirk were to be washed and sprinkled with lime. Three windows on the south side of the Kirk were to be glassed, the rest washed, and the rest of the doors completed.

John Ayton (elder) and Robert Nesbit, Bailey, were to go to Edinburgh as Commissioners to attend the Convention of the Burghs. The Provost would ride with them. There were two matters of concern to raise a) the wealth of the Burgh and the estate of merchants and b) what to do about bullion.

James Cockburn was loaned the great lintel stone from the chimney of St. Katherine's Chapel on condition he returned it when needed.

The Treasurer was instructed to pay £20 from the Common Purse to the Collector of Alms for the French Kirk.

22nd December

A qualified Reader and Exortar was sought, at 11 merks p.a.

1576

1st March

The Provost spent three days in Edinburgh, with John Thomson, copying the Burgh Accounts.

John Carkettle and Robert Nesbit were appointed Commissioners for Taxes.

James Baird, the locksmith, was to be paid 11s p.a. and provided with a new outfit and a Jeddart staff by the Council.

15th March

The Treasurer was instructed to have an iron dish made by the locksmith in which to assess all corn brought to the market to be sold.

All sacks of corn, due to be sold at stalls and booths, were to be brought to the market by 10.a.m. Whoever failed to do so would be legally charged 12d per load by the Council.

Katherine Richardson was to have the surgeon attend to her arm, and the Treasurer would pay.

4th April

The Treasurer would have the north and west side of the Kirk completed, the Pillar of Repentance demolished and rebuilt in wood.

The Saltmarket was to stand next to William Brown's yard, starting at his gate with the Mealmarket next to it, on the next market day. The Fleshmarket would stand where it previously stood, with stalls covered with boards, otherwise the stalls would be demolished. This was due to begin on the following Lammas.

15th April

Thomas Ponton was granted a licence to build a sepulchre, or burial place, within the Parish Kirk, ready for his demise. He was restricted to one flat gravestone on which his name could be inscribed, as a reward for good service.

26th April

The coalpit miners were ordered to carry on working until further notice. In the meantime, the Laird of Cockpen was asked to attend the Council meeting on 3rd May.

19th July

Lydgate was to be visited in the afternoon, and its occupants warned to change their meeting place for next Thursday, at which time the said gate would be restored to its former condition and walked over. The occupants were instructed to bring stones for the purpose of rebuilding.

The Treasurer was instructed to pay Laurence Burt 11s for drinking money.

6th September

The Treasurer was instructed to pay Laurence Burt 11s for his support in preparing Communion tickets.

5th October

The old and new Councils convened in the Council House to elect Provost, Baileys and Treasurer for the following year. Craft deacons also convened to vote but the Council disagreed, quoting an Act of the Convention of Burghs, 1541, which required deacons to attend in silence.

11th October

The Treasurer was instructed to buy a drum for the Burgh, and afterwards a taffeta flag; the cost to be shown in the accounts.

15th November

James Carmichael was told by the Council that, considering his work load as a Minister, another might be found to serve in the School, thus correcting previous failures of the Council to keep their promise to provide an assistant, which promise was neglected because of the frequency with which Councillors etc., were changed. Secondly, having already promised that the School would be based in the Burgh, and despite the false, malicious rumours raised by others, the progress towards this aim had been thwarted, therefore James Carmichael was not to blame for the disorder and inconvenience which has ensued. The Council would therefore take responsibility for dealing with the slander which has arisen. Nevertheless, the Council desired James Carmichael to heed their plea, and if he did, the Council promised to select a qualified man, free from fault, heresy, papacy or idolatry, following the public pronouncement of Christ the Evangelist in the Realm. James Carmichael would then surrender the position of Schoolmaster, together with stipends, School fees etc. The gift of the Abbey of Holyroodhouse, given by Adam, the holder of the benefice of the said Abbey, under the Common Seal of the Abbey, and with the King's confirmation, would be cancelled.

Whereby James Carmichael, his heirs and assignees, would be recompensed in travel expenses to the sum of £100. Further, a debt of £20, owed by James Carmichael to the Council, would be wiped clean. £40 would be paid on 25th December; a further £11 would be paid on WhitSunday, and the balance paid thereafter by James Cockburn, Treasurer. Adequate lodging would be provided for James Carmichael, rent free in the Burgh, for as long as he stayed on as Minister. He would continue to help out in the School when necessary, and until a Master is found for all the Schools except the High Grammar School.

Witnessed by Thomas Steven, Notary Public, Clerk of the Burgh of Haddington – in his own hand.

22nd November

Craft deacons were instructed to convene their craftsmen in order that rumours be dispelled; their response to be received within eight days by the Council.

William Brown was instructed to go to Edinburgh to find a Schoolmaster.

6th December

The Treasurer was instructed to prepare a room in the east wall of the Council House, in which to house the new Common Chest. Thomas Ponton, Provost, John Ayton (elder), James Cockburn, John Carkettle, Robert Nesbit, William Wilson and Cuthbert Simpson would attend the placing therein of the Burgh documents.

14th December

Lime and sand were ordered for St. Katherine's Chapel for the building of a School.

24th December

Fleshmongers had previously been allowed to sell meat etc., in the Fleshmarket on Christmas Eve, and this should be allowed to continue until such time as the Kirk dispenses with Christmas.

1577

11th February

Thomas Cockburn, whose new road was already partly laid, was instructed to take it up again by Matthew Bailey, because the latter had been commissioned by the Council to lay the road.

1st March

George Ayton, guarantor for John Hume, brother of Alexander Hume of Manderston, said that John Hume would present a silver bell to the Provost and Burgh worth seven English coins, i.e, one ounce of silver.

26th March

John Fowler was hired to be the Burgh miller. He was allotted two assistants, one for the West Mill and one for the Kirk Mill, at his own expense, for whose performance he would be responsible. He would be required to repair all the machinery etc., at his own expense, but the Burgh would provide timber, nails and iron. He would keep the Mill running and advise the Council of his expenses. He was not allowed to keep dogs or swine at the Mills. He and his assistants were to work in all weathers, including storms and frost, as was done previously.

He would receive 20 merks, payable at WhitSunday and Martinmas in equal portions, plus a dish of the best malt out of each mashing for his bannock. From each two bolls of wheat he would receive one milled dish of heaped flour, regardless of the amount of grist in it, as a reward for good and faithful service. Each man was required to grind according to his place of work both day and night. If they were absent then another would be found to take his place.

John Douglas declared himself to be a guarantor for John Fowler (younger) serving as an assistant in the said Mills. He promised to fulfil his duties and to be loyal. Thomas Ponton, Provost, and John Seton, Bailey, acting on their own behalf and on behalf of the whole community, promised to keep their part of the agreement. John Fowler (younger) agreed to release John Douglas from his guarantee in the near future.

15th April

James Panton was chosen to be the Schoolmaster at £10 per quarter, a free room and a stipend of 12d per child per quarter. His assistant was to receive 4d per child. Children from the outlying countryside were allowed to attend. The assistant was to have control of the children on alternate days. If the Burgh found any fault with James Panton, he would be dismissed at the end of the quarter. His duties were to commence on the following WhitSunday.

George Hepburn of Haucht renounced his own jurisdiction and declared himself to be a guarantor for James Panton for life.

10th May

Thomas Ponton, Provost, declared the commencement of the foundation of the Hospital of St. Lawrence, and asked the Clerk to make an official copy of his statement.

Sir Alexander Henderson was awarded the rent from the Kirk Colleges etc., which he was about to reform.

17th May

George Nesbit was hired to say prayers three days a week in the Kirk, excepting Wednesdays, i.e. Tuesdays, Thursdays and Fridays at 7 a.m. in the summer months and in winter at the appointed hour. He was also to serve as assistant Schoolmaster for one year at 11 merks p.a. plus the use of a room. John Ayton and the Clerk were to ride to St. John's Chapel on WhitSunday morning.

17th October

James Cockburn and John Gray were to go to Edinburgh on the following Monday to seek relief from the Regent for the forthcoming raid on Dumfries, scheduled for 1st November.

25th October

Council for the coming year: James Cockburn, John Ayton (younger), John Ayton (elder), John Seton, John Carkettle, Richard Wilson, Robert Nesbit, Adam Quentin, Patrick Hogg, Thomas Sydserf, James Kirkwood.

The Treasurer was instructed to take 200 merks in tax out of the Common Purse because of the great poverty present in the Burgh.

The Treasurer complained that Thomas Cockburn had not paid his customs due. The Provost had recently placed Robert Cockburn and David Forrest in the Tolbooth for the same offence, until next Martinmas.

Malt was to be sold for not more than £4 per boll; under penalty of a £5 fine.

No brewer was to sell ale for more than 8d per pint, until further notice; under penalty of forfeit of a barrel of ale. All bakers were to bake a 4d loaf to weigh 11 ounces; an 8d loaf at 18 ounces; again under penalty of forfeit. No bread was to be taken out of the bakehouse until 7 a.m. and then weighed by the baileys.

17th October

Thomas Ponton, Provost, and john Ayton (younger), John Seton and John Cockburn were to go to Edinburgh to speak to the Regent on the subject of St. Katherine's Chapel and the annual rent due to the Kirk.

22nd November

William Brown reminded the Provost and the Council that an annual rent was due from the Friars, plus two rents due from the Choir, according to Alexander Simpson's protocol.

27th December

John Carkettle, Adam Quentin and John Ayton (younger) were instructed to see Lord Yester about his complaint re Gifford Gate.

John Gray, Treasurer was instructed to pay James Panton £5 immediately and £% before Easter as a financial support because 1577 had been such an expensive year for him.

£20 in alms was awarded to the poor, with a further £20 due at Easter.

Thomas Ponton, Provost, James Cockburn, Robert Byres and John Ayton (elder) were to pass among the townsfolk every quarterday to consider the plight of the poor, and compile a list of names for the Council.

William Tweedie pledged not to molest John Fowler or his assistants in future; under penalty of banishment.

10s was given to John Thomson to cover the expense of riding to Stirling.

1578

7th February

The solemn oath of William Brown, lawful son of the late William Brown, former burgess, was received by the Council, following which he was received as a burgess, for the sum of 11s paid to John Gray, Treasurer. Robert Nesbit stood surety for him, provided that he set down roots in the Burgh as others did. William Brown then relieved Robert Nesbit of his guarantee.

21st February

Robert Henryson, of Tranent, swore, in future, not to buy old green hide, or salt hides, wool or skins in the Burgh on market day, under a penalty of forfeit of goods, unless he bought from a freeman.

Nungate travellers were required to pay a fee, as per usual custom and practice.

Al drapers were to pay a fee, as per usual custom and practice. The Treasurer would inspect the cloth.

19th March

John Gray, Treasurer, was instructed to pay Janet Hathaway £20 for the loan of her tapestry, which was used as decoration for the Council House at the time of the Justice Circuit Court, held in the Burgh in 1573, and for all the other claims arising from the demise of the late

Thomas Cumming, one time Schoolmaster in the Burgh, made upon the Provost, Council etc.

25th April

Lucas Wilson was appointed to be Reader of the Common Prayers during the daytime, and to serve as assistant Schoolmaster for six months, commencing at Beltane. He was to be paid 25 merks, i.e. 12 merks 6/8d per quarter, plus 4d per child.

20th May

David Forrest swore on oath and was made a burgess for 10 merks, payable in two terms, with 5 merks payable immediately and 5 merks on St. Angelus' day. Paul Lyle was to stand surety. A testimonial was required showing that his father and mother were married, following which a refund of 10 merks would be granted by the Treasurer.

27th May

The Setting of Customs, Firlots and Pecks for the Burgh of Haddington.

The Beer Market and Oat Market would be set up for one person to have 31 firlots to serve.

The Wheat Market and Pea Market would be set up for one person to have 6 firlots and 4 pecks.

The Mealmarket and Saltmarket would be set up for one burgess to have 3 firlots and 16 pecks.

Each firlot and peck would carry a distinguishing mark so that each trader would know his own.

If any firlot was altered, the trader would be punished.

Firlots and pecks would not be set up according to any trader's wish; under penalty of a fine of 11s, payable on the day of the market.

No burgess, baker or maltster shall loan their firlot to anyone else for their own use, so that they might defraud customers; under penalty of an 11s fine.

The firlots and pecks used by the Saltmarket and the Mealmarket were set up by Patrick Getgood's wife, for a fee of 10 merks, payable at Martinmas and WhitSunday, with John Gray standing surety for payment.

The 31 firlots of the Beer and Oats markets were set up by Thomas Blackburn, for a fee of 11 merks, payable at the aforesaid times. Should anyone wish to see them, they would be required to pay a surety to John Story of 22/4d.

6 firlots and 4 pecks for the Wheat and Pea markets were set up by Thomas Miller for 9 merks, payable at the aforesaid times, Surety was stood by Robert Cockburn and Thomas Miller, conjointly.

A pint of ale was to be sold for no more than 12d per pint.

10th June

John Gray, Treasurer, was instructed to give10 merks to James Panton, Schoolmaster, as financial support in view of the increased cost of living; a half immediately and a half in one month's time.

Townsfolk were summoned to St. Lawrence House at 5 a.m. to mend the gates, together with those at Lydgate and other gates in common use.

1st July

John Ayton (elder) and James Cockburn were instructed to ride to Stirling to the Parliament as Commissioners for the Burgh, and to be there for 15th July.

29th July

John Gray, Treasurer, was instructed to pay expenses to john Ayton and James Cockburn for their trip to Stirling, where they stayed for 20 days, to the sum of £51/6/8d, and for extra expenses incurred 34/6d. Expenses of 11s were also paid to Cuthbert Simpson for conveying the Abbot of Dunfermline across Lambert Moor and over the Merse (a district of Berwickshire lying between the Lammermuirs and the Tweed) to Berwick.

15th August

A nightwatch was ordered to patrol the Tolbooth at the Burgh expense, with another two watchmen on the street, starting this very night at 8 p.m. and lasting until 5 a.m.

The step at the West Gate was to be built up.

3rd September

Henry Chapman was appointed as Kirk Reader and assistant Schoolmaster for six months, starting immediately, for a wage of 25 merks, i.e. 12 merks 6/8d quarterly plus 4d for each child.

7th November

Nicol Clark, alias the Lord of Paddow Hall, was appointed the locksmith and gravedigger for the corpses of the condemned, for £4 p.a., I.e. 20s per quarter.

A boll of malt was to be sold for £3; a pint of wine for 4s.

28th November

The Treasurer was instructed to give as alms one peck of oatmeal per week to Margaret Wilson, and another to Magdalene Brown, to help cure her of her infirmities. A man was to be sent to her to offer medical assistance.

Thomas Wauss was ordered to repair the passage through his close, which was once a common venell to and from the Water of Tyne, according to old custom and practice, and to keep the gates open for anyone to pass through, from 5 a.m. to 9 p.m.; this to be completed within 15 days or else the gate would be demolished.

8th December

James Cockburn was chosen as Commissioner to go to Stirling on 15th January to attend the Convention of Burghs.

19th December

The Treasurer was instructed to pay Andrew Darling, the Beadsman (one employed to pray for others) in the Magdalen Chapel, the sum of £10/12s, in the name of James Ponton, in settlement of a debt, in return for which the said Andrew would discharge him of the debt and refrain from further proceedings.

The Council ordered everyone who kept a muck midden adjacent to the Tolbooth, to remove it within eight days on hearing the handbell, failing which the Treasurer would have them removed.

All burgesses, who currently reside outside the Burgh, were warned that they must reside inside, and were given 11 days to do so, failing which they would forfeit their freedom of the Burgh.

The Treasurer was instructed to distribute £30 among the poor, being the gift of John Ayton (elder), John Gray, James Cockburn, Archibald Kyle, Cuthbert Simpson and Robert Thomson.

No more was to be distributed among the poor until the following Michaelmas.

1579

29th January

All Deacons were advised to convene on the following Wednesday night, to agree on the building of a Schoolhouse, on which agreement was duly reached.

Nicol Mitchell agreed that, if, in future, he disobeyed the Provost, baileys and officials, or caused them an injury, he would surrender his freedom and his burgess-ship.

6th February

John Kerr, Minstrel, confessed to have had two children by Katherine Gray, one a maid of 14 and one a boy of eight. He was ordered to appear at the next daily meeting to receive the Kirk's injunction, failing which he would be banished from the Burgh forever.

23rd February

Provost William Brown, bailey Archibald Kyle, Henry Campbell, William

Wilson, John Hermiston, Robert Thomson and George Liddell, together instructed the Treasurer to obtain limestone, timber and scaffolding as quickly as possible with which to build a Schoolhouse beside the Chapel. Quarry stone was to be brought from Gladsmuir, and work was to start on the following Monday on the building of a slate roof.

13th March

John Yule of Garmilton complained to the Council about Thomas Stevenson, smith, saying that on Saturday, 21st February he openly blasphemed and swore at him in the open market, calling him a false gadabout and attacking him with a dagger to his great alarm. Wherefore he sought redress. The Council advised the plaintiff to attend on the full process of the law. Thomas Stevenson was summoned for the offence, whereupon he asked forgiveness and assured John Yule that he would offend no more under the threat of forfeiting his freedom.

27th March

Alexander Yule swore, on oath, whereupon he was created a burgess; Robert Sinclair stood surety for him. It was agreed that, if he married Alison Quentin he would pay the Treasurer 6 merks; if he did not, he would pay 10 merks for his burgess-ship.

10th April

All councillors were ordered to convene in the Council House when asked to do so; under a penalty for disobeying.

The Provost vowed to wager his person, goods and chattels against the intentions of the Laird of Herdmanston, in defence of the Common Moor of Gladsmuir.

Robert Thomson, representing the Fleshmongers' craft, protested that, if the Council acted against them by denying them their privileges, he would seek legal remedy.

The Treasurer was instructed to collect alms for the relief of prisoners in Africa, and to make it up to 20 merks.

No burgesses or inhabitants of the Burgh were allowed to buy skins or hides outside the Burgh; under a penalty of an 11s fine for each offence, with the added threat of incarceration in the Tolbooth.

5th May

James Cockburn, John Ayton (younger), John Douglas, John Buchanan (for J. Cockburn), Philip Gibson, Alexander Thomson, Adam Wilson, Adam Quentin, Patrick Hume, David Constance, George Ayton, James Wemyss, William Abernethy, James Douglas, William Douglas, Archibald Romanes, James Gray, Robert Panton, John Henderson, Henry Campbell, Robert Byres, Thomas Spottiswood, Thomas Barns, William Thomson (for William Brown, bailey), were all to go on the raid to Hamilton. Each would receive 10s per day and six pounds of powder.

9th May

John Kerr appeared before the Council and was offered 100 merks p.a., payable at, Halloween, Candlemas, Beltane and Lammas, plus 12d per child born in the Burgh, and an assistant who would receive 4d per child, with school and room rent free, with a Reader to assist in the same way as the assistant master did, all at the Burgh's expense, plus another assistant at 4d per child, payable at the usual four terms. This was to be confirmed by the Council before next WhitSunday.

The Treasurer was told to pay £4 expenses to John Kerr, plus wine.

11th May

The Treasurer was instructed to pay £100 out of the Common Purse as the first instalment of a total of £460 (allowing 8.7d for taxes) due as compensation for the raid on Hamilton, and the remainder to be taxed and taken from the burgesses and inhabitants as quickly as possible. The Taxman then set taxes at £79/8/7d.

Patrick Hogg, Henry Campbell, John Gray, Adam Wilson, Robert Nesbit and Paul Lyle were all imprisoned.

4th June

George Spottiswood, Patrick Moneylaws, William Howden, Robert Law, James Oliphant, John Seton and Thomas Aikman all forfeited their 'freedom' forever, because they had not fulfilled their oath that they would set up home in the Burgh; as was to be openly proclaimed by Andrew White, official, at the order of the Provost, Baileys and Council on 7th June at the Market Cross.

19th June

Thomas Ponton, Provost, William Brown and Alexander Thomson, Baileys, John Gray, Treasurer, James Cockburn, Robert Nesbit, John Carkettle, John Ayton (younger), Archibald Kyle and Robert Thomson ordered the Tron weights (stone, ½ stone, ¼ stone, ⅛ stone and one pound) be made of brass, and to be the same as the weights of Lanark, and to be stamped with the Burgh stamp, thus conforming to an Act of the Burghs made at Cupar at the Convention of Estates, held there on the 14th to 17th February and the 28th February 1579, as quickly as possible.

The Treasurer was instructed to pay James Cockburn 10s expenses for delivering the alms collected in the Burgh, for the captives in Africa, plus 7s for a quart of wine.

John Kerr's contract as a Schoolmaster was to be confirmed on 20th June 1579, in the Burgh of Haddington, as agreed by the Provost, Baileys and Council and Deacons, in the name of the whole community and their successors, on the one hand, and John Kerr, resident of St. Andrews on the other. John Kerr was to be the Schoolmaster for three years, commencing on the Feast of Lammas, which John Kerr accepted, to teach the children of the inhabitants of the Burgh, diligently and correctly, in Latin, Moral Virtues etc., as taught in other schools in the Realm; leading by good example as well as in his instruction and doctrine. He was not to be absent for more than three days without special permission. For these duties he would be paid £60 p.a. at the usual terms of year, in equal portions, starting the following Lammas. A sufficient Schoolhouse and room was to be found at the expense of the

Burgh. In addition, John Kerr was to receive, from each child, 4s .a. at the four usual terms, in equal portions. He had to provide an Assistant to maintain good order, at 4d per child, payable at the usual terms. John Kerr was allowed to include children from either within or outwith the Burgh as he pleased. The Reader of the Common Prayers at the Parish Kirk would assist him at the School and would maintain the premises. John Kerr, himself, wrote this contract, and the Common Clerk was to inscribe the names, date and place aforesaid, before witnesses Thomas Waterson, John Baird and divers others.

27th July

The Treasurer was instructed to pay Hugh Tod, for the agreement reached on the raid on Hamilton, the sum of £85/14/4d with £66 coming from the last tax income, and the balance from the Common Purse.

James Cockburn was chosen to ride to Stirling to attend the Convention of Estates to be held on the 4th August, as Commissioner for the Burgh.

Fleshmongers were told to produce their sample within a week so that the Council could see it. In the meantime the Council would taste samples taken from outlying fleshmongers, commonly available to Edinburgh.

14th August

Cuthbert Simpson, Deacon of the Fleshmongers, and Robert Thomson, were ordered to produce their sample, as decreed by an Act of Council, dated 27th July last. They declared they would not, Whereupon the Council stated that henceforth it would be legal for all fleshmongers to butcher meat, sheep, cattle, swine or lambs as they pleased. They could be sold, either as a whole carcass, or just legs or quarters as they chose, but they were not to be cut into small parts or sides; under penalty of forfeiture. They were also to pay a penny to the box, according to old custom and practice.

Robert Thomson, on his own behalf, protested that, if the Council caused any damage to the fleshmongers, by withdrawing privileges given previously, he would seek a remedy in law.

Cuthbert Simpson offered to produce the fleshmongers' sample within eight days.

Because bringing in mutton and beef carcasses to the market for sale, with no hide or skin, was very suspicious, it was ordered that no fleshmonger should do so; under penalty of forfeiture of goods and imprisonment; according to the Act of Parliament and Statutes of the Burgh.

10th September

An official was instructed to go to Edinburgh to order John Wilson, burgess, to appear in the Council House within 48 hours to face charges, or else he would forfeit his 'freemanship'.

13th October

Robert Nesbit was elected Provost, William Brown and Alexander Thomson elected Baileys for the following year.

Councillors' names: Thomas Ponton, John Ayton (younger), James Ramsay, Adam Wilson, James Cockburn, John Wilkie, John Ayton (elder), Thomas Barns, John Carkettle, Thomas Cockburn, John Gray, Adam Howden.

Representing the crafts: Patrick Douglas and Philip Gibson.

Thomas Ponton was granted permission not to attend the Council except when he felt able.

John Stevenson argued that, in the future, the Provost and Baileys should not be tenant farmers of the Mills, or taxmen of small businesses, or partners of the taxmen in the Mills, or Customs officials.

16th October

James Cockburn and William Brown were chosen as Commissioners to Parliament.

23rd October

If any official had cause to impound any land, property or house within the Burgh, or collect any rent or debt, or give out decrees, and are refused entry by the owners or dwellers, they were empowered to break down doors and to force entry.

No maltster was to sell a boll of malt for more than £3/10s. No brewer was to sell a pint of ale for more than 7d; under penalty of an 8s fine and an end to the brewing. There would be an additional fine of 11s for the maltsters, until further notice.

Bakers were required to bake good quality bread in sufficient quantity, being well dried and bearing the bakers' mark. The 4d loaf was to be made available once it had been weighed. The Deacon of the bakers' craft was responsible for the quality of the bread, as required by his position. The Baileys would weigh bread every Saturday morning.

6th November

Shoemakers were not allowed to sell shoes, boots etc., in the marketplace on Saturdays, except between the hours of 11 a.m. and 2 p.m., according to the law of Our Sovereign Lord. However, since this law would cause great distress, it was permitted that all such traders could come to the market at 8 a.m. and stay as long as they pleased.

20th November

The Treasurer was instructed to pay James Cockburn his expenses incurred while attending Parliament for 23 days, William Brown for 13 days and John Thomson for 24 days, at the rate of 5s per day.

The Assistant Schoolmaster was to be paid for boarders, as well as school-children from the Burgh, at 4d per head.

Hugh Mathieson was to be given 20s and told to leave the Burgh within five days.

11th December

All swine were to be removed outwith the Burgh; under penalty of slaughter.

The Treasurer was instructed to pay Alexander Simpson 100 merks, as a reward.

1580

8th January

Robert Nesbit was elected Provost, William Brown as Bailey. John Ayton (elder) and James Cockburn to go to Edinburgh to pursue the action against Dunbar.

3rd February

Three or four honest men were sought, to speak to Robert Young, in a bid to persuade him to be the Burgh agent in all actions pertaining, and to appear before the Lords, especially in the forthcoming action against Dunbar.

John Carkettle and John Wilkie were selected to attend the said actions, together with four others, acting on a week on, week off basis, along with the agent. The Provost, therefore, ordered six to ride, taking with them one, fit child ; all at the Burgh expense.

The Treasurer was instructed to give the Provost £20 to £24, to go to Edinburgh, to spend as he please on the Burgh Advocates etc., and to deliver the Coquet (the distinctive seal of the Customs House) to the Controller.

8th February

Shoemakers were found to be guilty of an offence of collecting box-pennies, from shoemakers who came from outwith the Burgh, on market day and disposing of them contrary to the Act of Parliament. To remedy this fault, it was ordered that, in future, this money would be given to the poor, especially those operating in the same craft.

6th March

Robert Nesbit, Provost, Alexander Thomson, Bailey, John Ayton (elder), John Ayton (younger), James Cockburn, John Wilkie, John Carkettle, Treasurer, all agreed that the four men, or any two of them, as nominated in the Act passed in Glasgow by the judges in the action between the Burgh and Dunbar, should go to Edinburgh to inform the judges there of the decision.

26th May

Elizabeth Mildison on the one hand, and Elizabeth Wilson on the other, agreed that, in future, if either offended the other, then the offender should stand in the iron bridle on three market days, in full view of the entire market.

30th September

In the presence of William Brown, Bailey, Peter Campbell, tinker, agreed that, if he was ever arrested in the Burgh in the company of someone suspected of theft, he would be put to death.

Agnes Anderson agreed that, if she was ever arrested in the Burgh and stood accused, she would be put to death.

Similarly, Andrew Browhouse, Janet Blackadder, Janet Young and John Shiel.

Henry Hepburn of West Saltoun, and Robert Cockburn, his guarantor, were required to pay John Douglas 31/4d for a new pair of boots and a new pair of shoes.

15th June

Robert Nesbit, Provost. William Brown and Alexander Thomson, Baileys.

The case of John Stevenson, introduced by James Cockburn and Alexander Simpson, was deemed to be answerable in law. John and Alexander Henryson appeared before the Council, arguing that this was not a usual day for the administration of justice, and that what had gone before in no way meant that they had committed any crime; nevertheless they were prepared to answer any charges laid by the said John Stevenson or anyone else. The Provost and Baileys proceeded with the case of the alleged slaughter of the late John Stevenson for which his son John was bent on pursuing, arguing that if the judges and Procurator Fiscal refused to place the accused before an Assize, they would be set at liberty, according to the laws of the Realm. He further argued that, if the Provost and Baileys were to set the accused at liberty, then they should be made answerable to him and his supporters, his son John Stevenson, Michael Forrest, Alan Brown and Thomas Stevenson. John Carkettle, Treasurer and Procurator Fiscal, argued that none of these submissions would be allowed to prejudice the accused's liberty. John Stevenson argued that his presence did not stop him from pursuing an action against the said Henrysons anyway, who, for their part, argued that they should be made to stand before the Provost and Baileys who were about to hold an inquest. Therefore, the judges allowed Messrs. John Stevenson, Alexander Brown, Michael Forrest and Thomas Stevenson, to appear in order to accuse John and Alexander Henryson of the alleged slaughter of the late John Stevenson, by open proclamation at the Market Cross. It was argued that the case should not be heard by the Provost and Baileys, since they included relatives and friends of the deceased. Nevertheless a date was fixed for the 12th July by Thomas Steven, Notary Public, for the case to be heard, leaving it up to John Stevenson, the son, if he wished to pursue the case elsewhere. John Stevenson argued that, since the slaughter was committed two months ago, the case should not be delayed for a further three weeks, as suggested. The Henrysons and John Carkettle argued that the Provost and Baileys were competent to judge the case under the new Commission granted by the King's Grace. John Carkettle, therefore, duly summoned John and Alexander Henryson by indictment for the alleged slaughter of the late John Stevenson, and required them to appear before the Assize. The Henrysons nominated Edward Henryson, Harry Balfour, William Hay in Winden, John Provan, John Henderson of Dryden, and Andrew Home of the Laws, as advocates.

Assize: John Douglas, Robert Byres, Paul Lyle, Adam Wache, Andrew Thomson, Patrick Hogg, William Douglas and Archibald Kyle.

The date for the hearing was fixed for 23rd November. The Henrysons disagreed with this delay and asked to be freed.

12th July

John Campbell and Margaret Heron, his wife, were summoned for disobedience and for swearing at the judges, calling them false, common thieves.

The Assize, comprising Cuthbert Simpson, Henry White, John Gilzean, Thomas Thomson, William Nesbit, John Kay, John Storey, Patrick Wood, John Richardson, Robert Anderson, James Wilkie, John Rammache and Thomas Stevenson, found Margaret Heron guilty as charged, but acquitted John Campbell.

13th July

William Purves pursued Alexander Learmont of Whitekirk for not repaying £20 due for healing him of spear wounds to the belly. The latter asked for time to prepare a defence to the charge. 25th October was assigned for the hearing.

20th July

The freedom and Sheriff-ship of Haddington was granted to Adam Brown, Bailey, and Alexander Simpson; the investiture document was to be returned to the Common Chest pending their return from St. Johnstone. They were asked to appear before the Secret Council.

No one from Haddington was allowed to prepare and pack herring at Dunbar harbour, or seek a licence to that effect, without permission; under penalty of surrendering their 'freedom' and thereafter banishment.

28th July

All parents of schoolchildren were asked to provide a daily meal which the assistant master could give to the children. Those who refused would be charged 18d instead.

5th August

John Carkettle, Treasurer, was instructed to go to Stirling on 24th August, to consult the Commissioners about the tax levied on the Burgh by the seamen of Leith.

Thomas Cockburn was summoned for disobeying Thomas Paterson, official, who was acting in the performance of his duties, on 17th August, which show of contempt the said Thomas Cockburn denied. The charge was proved and he was ordered to be detained pending the decision of the judges.

29th August

Thomas Cockburn was found guilty and warned that, if he ever offended again, he would be banished and his goods forfeited to the Burgh.

11th October

James Cockburn was chosen as Provost, and William Brown and Alexander Thomson as Baileys, for the following year.

Council: Robert Nesbit, John Carkettle, John Ayton (elder), Robert Learmont, John Wilkie, Paul Lyle, Thomas Sydserf, Thomas Ponton, Thomas Spottiswood, James Richardson, Adam Quentin and Nicol Marshall.

Craft Deacons: Patrick Hogg and Patrick Wallace.

24th October

Bakers were instructed to bake their 4d loaf, well dried, to weigh 19 ounces; under penalty of a 40s fine.

A boll of malt was to be sold for no more than £3/10s; under penalty of an 1s fine.

Brewers were to sell ale for no more than 7d a pint; under penalty of an 11s fine.

Council members were warned that, if convened, they must appear in the Tolbooth by 11 a.m. All absentees, who did not have permission, would be fined 4s.

All council statutes were to be implemented before the following Council meeting.

All Tron weights were to be regulated.

No staple goods were to be sold on the high road on market day; under penalty of forfeiture.

No half measures were to be used; under penalty of being broken.

No freeman was to attempt to sell any staple goods from a pitch in the gutter, or the water channel adjoining his booth door; under penalty of imprisonment and forfeiture of goods. A bailiff was appointed for this purpose.

Because of the long period of time during which the Cornmarket has operated, causing great upheaval and the law to be broken, it was decided to sell goods in future from a site adjoining the Tolbooth, which would be called the Bearmarket.

4th November

John Carr, Schoolmaster, was to have £10 taken from his rent and 10 merks awarded to him.

The Treasurer was instructed to pay the assistant schoolmaster £5 for the next quarter, and to provide a daily meal for him.

9th December

Burgesses complained of harassment by bakers, claiming that they baked their own bread at home for their own use. It was decided that burgesses could bake their own bread provided that it was only for their own use and in no way infringed bakers' rights.

1581

15th January

Alexander Thomson, Treasurer, was instructed to buy an oat mill and a kyle, containing 12 bolls of oats, before Martinmas. He was also to find a roadmaker to repair all of the roads of the Burgh as needed. He was also to buy timber, lead, stones, lime and sand for repairs to the School and the Schoolmaster's house.

The action pursued by Thomas Wauss against the Sybbo men, would be at the Burgh's expense. Alexander Simpson was instructed to go to Edinburgh for that purpose.

Andrew Main, baker, was summoned for swearing at John Ayton who was carrying out his duties in questioning Main about certain clay found in the Burgh's outlying districts. In answering with many evil words, Main threatened to cleave him with the spade he held in his hand. He confessed, and was ordered to seek forgiveness from the Bailey at the Market Cross, and thence the whole Council's forgiveness. Any further offence would result in his 'freedom' being forfeited, his house demolished and banishment.

Alexander Speir, slater, was instructed to slate and thatch Patrick Hepburn's house.

1582

8th December

The Treasurer was instructed to give 11s as financial support to Archibald Romanes, and to give Alison Cockburn a new cloak. Also £10 to Hugh Chapman, 20s to John Mann's daughter, 10s to Alison Carrick, her mother, provided she handed over a tin basin belonging to the Burgh which she received from Sir William Wilson.

1583

17th June

Present: William Brown, Provost, James Gray, Bailey, Robert Nesbit, Alexander Thomson, Philip Gibson, Adam Veitch, Robert Paterson, James Cockburn.

For the crafts: Robert Thomson and George Liddell.

Deacons: Henry Nesbit, William Cockburn and John Baird.

It was decided to open a Choir School with John Buchan as Choirmaster at 80 merks p.a., commencing at Lammas. He was also required to attend at baptisms and communions as needed. A house would be provided for him.

Neither swine or geese were to be let loose from anyone's property. Any which strayed would be slaughtered legally by whoever found them.

No one was allowed to bring in mown corn by horse at harvest time; under a penalty of 11s.

17th September

Alexander Yule was ordered to be detained in custody for 18 hours, and fed only on bread and water, for denouncing John Baird, official, acting in the execution of his duties, and for drawing his sword to strike him. He was ordered to stand at the Market Cross, holding his sword by the point, and to seek forgiveness from John Baird. Any further offence would result in his banishment, his house demolished, and never to serve as official or burgess in the Burgh any more. This punishment was to be extended to apply to any others who sought to pour contempt on Burgh officials, or to hinder them in the performance of their duties.

Janet Congilton was found guilty of stealing and reselling blue wool, belonging to John Manuel and Harry Burn, son of Patrick Burn, as well as the theft of other men's clothing. She was ordered to be put in the stocks, and then banished forever.

'Unfreemen' were liable to a fine of 11s for practising as burgesses or traders. Burgesses were ordered to show their burgess entry in the Council Book at the next Head Court. Burgess-ships were to be written on parchment, at their own expense, having already received 3s for this purpose. The Treasurer was instructed to buy one for Alexander Howieson and to present it to him as alms.

9th October

Alexander Young, fleshmonger, having sworn an oath, was made burgess for the sum of 20 merks. He paid 10 merks to the Treasurer, the other 10 merks being waived because of his good, quiet conversation and manner.

1584

3rd January

Any disorderly person who drew blood, was to be imprisoned for nine days and nights. Others, including those who slander neighbours, and any who disturb the peace of the Burgh, were to be imprisoned for 24 hours on being found guilty. This action was to be extended to all noisy folk in the streets at night, drunks, those disobeying magistrates, and those breaking the 10 p.m. curfew.

23rd May

Present: John Carkettle, Provost. John Ayton, Bailey. Robert Paterson, Bailey. James Cockburn, Adam Young, William Brown, Patrick Thomson, Paul Lyle, James Gray, Alexander Thomson, Treasurer.

Crafts represented by Philip Gibson, William Cockburn, Henry Nesbit and Thomas Barns.

Adam Millar, cutler, was arrested for twice striking James Reid, Minister, with a sword, thereby drawing blood and causing him injury, which was admitted.

13th October

Alexander Cook, Messenger for Our Sovereign Lord the King, who signed the message together with the Lords of Arran and Thirlestane of the Secret Council at Holyrood, 6th October 1584, which desired that, under accusation of rebellion if refused, the following be chosen as Provost I.e. Francis, Earl Bothwell. James Cockburn and John Seton to be Baileys and William Brown, Treasurer.

The Council: Philip Gibson, John Ayton, Thomas Spottiswood, John Wilson, Thomas Cockburn, James Ayton, John Carkettle, John Wilkie, David Forrest, Andrew Gray.

Crafts: John Douglas and William Swinton.

The above were ordered to accept under penalty of imprisonment. James

Cockburn argued that this was to be a foretaste or precedent of the time to come, and that he hoped that there was no intent to condemn his own term as Provost.

Francis, Earl Bothwell, was made a burgess and freeman of the burgh. He swore an oath to preserve and defend the freedom of the Burgh, and to offer faithful administration in his official duties. Baileys, Treasurer and Council gave their oaths to similar effect.

Having argued that, in order to choose a Deacon, there should be at least seven practising craftsmen, and that the Deacon of the various crafts should be virtuous, peacekeeping, law abiding householders, the Provost and Council appointed the following for the coming year:

William Main for the joiners,

Patrick Vallance for the masons,

James Douglas for the bakers,

Robert Thomson for the flesh mongers,

Robert Byres for the tailors,

John Henderson for the skinners.

They were all duly sworn in. Since there were not sufficient wrights in the Burgh, the above waived the need to appoint a Deacon.

20th November

Present : Earl Bothwell, Provost. James Cockburn, John Seton, Baileys. William Brown, Treasurer. John Wilson, John Carkettle, Philip Gibson, Thomas Spottiswood, John Ayton, Andrew Gray.

Crafts: John Douglas, William Swinton.

Deacons: Robert Byres, James Douglas, John Henderson, William Main, Robert Simpson. Robert Thomson, Deacon of the Fleshmongers, appeared before the Council, pleading that because the Fleshmongers' craft of Edinburgh were granted a statute forbidding 'unfreemen' from practising their craft, then the Burgh of Haddington should do likewise. Saying which he produced a Charter from the late King James V which granted the Fleshmongers of Haddington the same rights as their kindred craftsmen in Edinburgh. After due consideration, The Provost and Council granted the rights claimed by the Fleshmongers, and ordered officials to make this known to all 'unfreemen' in the Burgh.

Alexander Young, Fleshmonger, William Cockburn, baker, and William Straughan, baker, all burgesses of the Burgh, were accused of unseemly behaviour at night by firing a pistol. They were forbidden to do the same in future; under penalty of an 11s fine for a first offence and banishment thereafter. Andrew Gray agreed to act as guarantor for William Cockburn and William Straughan.

1585

19th February

William Maclennan, Minister of Lewis, or so he claimed, was accused of causing an unlawful marriage between James Storey and his beloved, who is a blood relative of his former wife, which is forbidden by law. He was also accused of baptising children born of the supposed marriage. He claimed not to know the names of the couple he had married. He was imprisoned and ordered to be banished from the Burgh thereafter.

13th March

Having regard to the faithful service carried out by the late Mungo Thomson, slater, father of Bernard Thomson, the present slater to the Burgh, the latter was commissioned to carry out work at the following prices: 10s per rood of pointing; for inserting one slate 1d.

27th April

William Brown, Treasurer was instructed to pay £40 to Alexander Simpson as payment for the half tun of wine given to Earl Bothwell by the Burgh last Martinmas.

28th June

David Forrest, (alias Laird Forrest), was accused of striking Thomas

Cockburn's wife, breaking down Thomas Cockburn's gate, and ransacking his house while carrying a sword and bent on slaughter. He was also accused of ridiculing John Seton, Bailey, while in the performance of his duties, and of breaking the Council House window when he was arrested. He confessed, whereupon he was warned that, if he re-offended in future, he would be fined £10, and, for any further offence, relieved of his 'freedom' of the Burgh.

The Treasurer was instructed to erect a wooden gate in Sidegate, exclusively for the Baileys' use in visiting the Mills during the plague. No one else would be allowed to use the gate.

John Sydie, John Waite or any other who lacked land an which to graze cattle, sheep or horses, should not attempt to do so anywhere else; under penalty of banishment. They were each allowed to own one nag, to use in winter only.

Because of the current influx of plague it was ordered that the West Port and the other Ports be placed under a strict watch. Men were appointed for this purpose at 15s per week.

James Stevenson, wright, was arrested and accused of causing distress to John Quentin by nailing his door shut, and also of swearing at the Baileys. He was ordered to be imprisoned and kept in irons for eight days.

10th July

The Baileys, Council and Deacons, concerned that the plague was increasing in intensity every day throughout the Burgh, ordered the market to cease trading in all items, except for wine, for 20 days. No one was allowed to go to Market from any suspect place: under penalty of death. All customs duties were nevertheless to be paid by the following Tuesday.

The Baileys and Council ordered a banquet for the forthcoming Convention of Burghs to be held in Haddington. Alexander Simpson and John Clark were appointed as Commissioners to the said Convention.

29th July

Statute for the plague – four Quartermasters were appointed, for each quarter of the Burgh. Robert Paterson, James Gray, John Wilkie and Willie Main for the West. John Ayton, Patrick Hume, James Ayton and Thomas Wauss for the North East. John Wilson, John Douglas, Thomas Cockburn and James Douglas for the East. Philip Gibson, Richard Wilson, William Wilson and Andrew Gray for the South. None of these men were allowed to leave the Burgh without special permission from the Provost, Baileys and Deacons; under penalty of an 11s fine which would be given to the poor.

Each householder was responsible for himself and his own, from 8 p.m. until 6 a.m.: under penalty of a 30s fine. No one was allowed to cut any corn other than the Burgh's own. If they did they were not to be allowed in again. No carter was allowed to travel to Leith unless he had a quartermaster with him; at his expense plus the hire of the cart. If he refused to be accompanied he would be fined 30s.

A small shed was to be built at each Port for the watchman, with a fire in it and a candle, to provide comfort through the night.

30th August

Act: for those sick with the plague.

William Wilson was ordered to bake bread for the nourishment of the poor wretches put out on the moor, or other parts of the Burgh, at 140 loaves per boll. Twenty gallons of ale were ordered to be brewed, to be distributed in the same way. Every man and woman was to receive one pound of bread and one pot of ale every day. Children would get a half pound of bread.

A watchman was appointed to keep watch over these poor folk.

100 crowns were advanced to Earl Bothwell, as requested in his letter. In case the plague continued, he was granted 500 merks to sustain him; to be taken as rent from the houses in the Burgh, or the Mills at a sasine of eight per cent.

Received from Patrick Congilton, on behalf of Margaret Congilton, his daughter, the sum of 500 merks, as the allowance granted to the same Margaret, from the annual rent received from the sister Mill called the Kirk Mill.

1st September

The Treasurer or Baileys were to collect money from the tenant farmers to sustain the poor in current necessities.

William Brown, Treasurer, was instructed to take 125 merks from the Common Chest, for the poor.

6th October

John and Adam Wilson applied for money to make repairs to the Mills for damage which occurred during the raid on Stirling which lasted for a month. £20 was awarded out of the £29/6/8d claimed.

8th October

Present: James Cockburn and John Seton, Baileys.

Old Council: John Wilson, David Forrest, John Ayton, Thomas Cockburn, Andrew Gray, Philip Gibson, John Carkettle.

For the crafts: John Douglas.

New Council: Richard Wilson, Mungo Geddes, Adam Howden.

For the crafts: Robert Byres and William Wilson.

A short leet of candidates was drawn up for officials for the following year:

Provost: Francis, Earl Bothwell, James Cockburn, John Carkettle.

Baileys: John Ayton, Richard Wilson, John Seton, Philip Gibson, Thomas Cockburn, Thomas Spottiswood.

The following Tuesday was the date set for voting and the choosing of magistrates. In the meantime, a group of four, selected from the above, were to go to Kelso to seek the advice of Earl Bothwell.

The Treasurer was instructed to pay Richard Wilson four days wages so that he could ride to Kelso.

12th October

Cuthbert Aitcheson, Messenger-in-Chief for Our Sovereign Lord the King, appeared to give effect to the following, (under the signature of Our Lord the King and those of Lord Thirlestane and the Justice Clerk, Two Lords of His Majesty's Secret Council, at the castle of Stirling on 9th October).

It was ordered that John Seton, Thomas Spottiswood, Thomas Cockburn, Andrew Gray, Mungo Gillies, Adam Howden, David Forrest, John Wilkie, Robert Paterson, William Brown, William Wilson, William Swinton and Robert Byres were to be appointed as Councillors for the Burgh.

Deacon for the joiners: William Main.

Deacon for the bakers: William Cockburn.

Deacon for the Fleshmongers: Robert Thomson.

Deacon for the Wrights: Lawrence Yule.

Deacon for the tailors: James Kirkwood.

Deacon for the masons: David Coustane.

Deacon for the skinners: Philip Gibson.

Provost: Earl Bothwell.

Baileys: James Cockburn, John Wilkie and Robert Waterson.

Deacons: Thomas Spottiswood, Paul Lyle, Patrick Hume, Andrew Gray, Alexander Thomson.

Treasurer: William Brown.

For the crafts: Thomas Wauss, John Carkettle, John Ayton, William Wilson, Thomas Barns.

Clerk: James Gray.

John Seton, Thomas Cockburn, John Ayton and Thomas Spottiswood declared they would not stand for election and left the Council House.

The remainder agreed with the selection unanimously.

15th October

Bearing in mind the great age and poverty of Patrick Allen, one-time friar, the Treasurer was instructed to provide one of the small, one-roomed houses at the East Port for him.

All Acts and Statutes made previously for the welfare of the Burgh were ratified and approved.

24th October

The Baileys, Council and Deacons chose John Ayton, Alexander Thomson, Paul Lyle, William Wilson, Robert Byres, John Carkettle and James Robertson to be tax assessors and gatherers to enable 24 arquebusiers to be sent to Stirling to join the King's army. £160 was to be raised as a levy. No men could be found to serve as arquebusiers, or soldiers, up to three or four days prior to the raid on Stirling, unless fully paid beforehand, plus one month's victuals as well. Therefore the Treasurer was instructed to gather in as much money as possible from any source.

29th October

Absent: Earl Bothwell, Provost.

Robert Thomson, Fleshmonger, gave £100 in order that 24 arquebusiers could be sent to Stirling to serve in the King' army, in return for the interest on an investment of £12, to be gathered at the usual terms, Whitsunday and Martinmas. The arquebusiers were to be raised as quickly as possible, and were to be given £7 in their hands, with the remainder to be forwarded to them. Captain Thomas Cockburn would lead them.

Complaints were raised that the townsfolk were not taxed in the same way, or to the same amount, as the Provost, Baileys and magistrates. It was agreed to adjust this situation in the near future in view of the poverty in the Burgh, regardless of the fact that those in debt were commonly the most prosperous.

1st November

Hearing that the arquebusiers would not obey Thomas Cockburn, John Wilkie was despatched to follow them as quickly as possible.

8th November

With regard to he plague, which had persisted in the Burgh since 20th August, and the distress caused to Adam Veitch, Patrick Hume and Alexander Thomson, tenant farmers of the Burgh Mills, it was agreed that they should be allowed to waive 40 merks in tax, which would be shown in the accounts by the Treasurer.

William Watson was appointed nightwatchman for the Tolbooth roof, at 10s per week.

27th November

James Cockburn and William Brown were chosen as Commissioners to ride to Linlithgow to the Parliament there.

William Wilson was paid 47s for assisting the poor on the Moor in the time of the plague.

9th December

On realising that there was no possibility of Alexander Simpson surrendering the Burgh books or 'protocols' belonging to the late Thomas Steven, The Baileys were ordered to serve a writ of outlawry on him.

On receipt of Our Lord's missive requiring payment of £30 for non-attendance at the Convention of the Burghs, a letter was sent to John Guthrie requesting this demand be withheld until documents were prepared against John Ayton, who was Commissioner to the said Convention, and in whose default the Burgh was outlawed. January 13th was set as the date when the Treasurer would pay £20.

Alexander Simpson handed over six books, including three 'Court' books, and written scrolls plus one small 'Court' book in his own handwriting, which he swore, on oath, was genuine, having been written at the time of his Clerkship.

Alison Quentin, widow of the late Alexander Yule, who had previously washed all dirty clothing in a cauldron at the time of the plague for £8, agreed to carry on the service provided the money be paid to James Lockhart, in part payment of a small debt. This was agreed.

Mr John Kerr, Schoolmaster, was paid £15 for having served for two years.

1586

8th February

William Walderston, in Spittalrig, paid £6 for three bolls of oats, as promised as restitution for corn eaten by fowl on the Moor, and on Alison Quentin's land at the time of the plague.

12th April

Marion Lindsay, wife of James Cockburn, was hired for one year, to teach the special needs children. She was to be given eating expenses in the same way as Isobel Spence, her predecessor.

William Tait, of Nungate, burgess, claimed he wished to be a burgess so that he might be safe from the King's raids for serving men, as did his customers in Edinburgh. He had worked as a man from the countryside in the Mills, with a room rent-free and no duty payable to the Mill owner. He was now required to pay duty, and his room was no longer rent-free, so his burgess-ship acted to his disadvantage. He asked to be restored to his previous status. The Council said, that if he paid 20 merks for his burgess-ship, they would instruct the tenant farmers not to demand duty, and to restore his room as rent-free.

George Burnhill, cleaner, was paid £6 for month's wages.

Margaret Thomson was given £4 to help her rebuild her house which had fallen down.

Hugh Chapman, Reader, was paid £10 for new clothes.

6th August

The problem of corn which was stolen by children etc., was considered.

An order was passed that anyone arrested for burning peas or beans or stealing corn, would be kept in custody for 18 hours, for a first offence, and banished for any further offence. If the children responsible are not to be found, then their Master or parents would be answerable for them and punished in the same way.

Helen Bell was given an appropriate sum of money for the great honesty she had shown.

In response to an application by James Horn, Henry Nesbit, David Constane and various inhabitants of the Hardgate, Thomas Wauss was instructed to keep his gate to the common venell to the Tyne open from 5 a.m. to 9 p.m. – as per the Act of 17th October 1578.

29th August

Present: Earl Bothwell, Provost. William Brown, Treasurer, James Cockburn, Thomas Wauss, Robert Paterson, Paul Lyle, John Wilkie, John Ayton, Alexander Thomson, Andrew Gray, Patrick Hume, William Wilson.

Deacons: William Main, William Cockburn, David Allen.

Notwithstanding the distress caused by the abuse of the selection system for Provost, Baileys, Councillors and Deacons in previous years, it was decided that none should be allowed to do so in the future: under penalty of forfeiture of 'freedom'.

14th October

Since beer was commonly sold for 4d per pint, no maltster should sell malt for more than £4/10s per boll: under penalty of a £5 fine. Ale was not to be sold for more than 9d per pint and was to be of good quality: under penalty of an 8s fine for a first offence and double that thereafter.

Since a boll of wheat commonly sold for £8, a 4d loaf should weigh 6 ounces while the 6d loaf should weigh 9 ounces and be of good quality: under penalty as aforesaid.

For all bread coming for sale to the market from outside, the 4d loaf should weigh 8 ounces. 'Outside' bread should weigh more than Burgh bread because of its comparative scarcity.

A pound of candles should be sold for no more than 2s for ragwort, and 26d for any other sort: under the aforesaid penalty.

No hawkers should buy any type of daily produce, such as butter, cheese, chickens, soap or eggs. on market days for resale before 7 a.m. No unfreeman was to sell any type of daily produce: under penalty of confiscation.

No inhabitants of the Burgh should harbour, or give lodging to, any person suspected of theft or pilfering: under penalty of replacing the stolen goods or the value thereof. Such people were to be banished forever. No person should buy anything from them without a guarantee, otherwise they would be regarded as having stolen the goods themselves.

No Fleshmonger should bring any type of rotten meat to the market. They must also bring the skin and head of every carcass to the market, according to the Act of Parliament: under the penalty contained in the same Act and confiscation of the goods. All outside Fleshmongers should sell their goods outwith the freedom of the Burgh.

Only burgesses living in the Burgh could buy cattle hides, sheepskins or wool at the market. No one else could sell any staple goods: under penalty of confiscation and imprisonment, pending the decision of the judges.

No one coming to market should secrete any corn, either in a sack or in their arse or mouth: under penalty of confiscation. All corn should be sold only in the market: under the penalties aforesaid.

No staple goods, such as velvet, cambric, canvas or silks, should be sold in the roadway on market days by hawkers, traders and others: under penalty of confiscation. No half measures were to be used: under penalty of having them destroyed and imprisonment for the user.

No freemen merchants should sell staple goods from stalls set up in the gutter: under penalty of confiscation. All merchants' weights should be made of lead or other metals.or else ringed with iron, as per previous Acts of the Burgh.

No freeman should allow any 'unfreeman' to act as a fleshmonger, fishmonger, trader or wool buyer in reselling any merchandise to the distress of the rest of the inhabitants: under penalty of confiscation and imprisonment of offenders.

All Acts so made were to be ratified, proclaimed and implemented.

1587

2nd April

Ten arquebusiers were to be raised at the Burgh's expense, to go on the Dumfries raid, thus satisfying the King's proclamation. £5 was to be given to each man, with more to come as needed. Thomas Cockburn was instructed to go with them; the Treasurer was to reward him accordingly.

The Treasurer was instructed to pay William Hardie £10 because of the great scarcity, and to buy George Wilson one coat, hose and shirt, plus one pair of trousers of grey cloth. These items were to be shown in the accounts. The Treasurer was also instructed to provide as much in the way of alms as possible for all the poor, honest people, including burgesses and their wives, listed.

22nd September

With regard to the cruel situation faced by Thomas Cockburn, Captain, presently poverty stricken, and as a fair reward for good service, the Treasurer was instructed to give him £20, both as financial support and to pay off the barber/surgeon.

The Treasurer was instructed to pay William Peris 20s to cover feu, and the same for Janet Forbes' impounding. He was also to pay Robert Livingston, a poor fellow, 20s as alms.

13th November

In order to counteract the onset of plague, any person from Edinburgh or Leith, or any other suspect place who wanted to stay in the Burgh, had to arrive within 18 hours of permission being granted. Once admitted, they would not be allowed to leave without the permission of the Baileys, and had to have a quartermaster to accompany them, paid for at their own expense. No licence would be given unless an appropriate testimonial was provided by the Provost or Baileys, in their own handwriting, that the part of the Burgh they came from was clean and unsuspected of plague.

1st December

Francis, Earl Bothwell, Provost. John Wilkie, Thoams Cockburn, Thomas Spottiswood, John Carkettle, James Cockburn, William Brown, Paul Lyle, Robert Paterson, Patrick Hume, Andrew Gray, Adam Young.

Deacons: William Swinton, Alexander Young.

Crafts: David Coustane, George Liddell.

James Cockburn, tailor, was chosen to serve as jailer for a year, for 10 merks plus 6d per night for every local in custody and 12d for outsiders. He accepted and gave his oath of loyalty. He was instructed to spend all his time in the Tolbooth, and 'keep the bar' every Court day. He was held responsible for everyone in custody and for the recompense of all who suffered because of any default of his.

11th December

John Carkettle, Treasurer, was instructed to pay masons for building a Port at the southern end of the Burgh, leading to the Mill. He was also to find lime, stone and sand for the purpose, or as the craftsmen requested.

James Carmichael, Minister of God, was due to return to practice as previously. He was formerly accustomed to having his rent paid. The Treasurer was instructed to pay him 20 merks p.a. and he was to find lodgings himself.

Henceforth Commissioners were to be granted 20s per day, for their horses and themselves, in a bid to counter the previous abuse of the system. No one was allowed a boy's wages as an extra anymore. The Treasurer was instructed to keep strict accounts.

1588

28th February

Sundry unmarried and licentious young women, having quit their positions or arrived from other places, had set up house in the Burgh, without any lawful occupation, so that they could live easier and with more freedom than they could while in service. Wherefore they were prone to exercise diverse, ungodly means to sustain themselves, and to offer their bodies to be sold if they could find buyers. This resulted in fewer servants, and the Burgh was full of beggarly whores and harlots, which, it is feared, would eventually destroy all civilisation, and make the townsfolk odious and detestable to all, besides bringing on God's plague on the Burgh for allowing such a disgraceful situation.

Therefore the Baileys, Council and Deacons, both for themselves and everyone else, ordered all such unmarried women to seek service in some honest house before WhitSunday, there to stay and act as a servant for a living. If any was arrested after eight days, having remained in any house alone, or not being in service for any Master, or otherwise had contravened the Act in any way, they would be banished forever. No other active, 'unfree' women should set up house under any pretext, without a special licence, to be produced when asked. If, in future, they allowed their houses to be used by suchlike forbidden persons, excepting lawfully hired servants, especially those found guilty of a notable offence or crime, such as adultery, incest, fornication, theft or suchlike, or keep company with them, knowing that they permitted abuse of their bodies, they would be imprisoned until they pay 11s – to be given to the poor. In order that the action could take effect, any person offering lodging to one of the forbidden persons would be fined £10 and any rent charged would be confiscated. When the forbidden persons were banished, no further imprisonment or impounding of goods would be allowed.

This Act was openly proclaimed through all the streets of the Burgh by the sound of the handbell, so that no one could plead ignorance.

4th October

Present: John Wilkie, Patrick Hume, Thomas Cockburn, Andrew Gray, Thomas Spottiswood, Paul Lyle, John Carkettle, Robert Paterson, William Brown, Richard Wilson, Alexander Thomson, James Cockburn.

New Councillors: James Kirkwood, David Veitch, Henry White.

Crafts: Thomas Barns, George Bain.

Provost leet for the following year: Francis, Earl Bothwell, James Cockburn, Thomas Cockburn.

Bailey leet for the following year: John Wilkie, Thomas Spottiswood, Richard Wilson, Paul Lyle, Philip Gibson, Robert Paterson.

8th October

Provost absent.

Francis, Earl Bothwell, was chosen to be the new Provost. Thomas Spottiswood, Paul Lyle and Robert Paterson were chosen as Baileys. John Wilkie was chosen as Treasurer. Baileys and Treasurer swore an oath of loyalty.

The craft Deacons requested that two honest craftsmen should be allowed on the leet for Baileys. The Council agreed that, in future, this would be allowed but that the Baileys had already been chosen.

One pound of candles, either hard wick or ragwort, should be sold for no more than 26d per pound, and the cotton wool wick for 26d per pound. Every candlemaker in the Burgh should have a Tron scale on which to weigh his candles with brass weights. On every market day he should erect a gallows beside his stall and hang his best quality products on them, and not hold them in his hands as he is prone to do: under penalty of 11s, not refundable.

The Treasurer was instructed to pay the Baileys, in the name of William Brown and Janet Hathaway, his spouse, the sum of £6 which had been spent by My Lord Bothwell and some of the Council last December, plus £14/11/8d for Hercule Stewart's expenses incurred while attending the execution of John Tweedie, Adam Miller and James Lister, as the Burgh representative. The same was to be paid to James Ayton, in the name of the said William Brown and his spouse, as repayment of two judgments amounting to £20.1.8d obtained by the said James Ayton against them for wine etc. The Baileys were obliged to carry out these judgments provided that the money was not spent by them without the consent of the Deacons.

6th December

James Robson, Dirleton, and George Ford, Thorntonloch, were accused of transgressing the Act by selling fish to traders, I.e. five fish to Alexander Aitken who resold them immediately. They were told never to do the same again: under penalty of confiscation of the fish sold by them. The said Alexander Aitken confessed to receiving and reselling fish, which he was found to do regularly. He was forbidden to deal in fish in the future in the market place: under penalty of confiscation of the fish and eight days imprisonment.

John Wilkie, Treasurer, was instructed to pay 100 merks to John Kerr, Schoolmaster, for services rendered as Minister of the Kirk. This sum was to be paid only when the Treasurer felt was the best time to do so.

24th December

The Treasurer was instructed to refund James Carmichael's wife for expenses incurred while preparing a banquet for the occasion of the Kirk visit by Gentlemen and Ministers.

The Treasurer was instructed to pay Alexander Wilson, surgeon, 52s as payment for curing John Smyth.

A vacancy arose for parish Clerk following the death of William Wilson.

John Buchan, Master of the Choir School, was appointed on the same terms as his predecessor.

The Treasurer was instructed to give Patrick Fairlie, of Leith, one boll of oatmeal for his wellbeing.

1589

7th March

Acting on the advice of Earl Bothwell, Provost. It was decreed that whoever took his neighbour's land or property because of envy, thereby causing great distress, and even bloodshed, or created a disturbance by setting half of the Burgh against the other, with magistrates being disregarded, such a person should pay £20 per acre, or have his goods impounded with three days warning; this announcement to be made at the Market Cross and other places so that none could plead ignorance.

11th March

Andrew White and Bernard Tweedie, officers, proclaimed the Land Act (see above) from the Market Cross, in the presence of Paul Lyle and Thomas Spottiswood, Baileys, with Gilbert Henderson and William Abernethy, officers, serving as witnesses.

10th November

William Brown, John Ayton and Philip Gibson, Baileys, fixed the customs dues of multures (a duty consisting of a portion of grain payable to millowners), perks going to the miller's assistant, payment for mills, the grist gained from the mill haughs, and customs firlots, following the Act of 13th October 1581.

After the handbell was rung in all the streets of the Burgh, burgesses and freemen were warned that customs dues were to be set at the appointed hour of 1 p.m. Granted to David Veitch and C. Johnston of the West and East Mills, was the duty paid to the millowner/tenant, the perquisite paid to the miller's assistant, the bond to a particular mill, payment for the use of a mill, dams, watergates, etc., for one year, starting at 12 noon, 11th November. Messrs Veitch and Johnston, together with Douglas and John Bartram, burgesses, acting as guarantors, should pay 1425 merks to the Treasurer, I.e. 100 merks in his hand now, and the remainder in regular payments as agreed.

12th December

William Brown, John Ayton and Philip Gibson, Baileys, received the solemn oath of William Ayton, glazier, son of William Ayton, mason, whereupon he was made a burgess of the Burgh for the sum of 20 merks, of which 5 merks was waived, and the rest paid to the Treasurer, or allowed as tax paid in return for glazing the Kirk windows. He agreed to set up home in the Burgh, or else to relinquish his 'freedom'.

Mungo Geddes was chosen to sit on the Council until Michaelmas as a replacement for Philip Gibson who had departed this mortal life.

1590

9th January

Robert Kyle, Deacon of bakers, appeared before the Council, along with John Bain, William Cockburn and John Hogg, bakers, complaining of those who falsely baked and sold flour, cakes and bread, to the detriment of all bakers in terms of quality, weight and impurities. They sought a remedy from the Council, who decreed that, in future, all bread, loaves, etc… should conform to the bread of Edinburgh in all things.

The Deacon was instructed to inspect bread in the market place. No one but freemen bakers were allowed to bake bread etc., under penalty of an 18s fine for everyone without exception conforming to the statutes passed in Edinburgh.

14th April

The arable land of Gladsmuir was to be tilled, harrowed and sewn at the Burgh's expense. The cost of the corn to be grown would be borne by the Common Purse; the cost of horses would be shared by the whole Burgh, and every inhabitant would contribute to the wages of the workforce. All ploughmen's harrows would be borrowed, and every man who owned a horse would be required to loan it. Every man who did not own a horse would instead pay 6/8d. Every horse would be fitted with a plough and would be in use for a day.

1st October

Present: William Brown, Andrew Gray, Alexander Thomson, Paul Lyle, Treasurer, Mungo Geddes, Thomas Spottiswood, James Kirkwood, Adam Veitch and John Wilkie.

Deacons: Henry Thomson, Robert Anderson, John Hay, James Horn, Thomas Stevenson.

Crafts: Robert Byres.

£2000 was awarded by the King's Controller – to be invested so that it might produce £200 profit.

Paul Lyle, John Wilkie, Andrew Gray and James Gray were appointed as Commissioners to go to Edinburgh to receive the said sum.

4th October

The Council convened to receive £2000 from the King's Controller, who retained £100. £1900 was to be distributed as follows: the Treasurer was instructed to accept, as recompense for unpaid annual rents, 500 merks. James Cockburn was to receive 350 merks as recompense for unpaid annual Mill rents of 13 merks. 2000 merks remained untouched. James Cockburn was to receive 500 merks, with 100 merks each going to Paul Lyle, Thomas Spottiswood, James Ayton, John Henderson, Andrew Gray, Robert Paterson, Adam Veitch, David Veitch, Henry White and Robert Anderson, burgesses. Each amount was to be registered in the Council Book, and each recipient was to give sasine of their lands or properties for an annual rent of £10, beginning at Martinmas. The terms of sasine were to be reviewed in case of any further demands from the King, with six months or less, if more annual charges were placed on the Burgh. No redemption was allowed without a charge being levied, but the redemption could be suspended for seven years. All recipients were obliged to find surety.

16th October

Because of the disorder and fraud associated with candlemakers in their use of weights etc., without regard to conscience or punishment, it was ordered that they should remove their market stalls to the west end of the Tron. The Treasurer was ordered to provide steel weights with brass edges for one quarter, one half, one pound and two pound for weighing candles at the Tron every market day by the Customs Officer, who would receive 4d per day from each freeman for carrying out his duty, plus 8d from each 'unfreeman'. Each candlemaker was to have a set of weights in his house to match, and no other would be allowed. None of them were allowed to set up a stall or sell candles in the old or new market: under penalty of an 11s fine.

Tanners of hides and leather were instructed to remove the horns of the beast upon purchase; under penalty of confiscation of all hides and leather.

1592

12th January

James Cockburn, Provost. Robert Paterson and Robert Byres, Baileys.

The solemn oath of James Weir, tailor, was received, following which hae was made a burgess. He was told to serve for three years, by displaying his cloth patterns between 4 a.m. and 8 p.m. throughout the Burgh; under penalty of a 2s fine. He was allowed one cloth garment or the rent of a house by the Treasurer.

7th March

John Buchan, Master of the Choir School, pleaded for recognition of his services, and, especially, with regard to the offence he had committed by slandering the Council. He claimed he had spoken inadvisedly in grief, and asked to be pardoned. He asked for his stipend and associated benefits.

25th April

The Council removed John Buchan from the post of Schoolmaster, and instructed the Treasurer to pay 11 merks to his creditors. John Ayton added £3.

With regard to the frequent disturbances and bloodshed in the Burgh, which caused great disquiet to others, it was decreed that, in future, any-one causing trouble in the Burgh would be fined 11s. Anyone convicted of bloodshed would be fined £10. This would not apply to burgesses except in the committing of a felony.

9th August

Merchants requested that they should be granted a Dean of Guild. This was agreed.

George Sprot, son of the late Richard Sprot of Jedburgh, was appointed Doctor to the School. He was also required to lead the Psalms in the Kirk for one year, beginning at Hallowmass. He was to serve under John Callender, Master of the Grammar School, in teaching all the school-children. He was to be paid 50 merks at the usual terms i.e. Hallowmass, Candlemass, Beltane and Lammas, in equal portions. William Henderson stood surety for him.

20th October

David Veitch, Patrick Vallance, James Horn and Bernard Brown, burgesses, were summoned to answer charges of taking cornmeal and malt, which did not belong to them, from the Gimmer Mills, on their horses, as well as preparing malt for sale outside of the Burgh, and sending the same to the Mills to be ground, and thus hindering the working at the Common Mills. In doing so, they broke the oaths they had made as burgesses. James Horn and Bernard Brown confesses to sending malt to the Gimmer Mills to be ground. This, and was found to be against the common good, and contrary to the duties of burgesses. The accused were told to remove themselves from any association with the Mills before Martinmas: under penalty of forfeiting their 'freedom'.

1593

25th October

The disquiet, caused by 'unfreemen' practising as if they were freemen of the Burgh, was voiced, especially with regard to maltsters who, it was alleged, bought their beer from others and sold it at a profit, becoming, on the one hand, the equal of freemen, and on the other, makers of malt for profit, selling it as if it was their own. It was decreed that no 'unfreemen' would be allowed to practise any of the freemen's privileges: under penalty of having their property impounded, and booths, barns and other trading places, houses and the dues thereof, surrendered.

6th November

The tenant farmers of the Common Corn Mills complained that certain persons in the summer season laid their lint to be dyed at the back of the weir, and covered it with weir stones. This practice was declared unlawful: under penalty of an 11s fine and the lint confiscated.

24th December

William Purves, barber and surgeon, burgess, produced a document he claimed was prepared by the Council, dated 10th July 1581, showing 11 merks stipend to be paid annually at WhitSunday and Martinmas, in equal portions, so long as he remained in the Burgh. He complained that he was forbidden to cure James Hislop, a good man injured in the Burgh's cause, which he claimed was contrary to the law. Therefore he renounced the law and was prepared to forfeit last year's pay.

The Provost, Council and Deacons, bearing in mind the age and long-standing in the Burgh of William Purves, as well as his action in refusing 10 merks, nevertheless instructed the Treasurer to pay him an annual stipend of 10 merks at Martinmas and WhitSunday in equal portions in future, so long as the said William dwelt within the Burgh and kept both house and shop there to practise his craft for all townsfolk at reasonable prices. He would be required to attend any person in the Burgh who was hurt, or had a disease, or had a leg or arm or any other member broken – subject to the discretion and further modification proposed by the Council.

1594

2nd October

Harry Burn was chosen to be locksmith to the Burgh, and to act as grave-digger for all those executed for crimes. The Treasurer was instructed to pay him 11s expenses and £6 p.a. fee plus 10s for each person executed that had to be buried.

23rd November

Patrick Campbell, Deacon of masons, Daniel Cockburn, Deacon of wrights and Bernard Brown were summoned to answer a complaint laid by the Baileys. Thomas Nemo accused them of striking him on the hand, causing blood to flow, although he had never caused them any offence, he being a simple, pure man willing to live in peace. Daniel Cockburn was accused of striking him in the face with a knife, after which the accused trio refused to be detained, but continued to pour contempt on Thomas Nemo and the Court officials. Daniel Cockburn admitted the offence, and placed himself at the mercy of the Court, but Patrick Campbell and Bernard Brown denied all charges. Because no words of remorse were uttered by the accused, nor any offer made to make amends, they were told that, if they continued to act in such a way until the next Council day, judgment would be made against them and sentence pronounced as the judges thought fit.

29th November

Present: William Seton, Provost. John Wilson, Thomas Cockburn, Baileys. Andrew Gray, William Swinton, Henry White, Paul Lyle, George Slaith, John Wilkie, Robert Paterson, Patrick Home, William Main.

Deacons: William Cockburn, Alexander Thomson, David Allen, Henry Thomson, Robert Bailey.

Alexander Simpson, burgess, was accused of being in the possession of the letters of Our Sovereign Lord the King, and thereby causing a change in the last craft representative elections. He had named Robert Oliphant to be Provost, Himself to be Bailey, and others to be councillors and magistrates. He had obtained the documents by giving false information, acting contrary to the freedom and liberty of the Burgh, as granted by Our Sovereign and his predecessors. Therefore, in violating his oath of burgess-ship and falsely seeking office, he had acted against the common good of the Burgh. Alexander Simpson confessed, but obstinately upheld his right to act as he did, saying he would do it again if need be, and others would have done the same, naming Philip Gibson as one. He was unanimously found guilty and thereupon revoked his further opinion, saying he would not do the same again.

Sentence was deferred pending further legal advice.

7th December

Officials were denied promotion, or any increase in wages, but were allowed an advance on wages as had been awarded to officials previously, when it was granted for extraordinary service in keeping watch on witches, for which one boll of victuals was awarded ,which the current officials claimed was now their annual right.

1595

7th January

Because of the abuse and contempt now shown towards magistrates and other Court Officers by certain people, it was decided to apply he following penalties: £10 for a first offence committed against a magistrate, £20 for a second offence, and, for each further offence, a doubling of the fine. For any other member of the Court, a 10 merks fine would be imposed which would be doubled for each successive offence.

Thomas Richardson, son of the late Thomas Richardson, was accused of abuse, slandering and blaspheming against James Kirkwood and William Swinton, Baileys. He confessed and placed himself at the mercy of the Court. He was cautioned and told never to repeat the offence, or to hinder officers in the performance of their duties, or he would incur the full penalty.

1596

20th May

Some burgesses openly criticised and showed contempt towards magistrates and Court officers, saying they lacked authority and were prone to commit similar offences themselves. Any person committing similar offences in future by showing contempt, or breaking wind or suchlike, would be put in irons. Any person who sought to defend the transgressor would be treated likewise. This Act was to be made public throughout the Burgh by ringing the handbell, so that no one could plead ignorance.

21st July

From propositions put to them at the time of the Kirk visit on 20th July about finding a second Minister, bearing in mind that Hugh Chapman, the Reader, was old and frail and unable to carry out his duties any more, it was decided that the work could be done by two Ministers. Therefore, James Carmichael and a second Minister would remain at the Kirk to perform their daily service, and parishioners would be approached to make up a stipend for a second Minister. No Reader was to be appointed in future, and no glebe, house or manse would be needed, or any claim to such made on the Council by a second Minister. His stipend would be borne by the parish rents, amounting to 100 merks.

James Currie, gunmaker, was made a burgess, having sworn of loyal service to the Burgh.

1st September

No one was allowed to bring in sheaves of corn to the Burgh, and mix it with other corn, either their own or someone else's; under penalty of a 40s fine. Only corn brought in on carts was to be allowed. Anyone who stole corn would be branded on the forehead and banished forever.

With regard to the slaughter of swine found in other men's cornfields, none were to be set at liberty until the corn was cut. This Act was also to be applied to geese.

8th October

The Treasurer was instructed to buy six or seven stone of powder for the arquebusiers; the Provost to pay for one third and the other two thirds to be laid at the Burgh's expense.

1597

9th August

Plague having been found in various parts of the Realm, no one was allowed to travel to the Merse, Teviotdale, Leith or any other suspect place, except under licence granted by the Provost or the Council. Those so licenced had to report on the place they had visited or come from. Those who failed to do so would not be permitted to enter the Burgh or stay there in future.

No vagabonds or beggars would be allowed to enter the Burgh, but instead would be kept outside: under penalty of branding and burning.

No one was to accept pledges from strangers or madmen. Any that offered such would be punished at the discretion of the judges.

26th August

The Provost, Baileys, Deacons and Quartermasters, who had been elected to keep order during the time of the plague, ordered that, which ever magistrate refused to carry out his official duties in the meantime would pay 6/8d.

Suspect houses were not to be visited without a Baileys' licence, otherwise, he who did so, would not be allowed to visit the Burgh again.

No stranger from a suspect place was to be allowed into the Burgh without a licence granted by the whole Council and magistrates. If admitted, they were to stay indoors for 20 days. Those who wished to return again were to gain a new licence.

One man, from each of the quarters of the Burgh, had to visit every house every morning, to see if any were ill. All sick persons had to be reported to the magistrates; under penalty of death.

A weekly Council meeting, requiring six or more to constitute a quorum, was to be held to determine how to keep the Burgh free from the plague.

5th September

Whoever fired a pistol or arquebus, either from indoors or at their gate, between the hours of 8.p.m. and 6 a.m., would pay 10 merks, and the householder 10 merks also. Any others accompanying would also pay 10 merks.

5th November

The Burgh, which was without either walls or ditches, had suffered great unrest by the theft of cattle, horses etc. In the time of plague it was impossible to keep, out strangers and suspect persons. Therefore it was concluded that the Burgh should again be enclosed by a substantial wall.

2nd December

Sir William Seton was chosen to be the Commissioner to Parliament. James Gray was to go with him to pay lawyers' fees and to seek advice on the dispute with Lord Lindsay. He was also to purchase a customs levy agreement, and a document for the walling of the Burgh.

1598

14th April

William Straughan, burgess, was chosen as town crier for one year at the same fee as previously.

He was to call out the hour between 4 a.m. and 8 p.m. every day through the Burgh. For every day that he failed to do so, weather permitting, he would be fined 11s. William Cockburn, baker, stood surety for him.

23rd May

James Carmichael, Minister, was to travel to see the King, and the Officer to the Burghs, and other nobles, to seek support for the repairing of the Burgh, which was partly burnt down on 18th May. Thomas Spottiswood and Paul Lyle would ride with the Minister and Provost.

12th June

Sir William Seton of Kylesmuir, and Andrew Gray received the oath of James Carmichael, Minister of God's Word at the Parish Kirk, and made him a burgess.

4th September

Patrick Storey, skinner, stood accused of striking Harry Barn, locksmith, for which he was detained by the Baileys, at which he expressed great contempt, saying, before all those assembled in the market place, that the plague was as nothing compared to what would soon happen to the Burgh - meaning the burning of the Burgh last May. He confessed, and what he had said was verified and proven. The judges and Council were informed that he was the son of the late Marion, a known arsonist, who was burnt at the stake for this and other crimes. He was referred to the Minister of Session to be tried for the offence.

13th October

Thomas Cockburn, Provost. Alexander Seton, Bailey. John Wilson, Andrew Gray, Adam Veitch, George Cockburn, William Burn, Paul Lyle, Gilbert Edington, John Lyle, John Wilkie, Richard Chaplin, Robert Paterson, Daniel Cockburn, William Cockburn, Treasurer.

Deacons: Cuthbert Sadler, Andrew Painston.

No malt was to be sold for more than 10 merks per boll, since beer was commonly sold for £5/8/4d per boll; under penalty of a £5 fine.

No ale was to be sold for more than 12d per pint, either inside or out: under penalty of 11s per offence, plus it was to be of reasonable quality or the brewing would be stopped.

A 12d loaf had to weigh 11 ounces, and be made as per rules applying in other burghs; under penalty of a £5 fine and the batch of bread destroyed. Bread from outside had to weigh 16 ounces, and be sold for 12d.

One pound of candles was to be sold for no more than 32d; under penalty of an 11s fine.

It was understood that fleshmongers from outside the Burgh had been free to slay animals within the Burgh, and keep a lot of meat etc., in booths, and take some to market. It was ordered that all meat etc., must be taken to market, and not kept in booths: under penalty of confiscation.

Because the shoemakers' box was collected weekly, one Deacon and one official were to undertake the task in the absence of freemen of the craft, and then given to the Council for distribution.

Shoemakers were ordered to set out their shoes for sale each market day at 10 a.m.; under penalty of an 11s fine for a first offence.

18th October

No merchants were to open booths at prayer time on Sundays or weekdays. No idlers were to hang around the Gate at prayer time. Each household, of more than three persons, should have at least one at prayers; under penalty of 12d for a first offence and double for any repeat offence.

Each was to keep a ladder and bucket in case of fire; each ladder to be the height of the house and to be in readiness: under penalty of a £4 fine.

1st December

James Bowie was hired to ring the bells at prayers, preaching and Sessions. He was also to bury the corpses of the dead in graves seven feet deep. He was never to be found drunk, but to behave properly at work. He was also to dig graves for those executed. If he was found to be at fault, he would be first put in irons and then banished. He was to have the same fees as John Graham, his predecessor.

Because of the fear of fire, no one was to light fires near to the bridge pillars, under the excuse of washing or for any other pretence; under penalty of a fine of 11s per offence.

8th December

Henry White, Treasurer, provided the names of those to whom the sum of £1027, sent by Edinburgh Council as a collection raised because of the Burgh fire for those who had their house and property burnt last May. The sum was distributed among the following:

Katherine Cowan, widow of the late Patrick Vallance, mason, and her son	£60
David Veitch	£80
Beatrix Main, widow of the late George Ayton	£80
Janet Allen, widow of the late John Carkettle (elder)	£60
Helen Dunlop, widow of the late Mungo Geddes	£51
John Sydserf	£41
Adam Veitch	£40
Thomas Blackburn	£6
William Swinton	£50
James Cockburn	£11
Paul Lyle	£50
Patrick Campbell	£41
Adam Forrest	£30
Alexander Thomson (elder)	£30
Thomas Barns	£31
Patrick Miller	£20
Janet Fairlie, widow of the late Thomas Steven	£30
Patrick Hume	£30
Marion Cockburn, widow of John Carkettle, now Alex Simpson's spouse	£15
Patrick Young	£20
John Lyle	£20
Alexander Henderson	£20
Richard Spottiswood	£10
John Storey	£20
Gillis Douglas, widow of the late Thomas Sydserf	£10
George Simpson	£10
Thomas Guthrie	£10
Robert Hamill	£10

Daniel Cockburn	£10
William Lauder	£10
Isabel Darling, widow of the late William White	£10
Jane Haliburton	£8
Thomas Stevenson	£5
Patrick Thomson	£10
James Kerr	£10
Lewis Sadler	50s
George Robertson	50s

The money to be spent by each person solely for the purpose of restoring their property. Alexander Henderson stood surety for Patrick Hume to the extent of providing timber and other necessities for repairing four houses in Crossgate.

John Simpson stood surety for Marion Cockburn and Alexander Simpson, her spouse, for the sum of £20 for timber etc., for repairing the tenement and house of the late John Carkettle.

Everyone expressed themselves as well satisfied with the outcome.

1599

12th January

Nicol Brown, sadler, was accused of slandering Alexander Seton, Bailey, when William Cockburn, his godfather, was arrested; upon which the said Nicol Brown spoke recklessly and angrily in disdain of the Bailey. He was warned as to his future conduct, and told that any further act of contempt could result in his banishment.

6th April

William Walker, in Dunbar, and Robert Walker in Whittinghame, traders, entered into an agreement with the Council I.e. to supply 25 firlots of fine Danzig lint before WhitSunday; to be held, waterfree, in containers, with iron girders for support, for one year. William Arnot, town smith, would inspect them. The Treasurer was to pay 11s for each firlot.

The Treasurer was instructed to pay Cuthbert Stoddart £20 for his trouble in mending the bells; making an entirely new nut and spindle etc., and guaranteeing them for life, and for maintaining the bells.

13th June

Firlots have been broken into by traders and others at the Market Gate, to the great distress of the townsfolk. The west end of the Market, which was the most used spot for the sale of corn, was now in disrepair, with all stalls, booths etc., fallen down. Therefore 24 firlots, for the oats and beer market, will be placed to the east of Robert Thomson's gable end. Anything which is placed to the east of that spot would incur a fine of £10. This rule is to apply until next Martinmas. Sales are to carry on for one day only at the west end, but must be gathered in at night; under penalty of a £10 fine for each offence.

Only 2d was to be taken for rent for each firlot bag.

None of the wheat market firlots were to be mixed with oats or beer; Under Penalty of a £10 fine per offence.

25th June

Because of the controversy which might arise at the carrying of the Burgh flag at the general muster or the riding of the moor, it was decided that one merchant would carry it one day, one craftsman the next, one commoner the next and, thereafter, day and day about. Each would be chosen the previous day by the Council. Because Patrick Brown bore it on the last day of the last riding, William Swinton, sadler, would bear it on the first day.

22nd November

Malt was to be sold for no more than 7d per boll.

Ale was to be sold for no more than 14d per pint.

A 12d loaf must weigh 14 ounces.

William Lauder, burgess, was accused of disobeying the Baileys on last Saturday after he had struck Harry Burn and been arrested by Hector

Cabell. He dismissed the charge with contempt and ran away. He later confessed and asked for mercy. He was told not to repeat the offence, and was then discharged. Any further would result in him being fined double the amount and then deprived of his burgess-ship.

The Treasurer was instructed to have six packs made for the beer and oats market.

1600

18th January

Present: Thomas Cockburn, Provost. Hector Campbell, William Swinton, Baileys. James Kirkwood (elder), William Cockburn, merchant, James Kirkwood (younger), Alexander Seton, Paul Lyle, Andrew Gray, Henry White, George Cockburn, John Wilkie, William Gibson.

John Cockburn, wright, was accused of drawing his dagger at Henry White, proposing to stab him, having already stabbed William Campbell and been confined in the Tolbooth. He was fined £10 and detained until the fine was paid. He was warned that any repetition of the crime would lead to the fine being doubled.

4th June

James Kirkwood (elder) was chosen to be the Commissioner to attend the Convention of Burghs to be held at Kinghorn, as well as the Convention of Estates at Edinburgh this month.

10th July

The distress to neighbours caused by masons etc., in building houses with outside stairs, pillars, extensions etc., and, in so doing, breaking windows, doors chimneys etc., was considered by the Council. To effect a remedy, it was decided that, in future, no mason should undertake any of this type of work without first advising the Council, and being given a licence to proceed; under penalty of conceding their 'freedom'.

It was ordered that the Mylds Burn should be cleaned out from one end to the other. Each landowner, owning adjoining property, was to clean their own section; under penalty of an 11s fine.

The solemn oath of John Lauder of Tyninghame, son of the late Captain Robert Lauder, was received, whereupon he was made a burgess of the Burgh for 20 merks, paid to the Treasurer and subject to the following conditions: he was to bring his entire home and family to the Burgh by next Martinmas, and not leave thereafter; under penalty of forfeit of his 'freedom' and burgess-ship. James Kirkwood stood surety for him.

18th October

The Treasurer was instructed to give Jane Haliburton, teacher to the children with special needs, one grey/black garment on condition that she did not pass any bills on to the Burgh in future, and that she stayed away from David Ogill.

Problems arose when burgess-ships were granted free of charge, either by soliciting Gentlemen or being granted free burgess-ship by the Council. It often caused discord, nor were those appointed as loyal as they should have been. Therefore, in future, all burgess-ships would have to be paid for, and pledges made never to act prejudicially to the office of burgess.

1601

9th February

An account was rendered of the sums of money gathered in the Burgh by the neighbours of those who suffered as a result of the fire of 18th May 1598.

Alexander Seton received from the Commissioner for Aberdeen at the Linlithgow Convention – 60 merks.

James Kirkwood (elder) received from the Commissioner for Kinghorn – £20

He also received, from the Commissioner for Dunbar – £20, and from the Dunbar Ministry £10 which was given to George Maclaren for his trouble in writing to presbyteries etc., seeking financial support.

Andrew Gray had received from Perth – £10, from Dunfermline – £20, from Culross – £10, from Kirkcaldy – 11 merks 3/10d, and from Ayr – 50 merks.

Total (not including the Aberdeen amount) – £121/17/2d

Expenses incurred by Alexander Seton and James Winrames (agent) – £51/8/5d

Expenses so far received – 32 merks.

James Carmichael and his son Nathaniel had received 316 from Linlithgow plus £10/5s from Gullane.

There were also various items received by the Council from Alexander Seton, James Kirkwood and Andrew Gray amounting to £303/12/1d.

The Council ordered the money to be distributed amongst those, who received nothing from the previous Edinburgh contribution, equally according to their need. Andrew Gray, Thomas Spottiswood, James Kirkwood and George Slake agreed to carry out the task.

16th February

The Treasurer was instructed to have a new causeway made, stretching from Lord Home's place westwards to John Black's and to provide the workmen and equipment for the purpose.

24th April

It was ordered that Lydgate be repaired between Herdmanflat and the Butts; all relevant landowners were to be advised.

27th April

David Forrest, Abraham Wauss, Alexander Simpson, John Simpson, Daniel Cockburn, Patrick Brown, Henry Thomson, William Black, William Main, Nicol Brown, plus divers others, appeared, as ordered to repair the Lydgate.

23rd June

No unfreemen or women were to practice any freeman's trade within the Burgh in selling merchandise, baking, brewing, maltmaking etc.; under penalty of a £10 fine.

23rd December

Since the Council were required to provide corslets (a cuirass to cover the body) which were not readily available, £60 was provided to buy some, putting aside some for the use of the Burgh, along with pikes and other equipment.

In order to counter the abuse of expenses charged whilst going on the Burgh's business, it was ordered that no expenses be allowed except as follows: to the Provost for the daily hire of horse and boy – 11s. If no boy was available – 33/4d. For each Commissioner going to Edinburgh etc., – 33/4d. If travelling no more than 10 miles and returning home at night – 20s per day. To the Treasurer for riding to Broxmouth Quarry for mill-stones – 13/4d per day. To Aberlady for timber – 10s per day. To the miller who accompanied him – 10s per day. No other expenses were allowed.

1602

20th February

Because fears of the plague were increasing daily in the area, it was ordered that each person owning property that had a top storey should have them extended to take in people within eight days: under penalty of an 11s fine for each offence.

Quartermasters were to be chosen and watchmen placed at each Port, day and night. No creel men, fishermen etc., were allowed to travel to Edinburgh without permission.

1st July

It was ordered that, whoever brought timber or other merchandise from Aberlady harbour, or the road leading to it, would have the goods confiscated by the Treasurer, the guilty party punished and his good passed over to a freeman.

House at Gifford Gate

Chapter 4

Reign of King James I and VI
Part II
1603 to 1625

Throughout his reign, both while he stayed in Scotland and later when he ruled from his London palace, James was beset with financial and religious problems which were never entirely overcome despite his best efforts. He did establish a more direct relationship between central government and the regions and strove unceasingly for a new quest for order. He brought the authority of sheriffs beneath the scrutiny of central law courts and Privy Council for the first time. All told the Convention of Royal Burghs met for a total of 87 times between 1600 and 1625, and, even when he had moved south, an agent was sent to London as a representative.

Money, however, was desperately needed to run the country. Burgesses, lairds, lawyers and feuars of Kirk lands were the first, and hardest, hit by taxes. In 1621 a tax of five per cent was levied on annual rents which brought in a further £230,000 per annum.

James dealt even-handedly with the problems of his two domains, England and Scotland. There was a fair representation of Scots in appointments to the court, Privy Council and Knights of the Garter despite restricting himself to only one trip back north in 1617. But English suspicions abounded in Parliament about the perceived Scottish threat to markets, where fears of cheap Scottish goods were never overcome. Nor was there any reprieve in the Scottish Parliament. They feared being turned into a mere province, fit to be ruled by a Viceroy as was the case in Ireland.

The Border area became the 'middle shires' of the realm. A Joint

Border Commission was established in 1605 and sat for four years before deciding that the shires were quiet and all could go home. In 1609 they were recalled.

For the first time, subjects of the King were declared to be 'natural born' and as such, could purchase land and bring actions before the courts. However, James' efforts to resolve religious differences were not so successful or well received. James believed in a Common Church but his Five Articles (private baptism, private communion, confirmation by bishops, observance of holy days and kneeling at communion) proved very unpopular.

The reign ended in economic and social crisis. Harvest failures in the 1620s and an overall fall in trade, allied to English suspicion that Scottish goods would flood the market, meant that there was little appetite among either populace for a union of the two countries.

During all this time, Haddington did send a representative to the Convention of Royal Burghs. Local issues, however, predominated in the Council records, among which efforts to combat the spread of plague, the proliferation of beggars, vagrants and the like, and measures to improve buildings in the Burgh, were regular features.

Even though James spent the bulk of his time in England, his agents in Scotland were keeping a close, maybe even envious, eye on Haddington. The success of the many markets there attracted a lot of attention, not all of it welcome. Beggars, idlers, ladies of ill repute, flooded into the Burgh in the hope of finding easy pickings. The Council was frequently at its wits' end to know what to do with all of these people. Nor was the King's agent averse to taking unearned and 'illegal' (according to the Haddington Burgh Council) profits from the Crossgate markets.

The problem did not stop there. There was also unwanted and unwelcome interference in the election of Provost and other officials in the form of messages delivered by the King's Messenger, stating, in plain terms, who was to be chosen.

Nevertheless, King James was made very welcome on his visit to the Burgh in 1617 and everyone went to some length to demonstrate their loyalty.

Having finally achieved some form of agreement with the powers in Edinburgh, the Burgh was then attacked from an entirely unexpected direction in December 1622. No less than the Earl of Melrose, made aware of the possibilities in this town to the immediate north, laid claim to the Moor of Gladsmuir. Only subtle and protracted negotiations enabled the Burgh to escape his clutches, by achieving a settlement which gave the Earl that part of the Moor which contained the coalpits – which had always been unprofitable, any way!

Haddington Burgh Council Records
1603 to 1625

1603

9th February

Philip Gibson and Alexander Thomson, skinner burgesses, were confined in the Tolbooth for non-payment of taxes, and for expressing contempt and pouring derision on the Council, to all of which they confessed. It was ordered that they would never be allowed to take any public office in the Burgh again, and that they should continue to remain in custody until their taxes were paid in full.

The plant market was to be sited at the rear of the Smiddy Row.

4th March

John Cockburn, wright, stood accused of crimes committed by him in the Burgh, along with divers others, most recently in injuring John Craik and in fighting William Robson and the Laird of Forton, and latterly in setting upon John Thin – all occurring during 1603. On 25th February when apprehended by officers, he struck them and afterwards drew a dagger at Patrick Brown, Bailey, and would not obey commands to desist. Afterwards, while detained in custody, he broke the locks and the door of the prison with a mattock. He acknowledged all of this to be the truth. He was condemned as an outlaw and ordered to be imprisoned.

6th May

His Majesty's Secret Council complained that there were many rebels etc., residing in the Burgh, and said that, if they were not arrested and banished from the Burgh, they would instal a garrison of troops at the Burgh's expense. Such people were openly residing in the houses of David Day, David Craw, Bessie Liddell, Margaret Ayton and Bernard Brown, who, on being summoned before the Council, were forbidden to house any of the said persons, under threat of detention and loss of livelihood.

John Hogg, Treasurer, was instructed to hire workmen to build one seat at the east end of the Kirk, with a stair. He was also to provide sufficient timber for the task, all at the Burgh's expense.

8th June

Daniel, James and Laurence Cockburn, wrights, were hired to build one seat at the east end of the Kirk, stretching from the one already built by them at the north-east end of the Kirk, southwards to the southernmost pillar within the Kirk, with four rails in front to support it and one pair of brass supports fixed to the wall and sealed so that dust and dirt could not enter the Kirk. Each pillar would be three feet wide with three seats each – the two hindmost being raised by one foot and a half more than the third. The four faces of the pillar would be panelled with a fine wainscot, with a moulding covering each two panels, so that the overall effect would be as good as any of the College Kirks of Edinburgh or Leith, with mouldings above and beneath. The front part of the back seats would be covered with fine wooden planks, each moulded as above. Each seat would have a flooring of wooden planks around. One stairway and entry would be made of wood, and the entrance door would be fine oak wrought with panels, bands of wainscot, and with turned pillars at the top of each seat. Another entry door would be made at the north end for the Provost to enter through. All would be completed by 1st July 1604. All wood would be provided by the wrights, except for the four trees already provided by the Treasurer. The total bill would be £100, payable as follows: the minimum required to be paid for the timber and delivery thereof, to be paid in cash, and the remainder to be paid on completion. If the work was completed to the satisfaction of the Council and Magistrates, a further 50 merks, over and above the £100, would be paid to the wrights.

The southern entry would be a wooden stair, clad in oak.

11th June

No lodging etc., was to be provided for any person coming from a place where plague was suspected, or who was suspected of theft or pilfering: under penalty aforesaid and being banished forever. Nor was anything to be bought from such people, otherwise the buyer would be treated as part and parcel of the theft and treated accordingly.

Daniel Cockburn, James Innes and Lawrence Yule, wrights, agreed to carry out the restoration work in the Kirk to the agreed standards and for the same fee as previously stated.

24th June

Thomas Cockburn was elected Provost. Alexander Seton was chosen to be Commissioner to the Convention of Burghs, due to be held in the Burgh on the 5th July.

4th July

The west haugh was ordered to be ploughed and grassed. No horse was allowed to graze there except the Commissioner's. After this decision was proclaimed throughout the Burgh, following a ringing of the handbell, the ploughing was awarded to Alexander Seton for 10 merks in cash.

26th August

Plague having been found in the Pans and North Berwick, it was ordered that two watchmen be assigned to each Port, night and day. The Burgh was to be divided into quarters. Any person who failed to keep watch was to pay 6/8d. Each householder was ordered to extend his upper rooms to accommodate more people, within eight days; under penalty of a £10 fine. No stranger was to be offered lodging unless the magistrates were advised; under penalty of a £10 fine. All previous Acts, relating to the plague restrictions, were ratified.

6th September

Because of the increase of plague in other places the Council ordered that no one should enter any house where a sick person resided, unless the magistrates were advised. Where death had occurred, no wake was to be allowed. Anyone who entered a house where a plague death had occurred, would be forced to reside there for 15 days.

No inhabitant of the Burgh was to be allowed to go any place suspected of having the plague, or bring any merchandise from there to the Burgh, nor any kind of apples, pears, plums carrots or other fruit or vegetables; under penalty of death.

16th November

The extortion wrought on local inhabitants by Our Sovereign's Lord's lieges in taking extra profits from the Shoemarket, Ironmarket, Clothmarket, Fruitmarket and from shops on the King's Causeway, to which they had no legal right, plus the fact that the profit belongs to the Burgh in the same way as other towns caused great discontent. It was therefore ordered that all stalls etc., on the Crossgate would be destroyed and everyone advised of this on the 21st November. No unfreeman's goods were allowed to be sold, unless ti was some necessity such as a neutered ram. In future, stallholders should have the following duties on stalls: 4d per day for each hurdle in the Shoemarket, 4d per day for each stall in the Clothesmarket and the Buttermarket, 2d per day for each stall in the Iron market and the Fruitmarket.

Each chipman's stall -6/8d p.a.

Each stallholder was to look after his stall as was done previously in all markets.

It was decided that the town drummer and clock keepers' fees would not be paid until the end of the year, so that any poor service give by them could be taken into account.

Alexander Seton, Treasurer, was granted £8/1s which had been spent by him on Minister's dinners in Alexander Simpson's house at the time of the visit to the Kirk.

1604

30th April

Alexander Seton, Treasurer, was instructed to have a silver bell made, weighing 5 ounces, for the Gentlemen's Race.

30th May

Because of the increase in the plague it was ordered that the Ports be manned by honest men; under penalty of a fine of 6/8d for failure to comply with instructions.

No one was to travel to Leith without the leave of the Provost, plus he must take an honest man with him at his own expense.

No one in the Burgh was to take in anyone or anything from Leith; under penalty of death.

No one was to go to the Canongate for merchandise, or to any other suspicious place, without the permission of the magistrates; under the aforesaid penalty.

No one was to come to the Burgh from any suspicious place to sell fish, fruit or fowl, or to buy the same without permission; under the aforesaid penalty.

The Treasurer was instructed to buy shroud cloth of fine, black, French material, or Florentine serge, for both men and women, and it to be edged with black silk, with one half-size of rough cloth for the children – all at the Burgh's expense. The Burgh would fix the price that people would have to pay.

John Cockburn stood accused of many wrongs, injuries, and insults inflicted by him on others within the Burgh, especially the offence of violence on 9th May last. He entered John Anderson's house and struck both his wife and his daughter, then entered that of John Lander, wright, and smashed a pair of brand new wheels with a broad axe. The said John confessed the offence, and submitted to the will of the Court. He was ordered to be detained in custody until he had made due reparation to John Anderson, his wife and daughter, and repaired the wheels. If, in future, he was, in any way to injure or vilify any magistrate, councillor, Treasurer, or member of the Court, or any honest man, he would be automatically detained for 20 days and fined £20 per offence. If he harmed or hurt anyone he would be fined the same amount.

6th September

Alexander Seton, Treasurer, was instructed to provide for Alexander Thomson, traveller, whose house had been destroyed by fire. He was also instructed to provide for the many households, placed in quarantine where the inhabitants were not capable of looking after themselves, provided that they found surety. He was also to buy one boll of cornmeal to distribute amongst the poor, stricken by plague.

If those who were confined indoors, because of suspicions of plague, did not obey at once, they would be sent to live on the Moor, and remain there as if they were infected. In the case of those told to remain indoors and who refused to do so, they would be fined £10, plus £20 for any further offence.

For any magistrate, or official, who an outsider to the Burgh was absent for the three days of the election, there would be a fine of £5.

26th October

No bastard son of a burgess was allowed to become a burgess, or have the benefits accruing thereto, because it was extremely contrary to the laws of the Realm. Any bastard who was inadvertently granted a burgess-ship would pay the same as an outsider to the Burgh.

7th December

Alexander Seton, Treasurer, was instructed to mend the path at St. Lawrence House, whose stonework was provided by Patrick Hepburn. The waterway at the West Port was also to be mended.

1605

15th March

Alexander Seton, Treasurer, was instructed to buy timber for the scaffolding needed for the Kirk steeple as quickly as possible.

11th October

Because of the slowness of the workmen in repairing the Kirk steeple, Richard Wilson was appointed overseer to note how long they worked each day, how many days they were absent, and to report this information to the Council. The Treasurer was instructed to pay him 13/4d per week.

Anyone keeping swine within the Burgh, with enough feed to sustain them, should keep them in bounds when the corn ripened; under penalty of the swine being slaughtered. It would be legal for anyone who found swine in his field to slay them. All inhabitants, possessing dykes and yards, should maintain them in such a way as to ensure that no swine gained access ; under penalty of a £5 fine. Any owner of swine, which intruded on property, would be liable to restore it.

6th December

Since the bell-ringing and clock maintenance in the Burgh had not been kept up, because of the sloth of James Bowie, the incumbent keeper of the clock and bell-ringer, it was decided to find an honest man for the job.

The Treasurer was instructed to rewire the west window of the Kirk.

1606

3rd January

Because of an influx of uncouth beggars arriving from all parts to the Burgh each day, four men were hired by the Court Session to keep them out for a month, at 6/8d per man per week. The Treasurer was instructed to pay half of the men's wages for a month.

In particular, young women were coming into the Burgh who, although to work, instead took up house, with one, two or three of them together, and practised viilainy, whoring and beggary, whereby honest men were deprived of servants, and the gates of the Burgh swarmed with beggars. Although Acts had previously been passed that the women should enter service- under threat of banishment, while those with houses of ill-repute were to be fined 11s per offence, these Acts had not been implemented but had been neglected. Therefore, it was ordered that all able, young women, who were unemployed, should be told to leave the Burgh, or find masters or mistresses before WhitSunday. If they failed to do so, they would be banished. If anyone housed them, except as servants, they would be fined £5, or else themselves banished if they could not pay. All beggars, who were unable to provide for themselves or their children, who had entered the Burgh within the last seven years, should find provision within fourteen days or else leave the Burgh. None of the beggars or women of ill-repute, were to be housed by others, excepting those who were born in the Burgh, or had resided there for thirty five years; under penalty of a £5 fine per offence. Any outsider, who was housed, should be notified to the magistrates and surety found, so that no children would impose any burden on the Burgh; under penalty of a £40 fine.

All of the above was to be published so that none could plead ignorance.

James Maislet, town drummer, would broadcast the same throughout the streets of the Burgh.

11th June

The Treasurer was instructed to build two play areas – one for men and one for children, in such places as would be most convenient, all at the expense of the Burgh.

17th June

Sir William Seton of Kylesmiur, Provost, and Daniel Cockburn, Bailey, acting on the advice of the Council and Deacons, received the solemn oath of a potent and noble Lord John, Viscount of Haddington, Lord Ramsay of Barns, and thereafter made him a burgess for spice and wine.

The solemn oath of Sir William Home of Whitelaw was received, whereupon he was made a burgess for spice and wine.

The solemn oath of Sir Ephraim Witherington of Tuechar was received, whereupon he was made a burgess for spice and wine.

Ditto Sir William Reid of Fennon, Alexander Ramsay, brother of the Viscount of Haddington, and also Andrew Ramsay, his brother.

23rd June

It was ordered that the Moor be ridden and the Marches visited next Monday, with Patrick Edington carrying the Burgh Banner as a craftsman. The Treasurer was instructed to buy gunpowder to distribute among the young men.

The Treasurer was instructed to pay Nicol Brown £10 for mending all of the drums during the preceding year.

5th December

With regard to the complaint about weavers, made by neighbours, in providing very little yarn for cloth, it was decided that the weavers be given the chance to redeem themselves. First Barthel Low, weaver, tried and achieved very good, dry cloth without faults, whereupon it was agreed that he should prepare one weave of fine linen for Elizabeth Sinclair, wife of William Cockburn, which was found to weigh 32 ells, losing only one half pound in the weaving. Another was prepared for Marion Porteous, weighing 25 ells, which lost only one half pound in the weaving, plus one more which lost only twelve ounces out of 26 ells of fine linen.

26th December

Sir William Seton, Provost, Henry Cockburn and Richard Spottiswood, Baileys, Alexander Seton, Henry White, Andrew Gray, Richard Brown, John Lyle, Adam Veitch and George Cockburn – all present.

Great discontent was caused in the Burgh, during the time of the plague, by outsiders entering the Burgh and applying to become burgesses, some by supplication and request, others by payment, albeit it was not known who to believe. Therefore, it was decided that, in future, no burgess would be allowed in from outside unless he could offer surety; under penalty of a fine of £40. Nor would his wife and family be allowed to become a burden on the Burgh in time of sickness, plague, or any other such incidents.

Mr William Bowie, Schoolmaster, complained that a number of people in the Burgh, either out of ignorance or malice, had removed their children from his school, and had instead put them in a school in the Nungate, run by someone called Burnside, in order that they be better taught. It was ordered that no one would be permitted to place their child in the Nungate school, or any other school within one mile of the Burgh school; under penalty of a 40s fine for a first offence, £5 for the next, and banishment forever, plus forfeit of burgess-ship etc., forever thereafter.

1607

30th January

The great hole, called the Hell's Hole, in the East Mill haugh, was to be filled in at the Burgh 's expense.

It was unanimously agreed that, with regard to the pitiful case of Philip Gibson, co-burgess, who was robbed by Spanish pirates at Dunkirk, and his ship and merchandise taken while he was abandoned on dry land with the ship's company without money or clothing, he would be sent £100 by the Treasurer to assist him in his plight.

25th September

Patrick Brown, Bailey, was ordered to ride to Edinburgh to consult the Baileys and Council there with a view to preventing locals bringing any kind of merchandise to sell at the time of the fair. Inhabitants of the Burgh were told not to provide lodging for anyone coming from places suspected of plague; under a £5 penalty plus imprisonment for such people during the time of the fair and thereafter, at the discretion of the judges.

Four able men, not boys, were to be hired during the time of the fair, to man the Ports together with the four already in position; under penalty of a fine of 6/8d for failure to turn up.

The Treasurer was instructed to buy a new gown of grey-black cloth for Richard Wilson, plus a complete outfit for Robert Brown i.e. a jacket of grey-black cloth, a doublet and a pair of black fustian breeches.

26th December

The Council convened with the Deacons – John Hogg, John Vallance, Cuthbert Stoddart, Thomas Lyle, Henry Thomson, James Dawson.

Crafts – Daniel Cockburn, Alexander Speir.

The magistrates were required, according to a document from Our Sovereign Lord, to pay three taxes – a) a second term's payment of 400,000 merks, of which the Burgh was due to pay £211/2/2d – b) another for Dumbarton, to save it from being flooded, for which the Burgh was due to pay 15/9d, and – c) to James Winrame, for looking after certain sums due for the Burgh's affairs, amounting to 1,000 merks, plus £100 out of which the Burgh was due to pay £13/6s. All payments due before Candlemas.

Because of the poverty of the Burgh inhabitants, and because output from the Mills was down and customers were awaiting payment, it was therefore ordered that William Cockburn, Treasurer, would pay as much as possible out of the Common Purse, towards the due taxes.

1608

14th January

A great storm of frost and snow, which had lasted for a long time and was expected to continue, plus the fear of floodwater from the Mills at Mills Burn, Lothburn etc., convinced the Council to warn the whole Burgh to be ready with pikes, mattocks and other tools to break the ice and clear the waterways. The Burgh was to be divided into quarters. Each inhabitant was to be ready as agreed, either personally or by substitute, provided at their own expense. If they failed to do so, they would be fined 6/8d to pay for another man in their place.

24th January

The solemn oath of Richard Scowgill, legitimate son of Patrick Scowgill, tailor, was received, after which he was made a burgess for spice and wine. It was agreed that he would beat his drum through all the Burgh streets from Port to Port every day at 4 a.m. and 8 p.m. plus other times as required, both within and outwith the Burgh, at all proclamations, muster days, riding the Marches of the Moor, King's night, 5th August, 5th November, and at all other festivals etc. If it happened to be wet weather, he was to play the Great Pipe in the same places and at the same times. Should he fail to do so, the Treasurer would retain his fee. He would be expected to maintain the Burgh drums in good order, at his own expense. Patrick Brown and Alexander Speir stood surety for him.

28th March

It was observed that there were a great many of idle men in the Burgh who professed to be workmen without craft or industry. They would not work for honest men even when offered reasonable wages but would demand more, or else would not work at all. Therefore, it was ordered that, if they refused work in future at 4s per day to thresh six firlots, they would be apprehended or banished at the discretion of the magistrates.

Bessie Ayton, spouse to Laurence Sadler who had now left the country, was now in a state of poverty, with several children to support, although herself destitute. The Treasurer was instructed to give her £20 to assist her in her hour of need.

27th April

John Lyle, Treasurer, was told to prepare his accounts. Tenant farmers in the Mills, plus customs payers and others, were warned to pay their dues to the Treasurer straightaway.

An application was made by James Smith of Byres, with regard to his acquisition of a property at the east end of the north side of Crossgate, and on the west side of Strumpet Street, to restore a ruined building, by constructing it more securely, with pillars at the front, similar to George Hepburn's property to the west. He asked permission to erect pillars, and to place a turnpike, or stairway, at the east end, stretching for four feet beyond the present side wall which stands on the east side of his property. After visiting the property, the Council agreed that it was not prejudicial to the Burgh in any way, but instead added to the Burgh's appearance. Therefore licence was granted to proceed.

28th June

Harry Cockburn was chosen to be Commissioner to the Convention of Burghs due to be held in Dumbarton in July.

Patrick Brown was ordered to ride to Edinburgh with the Provost, to seek a release from the Gentleman's Order to alter firlots, and also the order/instruction for a raid on the Isles.

21st July

An Act was passed at the last Convention of Burghs which decreed that no middens were allowed to empty on to causeways, or any muck or filth be seen on the streets in future. Nor were swine allowed to roam the streets; under penalty for any failure on behalf of the Burgh. Therefore it was ordered that no one was allowed to leave muck etc., on the causeways or at the gates of the Burgh, or to place it at night outside doors and closes, but that the same shall be removed and taken away: under penalty of a 6/8d fine for a first offence, 10s the second, 15s the third ad 20s for each offence thereafter. If the magistrates were found to be remiss or negligent in carrying out this requirement, their goods would be impounded. If they complained they would be fined similarly, I.e.11/8d per midden which had not been cleared. If such was not cleared within eight days, the magistrates would be fined 20s per midden. This Act was to take immediate effect. No swine were allowed to roam the streets after 28th July. Harry Burns, locksmith, was instructed to kill any swine found roaming the streets without any further warning being issued. He was allowed to keep the swine carcass, and be paid 40d per swine slain. If he was found to be failing in his duties he would be put in irons and kept there for one hour for each swine running loose.

9th August

Sir William Seton, Provost. Harry Cockburn, Bailey. William Cockburn,

Treasurer. Thomas Spottiswood, John Lyle, Patrick Brown, Andrew Gray, Richard Brown, Henry White, Walter Seton, Daniel Cockburn, Alexander Speir.

Deacons: John Hogg, Henry Thomson and James Dawson.

A great multitude of people, of all ages and from all parts, were now residing in the Burgh, having little or no trading to do, nor any craft or vocation to practice, excepting for casual work. All of which placed a great burden on the Burgh as well as being especially dangerous at times of the plague. At harvest time, when extra workers were needed, these people proved to be very ungrateful, and would neither shear, bind or thresh , or do any other work, even though it paid well. Therefore, it was ordered that, in future, shearers, binders or other farmworkers, resident in the Burgh, should perform their tasks for anyone who lawfully employs them at harvest time, so that the Burgh's corn is sheared and bound. Any refusal to requests to work, properly made, by those who subsequently work for someone outside the Burgh, will mean that they have to pay to the original, potential employer, such wages as were available at the highest rate.

There were also many young and able-bodied people who preferred to spend their time idling, loitering, pilfering, stealing and reaping corn for themselves at harvest time, under the guise of being corn gatherers. Therefore, it was ordered that none of these people would, in future, be allowed to gather corn anywhere in the area at harvest time; under penalty of a 10s fine, payable to the landowner at the first offence; thereafter to be banished forever for any repeat offence.

3rd September

Since it was understood that there was plague in Linton and other places on the north coast of the Forth, it was ordered that no one should go outside the Burgh to work on the land or shear sheep; nor should shearers be allowed in from outside, nor should strangers be allowed in to houses in the Burgh: under penalty of a 40s fine per offence, then banishment and confined at the discretion of the judges. Anyone who found plague was to notify the Magistrates or Quartermasters as quickly as possible: under penalty of death.

11th October

Following His Majesty's instruction that no one, inclined to the Papistry, should be allowed to be Provost, nevertheless Sir William Seton, who was suspected of Papistry, was elected as Provost because of his good record in administering justice and keeping the peace in the Burgh for a good many years, thus failing His Majesty's agreement, and in which case all votes would be null and void and a new election would be called.

12th November

Archibald Bald, Messenger at Arms, in the King' name, charged the Council to choose one of their number to be Provost within six days. Sir William Seton, Thoams Spottiswood and Patrick Brown were placed on a leet. Thomas Spottiswood was chosen as Provost.

Robert Wallace of Preston, or some other craftsman, was to be approached with a view to mending the Burgh Clock, and hanging the bell in the steeple.

The Treasurer was instructed to buy four and a half ells of grey cloth for a coat and breeches for George Richardson, and to have them made for him.

1609

3rd March

Marion Redpath was paid to teach disadvantaged children to read and sew until next Martinmas, on condition that no other schoolmistress was allowed to set up school or teach any of these children. Elizabeth Donaldson, spouse of Andrew Patterson, had been asked to teach the children, on the same terms and conditions before Marion Redpath had been appointed, but had disdainfully refused. She had now set up school with a large number of disadvantaged children, to the great distress of Marion Redpath. Therefore, it was ordered that Elizabeth Donaldson desist, and that no others should have such a school so long as Marion Redpath, or her lawfully appointed successors, were in office; under penalty of a fine of £5 per offence, plus the person sending the child would be deemed an outlaw, or confined in custody at the discretion of the judges.

24th March

Since a large number of outsiders were still attempting to become burgesses, notwithstanding Acts of Parliament which had been passed against 'unfree' traders, and usually got nowhere, but instead became burdens on the Burgh, providing little in the way of revenue, it was ordered that no outsider, having no privilege in either rank or marriage, should be admitted as a burgess unless they paid 100 merks. This would not be applied to craftsmen so rigorously, who would only be required to pay 50 merks at least. Any defaulters would incur a fine of £20.

20th April

The Treasurer was instructed to have a new Pillar of Repentance built, at the west end of the Kirk, to cope with the increasing number of adulterers and fornicators.

15th May

A merchant was sought who could bring back a new Great Bell, weighing at least 400 weight, and who could agree terms with Robert Wallace of Preston to hang it, as well as mending and maintaining the Burgh Clock.

James Kirkwood, Bailey, was instructed to ride to Edinburgh to complain to magistrates and customs officials about the level of customs duties taken from the Burgh.

31st July

Any swine, found running wild, were ordered to be killed. The Treasurer was instructed to buy a Jeddart staff for Harry Burn, with which to slay the swine.

Owners of houses with a top storey, as yet not extended, were ordered to be detained, as per the Acts passed previously.

10th November

The abuse, practiced by women, of smuggling in cornmeal to be sold in the market, was countered by an order allowing them to be detained until they found bail; under penalty of a £10 fine, to be increased at the discretion of the judges. Any further offence would result in an increased fine.

No schools for disadvantaged children were to be allowed, other than that run by the appointed schoolmistress. All those who had such children of 13 or 14 were to send them to learn how to weave, knit or sew buttons etc.; under penalty as contained in the relevant, previously passed Act. If they wished to send them to any other school, they were required to obtain the permission of the magistrates, and to find surety to guarantee that they would not learn how to read or write; under penalty of a £5 fine.

20th November

David Forrest, standing as guarantor for James Borthwick, son of James Borthwick (senior), gave a silver bell to the Council, a prize which had last been won by the said James at the horse races.

1610

2nd February

Henry Cockburn, Provost, was chosen as Commissioner to ride to Edinburgh in order to convene with the Convention of Burghs, assembled by order of His Majesty, to decide what to do about the plea from the Flemings for freedom to fish in Scottish waters.

17th February

George Seton of Northrig requested some men to help work the coal mine at Morham, at which he was presently engaged. This was considered to be a reasonable request since it brought profit to the whole country, especially the Burgh because it was nearby. John Hogg, Treasurer, was ordered to pay £20 as a deposit towards as many men's wages as he could find, so that as much coal as possible could be extracted.

2nd March

The filthy and damnable vices of streetwalking, drunkenness, playing at cards and dice etc., increased daily among young, profane, insolent people, whereupon there follows rioting, swearing, whoredom, harlotry etc., to the dishonour of God and the slander of the whole Burgh. For the most part it was due to those owners of houses which sold wine, ale and beer. It was ordered that no tavern keeper, brewer, wine seller or beer or ale merchant, should, in future, allow people to sit in their establishments to be provided with meat, drink, candles, tables, cards or dice, under any pretence whatsoever, after 9 p.m. in winter and 10 p.m. in summer; under penalty of a £5 fine per person involved in the first instance, and double the penalty thereafter. Similarly any person supplying ale, beer or wine on a Sunday would be fined 11s.

7th May

With regard to the numerous complaints about the stealing of corn and grass in the Burgh, at least partly maliciously and wilfully, by horses eating at night, it was ordered that, if any beast, stallion or mare was caught on the Mill haugh, or on any other man's field, either at night or during the day, until such time as the corn was reaped and sheared, the owner of the beast should pay 40s per beast to the owner of the field.

15th June

Notwithstanding the many Acts passed restricting the movement of swine in the Burgh, including those Acts drawn up by His Majesty's ministers, the problem remained as bad as ever, to the great risk of incurring the displeasure of His Majesty. It was ordered that, in future, no swine would be allowed in the Burgh unless confined to their owner's property and not allowed to roam free, in which the landowner could kill them legally, or trace their owner and charge 11s per offence.

12th July

Marion Redpath, teacher and schoolmistress to disadvantaged children, declared she could no longer earn a reasonable living in her present job, and would therefore leave at Martinmas, which was accepted.

20th July

The Treasurer was instructed to give £16 to a Greek called Constantine Achilles, who carried a testimonial from the Archbishop of Constantinople, and who was captured by the Turks, his lands and goods confiscated and forced to pay a big ransom. A further £8 was donated by the Kirk Session.

26th September

John Wilkie, notary, was accused of showing contempt and the slander of magistrates, and of persuading others to stay with him in the Tolbooth, bringing in pipers to play all night. This was the result of failing to keep the keys away from him. It was ordered that the Tolbooth doors should be locked shut all night as well as all day. No one was to be allowed in, except by permission of the magistrates. John Wilkie was accused of showing contempt towards the magistrates on the 25th, after which he sat up all night in the Tolbooth, along with certain insolent persons, drinking and playing and bringing in Richard Skowgill, piper and drummer, and John Graham, piper, who played all night in the Tolbooth. He was referred to the magistrates for sentencing.

2nd November

The Reverend George, Archbishop of St. Andrews, was made a burgess of the Burgh following his solemn oath. Edward Hepburn of Haugh swore an oath, as did John Hepburn of Cranshaw, Peter Hewitt, Minister of God at Edinburgh, George Blyth, Minister of the Kirk at Holyroodhouse, Charles Lumsden, Minister of the Kirk at Duddingston, James Jardine, Minister of the Kirk at South Ferry, William Douglas of Rathobyres, David Wood, Chamberlain of St. Andrews, Mark Gladstone, burgess of Edinburgh. All were created burgesses of the Burgh.

1st December

Patrick Dunbar, musician, was appointed Master of the Music School for one year, to teach both men and children to sing and play upon virginal, lute, guitar etc. He was also to take up the psalms in the Kirk every Sunday and other days as necessary. He was also to take the Grammar School for Evensong and to teach children to read and write. If Richard Wilson, Reader, was taken ill suddenly then the said Patrick would take over his role each morning, at reading the Psalms etc., and take over entirely in the event of his death. He would be paid a fee of 100 merks plus 50 merks paid by the Kirk Session. payable at the two usual terms in equal portions. Every child, taught to sing, read and write, would pay 30s per quarter, while those who learn to sing and play an instrument would pay £3 per month. Children from outwith the Burgh could also apply to be taught.

10th December

James Thomson, candlemaker, and Archibald Weir, tailor, were accused of sheltering a number of thieves, plus stolen goods, including John Duncan and his young fool of an assistant, Isobel Grant, a whore and harlot, together with two young hussies, Helen Thomson and Janet Young, both common thieves who had been previously branded on the cheeks and shoulders. James Thomson, and his wife Marjorie Trotter, received a flagon stolen from George Simpson (younger), burgess, for which they paid 8s and from which they drank in their house. Archibald Weir admitted receiving one web of linen from Janet Young, belonging to Alexander Adamson in the Nungate, plus one bag of meal taken from John Simpson and one candlestick taken from William Main – all stolen by John Duncan and his companions. For these crimes, which were admitted, the said persons were accused, convicted and condemned. James Thomson and Archibald Weir admitted having the thieves in their house but did not know that any of the items were stolen ; therefore they asked for mercy. They were detained in custody pending the decision of the judges.

1611

25th January

Isobel Douglas, daughter of the late John Douglas, baker, and Barbara Gray, daughter of the late Robert Gray, were accused of receiving from Jane Logan, servant to Thomas Broderston, certain goods stolen from the said Thomas, for which Jane Logan was convicted, having freely confessed, on the 22nd January. The said Isobel confessed that she had received half an ell of linen, plus one English knife with sheath. Barbara confessed to receiving three quarters of an ell of linen, plus some damaged cloth and braid. Isobel Douglas and Margaret Douglas, her sister, confessed that the said Jane Logan, after she was condemned for the theft, scourged through the Burgh, and banished forever, returned that same night and was taken in by Isobel, Margaret and Janet Jackson, their mother, in her house, and stayed there all night. Isobel and Barbara were found guilty, by their own confession, of receiving stolen goods, and were ordered to be placed in the iron bridle and collar for one hour. If they ever re-offended, they would be scourged, banished or other such punishment, according to the degree of seriousness of the offence.

23rd March

The agreement between the Treasurer and Robert Wallace of Preston was ratified, with regard to the new works to be installed in the Burgh clock. The lettering was to be of fine gilt, similar to the clock in Edinburgh, and erected in the same way, and the hands and chains all repaired; all of this work was to be carried out by WhitSunday. Payment would be made out of the Common Purse.

13th June

Harry Cockburn, served as Commissioner for the Burgh at the General Convention of Burghs at Stirling at the beginning of the month, with particular reference to two Acts a) the appointment of a Postmaster and horse and b) the Acts against the purchases of suspensions by magistrates.

Expenses claimed by him amounted to £25, including his man and horse, for attending the Convention, plus two days in Edinburgh.

5th December

George Dick, inhabitant of the Burgh, who had behaved in a mad, fanatical way by committing several highly dangerous acts, including vowing to burn down Alexander Speir's house, was detained in the Tolbooth. On Saturday, he had set his cell on fire to the great alarm of all, and the likelihood of the Tolbooth itself going on fire, or maybe the whole Burgh if God had not intervened. On being released from custody, he continued, maliciously, and in a frenzied manner, to set fire to the roofing peats of Alexander Speir's house.

The Provost, Baileys and Council were not entirely convinced that the said George had done all of these things out of madness. It was thought to be expedient to have a pair of iron bands and keys made, so that he could be confined night and day to stop him from carrying out his evil intentions until he could be placed on trial.

1612

3rd January

James Blackburn and William Abernethy, tax and customs collectors, were found guilty of falsely passing on customs dues from the North Port to John Watson, unfreeman, this being contrary to the law. They were ordered to be detained in custody until they paid the relevant fine, and were forbidden to repeat the offence, either with John Watson or anyone else: under penalty already laid down.

The Treasurer was instructed to pay for the Kirk Bible £10/5/4d (Scots money).

28th February

William Cockburn, Treasurer, was instructed to pay a Gentleman in Fife, (who had a testimonial from several ministers, barons etc.), the sum of £4, with a further 11s. given by the Kirk Session.

The Treasurer was instructed to pay 18s to Richard Brown for two pints of wine – one to go to My Lord Thirlestane, the other to My Lord Burley – by order of the magistrates.

13th March

William Cockburn, Treasurer was instructed to send an unspecified sum to two Scotsmen, one called Francis Dumbarton and the other John Sinclair, merchants, from the town of Stinton in England, who had brought with them a testimonial from certain Justices of the Peace, testifying that they had been rendered destitute by a sudden fire which burned down both of their houses, killing two children, as well as other houses in the town.

The Treasurer was instructed to send to Robert White, traveller, £10 with which to buy a horse.

27th March

Patrick Dunbar, Master of the Choir School, was given 50 merks as stipend for one year, provided that he taught the children sent to him for one hour each day to write and sing. The Kirk Session gave him 25 merks.

The housing for the Clock was ordered to be erected and the Great Bell installed.

The Treasurer was instructed to send £30 to Robert Wallace as promised for making the works of the Clock.

The Treasurer was instructed to send £5 to Richard Brown, given by the magistrates for the Minister of Innerwick, plus £5 expenses for questioning one Grissell Howieson, detained in custody on suspicion of murdering the child of Margaret Alexander.

13th April

George Carkettle, of Over Liberton, swore an oath and was made a burgess, in deference to his late father-in-law, Patrick Brown of Colston.

19th June

The Treasurer was instructed to send £4 to Alexander Thomson, Messenger at Arms, as expenses incurred in fetching Grissell Howieson, suspected of murdering a child by drowning, to which he later confessed to Margaret Alexander from Dunbar.

8th October

Harry Cockburn, Provost. James Kirkwood, William Swinton, Baileys. John Lyle, John Vallance, Robert Spottiswood, Andrew Gray, William Wood, William Cockburn, George Hepburn, James Cockburn, Thomas Blackburn, Gilbert Edington, William Blake.

Deacons: James Cockburn, Daniel Cockburn, James Dawson, Robert Young, Alexander Blackburn.

Thomas Maislet was accused of wrongdoing against George Grier, Minister, by cursing and harassing him and generally misbehaving in the Parish. The said George had reproved the said Thomas for not ringing the bells, or preaching or praying or any of the other duties normally carried out by him, as well as for remaining in the Kirk during the whole of preaching time etc. The answer offered was that the said George was lying, which Thomas continued to argue. He was nevertheless found guilty of the offences and ordered to be put in irons and kept there during the magistrates' pleasure. Thereafter he was to be detained in custody until he had repented by public proclamation at the Kirk and the Market Cross or wherever George Grier decided; thereafter to perform further acts of repentance at the discretion of George Grier. – John Lyle, Treasurer, was instructed to ride to Edinburgh to buy that with which to strengthen the pinnacles of the Tolbooth, and to find brass for a fine weather vane, and to have the work completed.

19th October

James Cowper, a plumber from Dunfermline, was hired to line and strengthen the Tolbooth with lead. Materials for the job were to be bought for 6/8d per stone.

26th October

Harry Cockburn, Provost, was elected Commissioner for the Burgh to attend the Parliament, due to be held at Edinburgh at the month end. Expenses were allowed at the rate of 40s per day, of which £5/12s was owed to the clerks and heralds, with 12s to the doorkeepers. £16 was to be allowed for extraordinary expenses for attending the Convention of Burghs at Arbroath.

It was decided that, in future, wherever a Convention was to be held, no one would be granted expenses of more than 16s per day, but, if a boy were to accompany them, a further 6/8d would be allowed per day, so long as the boy was in attendance.

17th November

Because of the high price and the scarcity of victuals, it was thought that a contribution to the poor might help, especially those who are unable to ask for help for themselves. The Kirk Session would do likewise. The Treasurer would contribute £100 and the Kirk Session the same amount.

1613

25th January

The solemn oath of Francis Lyle was received, whereupon he was made a burgess in the hope that he would be able to help the poor and diseased within the Burgh.

The Treasurer was instructed to send to George Galloway, a student at St. Andrews, £20 to help him buy clothes; he was about to receive his degree and be made a Master.

With regard to the petition submitted by George Grier, Second Minister, who claimed that he had obtained a glebe from the Nungate Kirk, called St. Martin's, standing to the south-east of Nungate, and arranged a removal there at his own expense. Payment was no due to the feu holders and heirs to the Kirk lands in the Parish of Nungate. The glebe itself was to remain the property of the Second Minister forever, until such time as the Nungate had its own Minister, which was not likely in default of a stipend becoming available. He therefore requested relief from some of his expenses. He was advanced £100.

10th February

Harry Cockburn, Provost, was ordered to ride to Edinburgh to confer on the Suspension of Tranent, brought about by an Act of Parliament, which was passed against 'unfree' traders.

Because of the huge problems caused by cattle, swine, horses etc., belonging to those who did not own land, or keep corn, straw or grass with which to feed their animals, it was ordered that the Baileys take a stock check of the animals, so that action may be taken against their owners. In the meantime previous Acts were to be implemented.

Nicol Brown, saddler, was appointed to be th Burgh drummer for six months on the same terms and conditions offered to Richard Skowgill, the previous drummer.

Since it was understood that the drums were in a state of poor repair, lacking the skin for the drumhead, £10 was allocated to mend them.

In consideration for the work done by Alexander Simpson, Evangelical Minister from France, who stayed in the Burgh for a great while teaching God's word, and who, although born in the Burgh, was about to return to France to rejoin his family, it was agreed to acknowledge his efforts with a payment of £35 to cover the cost of the wine etc. he had used.

Also due to be paid for by he Treasurer were certain wines consumed by the Provost and others, including the Laird of Elphinstone, who requested the use of Burgh horses in order to visit the coalpit.

£6/6/8d was given to the Commissioner for Dunbar and North Berwick for attending the meeting of Justices of the Peace, who were discussing weights and measures.

£3/14s was given to James Nisbet, Bailey from Edinburgh, who was travelling to London.

Because of the prejudice widely held in the Burgh on the matter of disbursements or reckless overspending by the magistrates, despite sundry statutes passed to control the problem, it was decided that, in future, special consent of the Council would be required before such expenses would be allowed.

19th February

Henry Cockburn, Provost, Richard Brown and William Swinton, Baileys, received the solemn oath of Alexander Simpson, son and heir to Alexander Simpson (senior), former burgess of the Burgh and Minister of God's Word at Chastedoup in France, and made him a burgess for spice and wine.

2nd July

The Treasurer was instructed to send to David Auchterlonie, Bailey and Commissioner for the Burgh of Arbroath, £20 to go towards repairing the harbour there.

20th August

The Burgh cuirasses and helmets were given to the following for safekeeping: Harry Cockburn, Provost, – one cuirass and helmet. Richard Brown – one cuirass and helmet. They were required to look after them and return them in the same condition when requested.

6th December

Harry Cockburn, Provost, and Patrick Brown, Bailey, were chosen as Commissioners to attend the meeting of the Lords of Secret Council, to respond o the charge laid against the Burgh of not paying Patrick Gordon £600 expenses incurred in the pursuit and apprehension of a German called Stercovins, who had published an infamous libel against the whole Scottish nation in his book.

The Treasurer was instructed to provide William Brown, son of Nicol Brown, drummer to the Muster, one doublet of Lyons cambric, one pair of blue breeches, and one pair of shoes, to wear on his parade around the Burgh beating his drum.

1614

27th January

James Kirkwood, Treasurer, was instructed to give £100 to James Cockburn, Bailey, for his trouble, travel and other expenses, in providing documents for His Majesty's Treasurer relating to the bells promised to the Burgh by My Lord Chamberlain, plus certain other matters relating to the restoration of Aberlady harbour. Also needed was approval to obtain the metal with which to cast the bells, and to carry what was left back to his property.

22nd July

William Cockburn, merchant, was chosen to be Commissioner for Dunbar during the herring fishing, to see that the orders passed at the last meeting of the Commissioners of Burghs were carried out.

The contract, between Our Sovereign Lord's Treasurer and the Provost, Baileys and Council of the Burgh, with regard to the new wine tax of £4, was subscribed to by many magistrates and Councillors, with James Gray, Clerk, being asked to subscribe the names of those who could not write. Patrick Brown was despatched to Edinburgh to see that the subscriptions were registered.

The Treasurer was instructed to send 40s to a Frenchman called Matthew de Bouillon.

11th October

The Baileys of Tranent sent a petition requesting that a causeway be built at the Moor end of their town, next to the late David Seton's property in King Street, thereby affording an easy passage between Edinburgh and Haddington. The Treasurer was instructed to set aside £20 for the building of such a highway in the spring.

4th November

Harry Cockburn, Provost. Patrick Brown, John Lyle, James Cockburn,

Baileys. William Wood, Andrew Gray, Richard Spottiswood, Thomas Blackburn, William Hallens, James Barns, William Cockburn, Walter Seton, James Kirkwood, Thomas Geddes, Thomas Veitch, Patrick Young, John Vallance, James Bartram, William Main, Patrick Hogg, Alexander Gardner, Thomas Anderson.

An Act of 12th July 1613 was ratified whereby the bakers of the Burgh were ordered to remove their seat from the south side of the Kirk because it cut out the light; otherwise the Treasurer was instructed to have it removed.

The two old bells, one the old Knox bell which was broken and the other in good condition, were to be recast as one. William Main, potter, agreed to carry out the task.

Thomas Paterson was appointed for six months to teach children to read and write, at a fee of 6/8d per child per quarter. Children of the poor did not have to pay, for which he was recompensed by the Kirk Session and the Council at the half-year's end.

12th December

John Vallance (younger), complained of being surrounded by bakers on Saturday, 10th December in the evening. He was proceeding quietly to his own house from the house of his uncle, William Vallance (younger), now deceased, when two of the said craft came up to him from behind, one armed with a heavy staff and the other with a dagger, and attacked him, giving him several blows to the head before running off in the dark. He thought them to be John Kyle and William Main, bakers, who had been debarred by the rest of the craft. The two accused confessed, saying it was because the seat had been taken down by John Vallance, who, in their opinion, should have been pre-eminent in stopping this from happening. It was also stated that Walter Hogg and Mark Cockburn were lying in wait on the previous night to carry out a similar attack before James Cockburn returned home, this having been agreed by the four of them. More evidence was heard, following which, by a majority vote, it was found that Patrick Hogg, Deacon, Walter Hogg, Mark Cockburn, David Kyle, John Kyle, John Gray, William Black and

William Main, all bakers, were guilty of the crime committed against John Vallance. They were ordered to be detained in custody, pending a decision on the punishment to be inflicted.

1615

13th January

William Main and John Kyle were ordered to be placed in irons, following which a great number of young men took to parading up and down the streets at night, some armed with swords and some with heavy staves. Injuries were inflicted on passersby, who were not looking for trouble; after which it was ordered by the judges that John Kyle and William Main be forbidden to walk the streets at night, carrying any kind of weapon, unless on legitimate business, or going to and from their own homes. If they disobeyed they would be regarded as vagabonds and treated as such. No one was allowed to parade at night in the streets carrying a weapon, unless on legal business; under penalty of a £5 fine. Also, because of the great unrest caused in the Burgh by taking down the bakers' seat, it was ordered that, in future, no one should slander the magistrates for their action in this matter, or else they would be fined £10.

10th March

The weavers submitted a petition requesting that 'unfreemen' be refused from either bringing in work or taking it outside the Burgh, under a fine which would go to relieve the taxes placed on Burgh weavers. This petition was refused.

24th March

The Silver Bell was to be awarded at the next horse racing at a date yet to be confirmed.

16th June

William Stoddart, cutler, was accused of blasphemy and slander against George Grier, Kirk Minister, and his wife, harassing him and vilifying the magistrates in the course of their duties. On 13th June, the said William came to George Grier's house, in his absence, and called out, in a loud voice, that he was a swine, a bumpkin, a vagabond and other blasphemous words, vowing that he would stab him and kill him, as well as calling his wife a harlot and a whore, all without reasonable cause, excepting the removal of the carpenters' seat, which was carried out with their consent, as well as that of noblemen, barons, gentlemen and others, so that there would be more space in the Kirk. He turned on those who had arrested him and told them to go and hang themselves, in a manner which demonstrated contempt for Our Sovereign Lord, his laws and authority, as well as to his own oath of burgess-ship. He finally confessed, saying that he did not remember what he had said or done. He was ordered to be placed in the stocks at the Cross, as an example to others, and to offer public repentance in the Kirk, and to be detained in custody until he had paid all the fines he had previously incurred.

26th June

Because the gift of powder to arquebusiers on muster days was greatly abused, it was decided that, in future, they should provide powder for themselves, and that none would be paid for by the Burgh.

27th October

The long lasting illness endured by Isabel Fenton, widow of the late John Bain, which had resulted in her being bedridden, was addressed by the Council who instructed the Treasurer to give her 10s per week.

6th November

An action was raised by Edinburgh magistrates against those of the Burgh, preventing them from exacting any further customs dues. James Cockburn was ordered to ride to Edinburgh to consult the magistrates and find surety for the Burgh's release.

9th November

Harry Cockburn, Provost, and Patrick Brown were instructed to ride to Edinburgh to defend the Burgh's action in taking customs dues.

The Treasurer was instructed not to pay any further wages to Harry Burn, locksmith, because of his failure to keep out uncouth beggars.

1616

19th January

Harry Cockburn and Patrick Brown were instructed to store the documents received by them from Edinburgh magistrates, referring to the matter of customs dues, in the Common Chest, and to declare the expenses incurred.

8th March

William Sinclair, bellringer, was accused of breaking into fresh graves, especially that of John Ayton's sister while she was not yet fully decomposed nor fit to be seen, and for interring there the corpses of strangers and outsiders. He was ordered to be placed in the stocks for a full day, and thereafter to be held in custody pending sentence.

25th April

The Provost was chosen to be Commissioner to go to Edinburgh to confer with his counterparts from other Burghs.

20th May

The solemn oaths of John, Viscount Lauderdale, Lord Thirlestane, Thomas Seton of Oliestab, Christopher Cockburn, servant to the noble lord, and Peter Maitland, servant, were received. They were all made burgesses of the Burgh – gratis.

17th June

Harry Cockburn and James Cockburn were chosen as Commissioners to attend the General Convention of Burghs, to be held at Perth on the 1st of July.

24th June

The Provost and Patrick Brown were instructed to ride to Edinburgh to confer with Justices of the Peace about repairing the highways, and to resist, as far as possible, any further burden on the Burgh.

8th July

Harry Cockburn, Provost. Patrick Brown, James Cockburn, Baileys. George Hepburn, James Kirkwood, William Cockburn, Walter Seton, Andrew Gray, James Black, James Vallance.

Deacons: Daniel Cockburn, carpenter. Andrew Paterson, tailor. John Barns, skinner. David Kyle, baker. James Thomson, smith. Thomas Simpson, fleshmonger.

Harry and James Cockburn, Commissioners, reported on the Perth Convention viz: the Burgh was declared to be outlawed from the Convention at Kirkcaldy for failing to pay the tax due on harbours, I.e. Aberlady, which was to go to His Majesty in England.

All Burghs were told to remove the Act, relating to pewter and pewterware makers, from the Statute Book.

Every reel of linen was to measure one half of an ell ; a slip of yarn was to be five quarters length of double yarn and ten quarters length of single yarn.

No private individual was allowed to disregard a decree announced by any magistrate of the Burgh ; under penalty of a fine of £100.

No single Burgh should be allowed to set aside, or buy a suspension from, any Act, decree or ordinance passed by the Burghs at their Convention; under penalty of a £100 fine.

No eggs were to be exported.

22nd July

George Hepburn was elected to the post of Collector of imposts from merchandise, either going in or out, of Aberlady harbour by ship.

The Treasurer was instructed to send £20 to the University of St. Andrews, to help them to replenish their library.

No person, servant, belongings, horses or cattle, were allowed in other men's cornfields; under penalty of an 11s fine per offence.

Nobody was allowed to bring in corn, either cut or pulled, their own or someone else's, under a penalty of a £5 fine per offence for other men's corn, and 40s for their own.

No grass turf was to be cut on the lane leading from St. Lawrence House; under penalty of an 11s fine.

4th September

Thomas Bartilmo, burgess tailor, James Craik of Gullane and George Bartilmo were arrested for the murder of Thomas Bryson, burgess tailor, on 3rd September at 4 p.m. Acting on the advice of James Carmichael and George Grier, Kirk Ministers, the accused were referred for trial.

23rd September

Michaelmas Fair was scheduled for the last Monday in September. Six men were hired to assist the Provost and Baileys. All middens, especially at Crossgate, were to be cleared within the week; under penalty of an 11s fine. No customs duties were to be taken from the Dunbar burgesses during the Fair and immediately afterwards, except for 2d per sheaf of corn and for the Sheriff's gloves.

8th November

The abuse suffered by the customs gathering system was discussed, and it was agreed that it was because the customs officials were, for the most part, unskilled, wilful and indiscreet. It was ordered, therefore, that no one was allowed to defray any customs duties without the express permission of the magistrates ; under penalty of a £5 fine.

A dispute arose between the tax collectors at the Fishmarket and the Crossgate about the taking of profits. It was ordered that all onions, sybies, herbs, turnips, carrots, cabbage etc., and dry fish should be sold in the Fishmarket only, and not in the street outside, or in the Cross gate; under penalty of an 11s fine, with the appropriate customs due being paid to the Fishmarket Tax collectors. Similarly no apples, pears, plums etc., were to be sold in the surrounding streets on Market day, but at the Cross only, with the appropriate customs due being paid to the tax collectors of the Crossgate. This decision was to stand for all time to come.

James Vallance was to be prevented from allowing his water spout, on the west side of his property, from emptying into the street adjoining the Cross to the discomfort of passersby. Wooden spouts were needed to be fixed to his property to prevent dirt and water falling on those beneath; under penalty of a fine of £5.

25th November

Patrick Brown, Treasurer, was instructed to give to John Makmain, cowherd, his fee of 40s to buy a gray coat.

23rd December

James Cockburn, Bailey, was chosen as Commissioner to ride to Edinburgh to appear before the Lords of the Secret Council on 24th December, to reply to their summons re the lodging and stabling to be provided for Englishmen and other strangers next summer.

A response was sought to the petition lodged by Alexander Wallace, George Fraser and Bernard Brown, officials of the Burgh, who were seeking relief from the pledge of £100 lodged by Archibald Smith or David Forrest on behalf of Walter Kerr of Kokillmyln to ensure his secure custody. He had escaped through their negligence, therefore, the magistrates refused to acknowledge their request and ordered them to be detained pending the settlement of the surety.

1617

3rd January

John Young, merchant burgess, accused James Ramsay, burgess, of arriving at his house armed with a sword on Friday, 20th December, then striking at the door to gain entry, and disturbing the peace and quiet of the night time. The said John and his wife, who were in bed at the time, went to the window in time to see the accused attempting to break in, all the while shouting that he would be avenged of the insult to Janet Buncles, his wife. He was charged with this offence, and with disobeying Walter Seton, Bailey, by breaking free and hiding in his own house, thus contravening his own statement made, on oath, voluntarily, on 22nd April 1612. He confessed his guilt, and was ordered to be detained in custody until he could find those prepared to guarantee his good behaviour, pending sentence to be set at the discretion of the magistrates.

William Gibson, William Cockburn and Thomas Veitch were freed from the burden of Councillors' duties, along with James Vallance, lately departed.

8th January

Patrick Brown was instructed to ride to Edinburgh on the morning of 9th January, to appear before the Lords of Secret Council to produce a list of lodgings available for strangers due to arrive with His Majesty.

The Treasurer was instructed to give John Manylaws, son of the late Patrick, £3/12s to help him to buy clothes before he enters service.

The Treasurer was instructed to pay the Tolbooth watchmen 36s for guarding the prisoners held there.

7th February

The Provost and Baileys decided to set free Thomas Bartilmo, burgess tailor, held since 3rd September 1616, for the murder of Thomas Bryson, burgess tailor, on condition that he would never attempt to harm those who gave evidence at his trial, or their families, for a bail set at £100, after which the said Thomas agreed to be banished from the Burgh forever.

Alexander Hogg, legitimate son of John Hogg, baker, was made a burgess.

10th February

Walter Seton, Bailey, was instructed to ride to Edinburgh to seek a warrant for the two thieves who broke down John Richardson's shop door and stole his goods last Christmas. For this crime, John Hogg and Alan Main were held in custody.

Patrick Brown, treasurer, was instructed to give £20 to Tranent to help build a highway to Edinburgh. To this sum was added a further 10 merks.

10th March

Harry Cockburn, Provost, serving as Commissioner at the Convention of Estates held in Edinburgh on 5th March, reported that a voluntary contribution of 300,000 merks had been granted to Our Sovereign Lord, of which the portion due from all of the Burghs amounted to 50,000 merks.

John Mercer, who had set up school to teach children to read and write, was ordered to stop, along with others who sought to do so. Thomas Paterson had been appointed Master of the Grammar School for this purpose. No parents were allowed to send their children to any other school; under penalty of having the school fees remitted to the said Thomas. This order was made public throughout the Burgh, preceded by the sound of the handbell.

25th April

The statute of 8th May 1612 was ratified forbidding the tilling and cultivation of unploughed land and the penalty for disobedience was increased to £10.

The statute of 8th May 1611 was ratified forbidding 'unfreemen' to store goods for sale; under penalty of an 11s fine.

The statute of 7th June 1611 was ratified forbidding the keeping of geese in the Burgh: under a penalty of a £5 fine per offence.

No swine were allowed to roam freely in the highway during the visit of His Majesty.

2nd May

Richard Spottiswood was given permission to reap the grass between Hector Campbell's property to the west of the West Mill, along the north side of the Mill dam, for the entire summer season, at a cost of 20s payable to the Treasurer.

May 8th

Pending the arrival of His Majesty and his company in the week following, a document was presented to the magistrates pledging the provision of meat, drink, lodging and stabling. All victuals, excepting bread, were to be ready for sale in the Burgh, and meat made ready for the entire week. Bakers had made their own arrangements to ensure that sufficient bread was available.

George Fraser, Burgh officer, plus one other, was instructed to wait at the Cross between 3 and 4 p.m. on Market day, to see that good order was maintained, and the 'unfree' sellers of fowl, eggs, butter etc., were arrested and punished.

Three others were to serve as officials to attend magistrates for eight days during the visit of the strangers to the Burgh. £20 was made available to see that they were clothed correctly.

Alexander Henderson was accused of showing contempt towards James Cockburn and James Kirkwood, Baileys, while in the course of their duties, on Sunday, 4th May, which was Communion Day, between the forenoon and afternoon prayers, for detaining his son in custody on a charge of creating a disturbance during morning prayers. The said Alexander disdainfully replied "I don't give a fart whether I am detained or not" claiming that it would be nothing compared to the general envy shown towards him. He was ordered to be kept in custody for 48 hours, and told that, if he ever repeated the offence he would be punished and made to pay a fine.

David Forrest and Elizabeth Nicholson, widow of the late John Skowgill, were accused of ploughing up the common strip of land leading from

Lydgate and the southern end of the strip lying between Herdmanflat and the Earl of Congilton's property, leading to the new North Port, which has always been a common right of way. They agreed to four or five able men being hired at their expense to restore the said strip, and to insert marker stones on either side to separate the said strip from their own land.

19th May

The Treasurer was instructed to have a wooden gate made for the new North Port on the north wall of the Burgh.

Thomas Blackburn, John Hogg, baker, Henry White and John Anderson (elder) were chosen as four able men capable of restoring the strip of land between David Forest's land and Elizabeth Nicholson's, leaving them to decide on the correct width.

4th June

A report was received of a number of local, honest men, travelling through the Straits of Gibraltar to the Mediterranean in John Murton of Leith's ship, who were taken prisoner by the Turks. A voluntary contribution towards their ransom and release was sought, whereupon three Baileys – James Cockburn, James Kirkwood and John Lyle were appointed as collectors.

A request was received from the bakers and woodworkers of the Burgh, to build a seat at the west end of the Kirk, following the Act of Session, 27th May 1617. It was proposed that, if the Burgh would provide two long trees to be placed between the west pillars, and four wainscot pillars to hold up the crossbeams, they would build the gallery to match other galleries and not affect the Samuelston Gallery, all at their own expense. A third part of the gallery was to be dedicated to the Burgh, I.e. James Carmichael and George Grier. The Treasurer was instructed to provide the said four pillars in fir and fix the two joists at the expense of the Burgh.

No malt was to be sold for more than £8 per boll; under penalty of a £5 fine per offence.

No ale was to be sold for more than 16d per pint; under penalty of a 1s fine per offence.

11th July

The Queen's plea, made to all estates of the Realm, to help repair the harbour at Musselburgh, was heard. She has granted that £40 would be paid by the Treasurer for this purpose.

Twenty merks was awarded to William Cockburn, son of the late Thomas Cockburn, as expenses for his journey to Poland.

13th July

Walter Seton, Bailey, complained about John Gray, skinner and burgess, alleging that he spoke contemptuously to him. In return, John Gray complained that Walter Seton had struck him with a heavy staff and arrested him without any justification at all. The case was referred for trial and several witnesses sought, sworn in and admitted. John Gray was absolved of all charges and Walter Seton was deemed to have exceeded his duty.

The solemn oaths of William Ramsay, brother to John, Viscount Haddington, Robert Heriot of Trabroun, Robert Lawson, brother of the late Sir James Lawson of Humbie, and Alan Cockburn of Ormiston, were received, whereupon they were all made burgesses – free of charge.

3rd October

This was the usual day for preparing the leets for Provost and Baileys for the Burgh for the forthcoming year. James Cockburn produced a document from Our Sovereign Lord the King, asking that he should not be chosen as Provost or Bailey, but to excuse him from all duties. The Council took this to represent an intrusion into their freedom of choice, and declined to respond pending further advice.

10th October

James Cockburn appeared in person; his election to Provost was intimated by the magistrates and Council. He willingly accepted notwithstanding Our Sovereign Lord's document, and gave his oath of loyalty.

The Treasurer was instructed to pay James Veitch £10 as expenses incurred while serving as Constable to the Burgh, waiting for the carriages transporting His Majesty home and further afield.

24th October

James Cockburn was chosen as Commissioner to appear at the private Convention of Burghs to be held in Edinburgh on 31st October. He was also to confer with other Commissioners about their grievances felt about the book *God and the King* and about the transporting of merchandise by Scottish shipping.

A warrant was ordered to be issued to him under the Signet and Clerk's signature.

Patrick Brown, Treasurer, was instructed to distribute sums to the poor as follows: John Cockburn, to pay for a horse – 10 merks. Andrew Byres, beadle of the Kirk, £6.

Isobel Mow, widow of the late James Horn, £10 to help put her son to a craft and pay his apprenticeship fee. Bessie Wilson, widow of the late James Alan, 11s. Patrick Kerr, son of the late John Kerr, who worked as a creelman, four ells of white plaiding.

29th October

In response to the intention of the Laird of Preston, having obtained a Burgh of Barony for Preston, to hold a market day every week on a Saturday, and a Fair to be held on the morning after Michaelmas (which would clash with Haddington's dates), the Provost and Patrick Brown were ordered to ride to Edinburgh to consult lawyers about the best way to resolve the situation.

Beer being sold for £6 per barrel meant that no malt should be sold for more than £7 per boll; under penalty of £5 fine.

No ale was to be sold for more than 14d per pint; under penalty of an 11s fine per offence.

A 12d loaf of wheat bread was to weigh 12 ounces; under penalty of a 11s fine.

No candles were to be sold for more than 4s per pound of the best quality; under penalty of an 11s fine.

7th November

It was intimated to the Council that last Michaelmas, Thomas Anderson, tailor, was nominated as Deacon for that craft, whereupon, having previous experience of his behaviour in the past, they found him unsuitable and directed James Cockburn, baker, to inform the said craft, who then appointed James Bald to be Deacon. The said Thomas attempted to usurp the office by public declaration to the craft in the Tolbooth. He was summoned and informed that he was acting in contradiction of an Act of Parliament which forbade the countermanding of the authority of magistrates. Thomas Anderson, plus John Anderson and William Forrest, his supporters, confessed their error, whereupon they were freed on condition that they did not repeat the offence.

26th December

The Treasurer was instructed to provide Thomas Guthrie with six ells of gray cloth to make coat, cloak and breeches.

1618

13th February

The increasing problem of youths breaking down walls in yards and parks, leaving pools of stagnant water and cutting down young trees and shrubs, was considered by the Council. An order was issued that no one, young or old, should behave in this way; under penalty of a £5 fine per offence. Parents, guardians and masters would be made answerable for their children, servants and apprentices. This was to be published and proclaimed following the sound of the handbell through all of the streets of the Burgh, as per the Act of 7th February 1614.

William Sanderson, also known as 'sour Wullie', was arrested and charged as a common disturber of the peace at night, by playing at cards and dice and drinking, expressly contrary to the Burgh statutes, as well as offering a bad example to others. He was a young, insolent youth with little or no zest for work. He duly confessed and was told never to repeat the offences or he would face banishment. He was fined 11s for each offence.

24th April

John Bald, Deacon of tailors, was accused, together with Robert Trotter and Alexander Wallace, of pushing, shoving and abusing Rachel Hepburn in her own house, while pretending to be searching for George Miller, an 'unfreeman' tailor.

They finally confessed the offence and were released pending further consideration of their sentence.

1st May

James Cockburn, Provost. Andrew Gray and George Hepburn, Baileys. Harry Cockburn, Patrick Brown, James Kirkwood, James Dawson, William Cockburn, John Cockburn, Patrick Young, George Spottiswood, James Black, James Bartram, John Barns, Daniel Cockburn present.

Lydgate was ordered to be surveyed and the cobble stones lifted. The Treasurer was instructed to hire a strong, eight oxen plough for this purpose, and to ensure that the gate was made higher and stronger.

15th May

A common muster of troops was called, from freemen and citizens of the Burgh, for the Riding of the Moor, to be held on Monday, 8th June. James Kirkwood (younger) was to carry the banner.

Andrew Byres, Beadle of the Kirk, and Patrick Tait were both ill and bedridden. The Treasurer was instructed to give Andrew Byres £4 and Patrick Tait 11s to assist them in their dire situation.

9th November

It was the time to fix the Customs Rate for the Common Mills, haughs etc., and, following an Act of Parliament, it was also time to fix a uniform rate for corn stacks. Therefore, it was decided that weights, measures and yardsticks should be fixed to conform with Tron weights I.e. the merchant Troy weights and the Scottish weights which were called Tron weights, and should be brought together as one weight e.g. a Troy weight containing 16 Tron pounds to the stone was to be used for all commodities. Persons attempting to counter the system by weighing so-called 'country' goods I.e cheese, wool and butter, with old Tron weights would pay £10 – one half to the magistrates and one half to the Tron tax collectors.

Following the petition of James Carmichael and George Grier, Ministers, for the benefit due to Robert Cunningham, who stood in for them on several occasions, and because Robert Wilson, Reader, could no longer get about in the performance of his duties, it was requested that the said Robert Cunningham may be appointed in his place, and that if the Burgh would pay £20 for six months between WhitSunday and Martinmas, the Kirk Session would also pay £20. James Carmichael would collect 15 merks from each gentleman living outwith the Parish. The Council agreed, provided that Robert Cunningham would read the Chapters and lead prayers

20th November

George Hepburn, Bailey, appeared before the Council having collected from Edinburgh the deeds for St. Lawrence House and copies of the freedom of Dunbar. He claimed that Sir John Seton's action, taken before the production of the deeds, had been unnecessary, and that the Provost of Dunbar had already taken up the issue, promising to redress all wrongs. John Lyle showed two documents, the first referring to an Act written by the Clerk of Dunbar, which for bade them to levy customs duties, the other a copy ofan Act of Burghs made to this effect.

1619

10th June

James Cockburn, Provost. George Hepburn, Andrew Gray, John Vallance, James Kirkwood (elder), Richard Spottiswood, Robert Learmonth, John Cockburn, Patrick Brown, William Cockburn, James Kirkwood (younger), Walter Seton.

Deacons: Daniel Cockburn, John Bald, Thomas Simpson, David Lyle, Alexander Speir.

Crafts: Patrick Hogg, John Barns.

The General Convention of Burghs was due to be held in the Burgh on 6th July. Therefore, in order to be in readiness, the Deacon of bakers was asked to bake good bread and to keep the ovens hot, and the fleshmongers to have freshly slain meat ready daily, and all other victuallers to be prepared. The Treasurer was to provide one barrel of fine ale, with shortbread, for the afternoon drinks each day. All middens to be cleaned and all muck removed from the highway, and no swine to be roaming about; under penalty as laid down in the previous Acts passed for this purpose.

The Treasurer was instructed to give Nicol Brown, drummer, ten merks to wash his own clothes, and also to buy for his son, James Brown, one white pullover, a doublet, one pair of breeches, one shirt and one pair of new shoes.

24th June

The Treasurer complained that, although he was due to pay 500 merks to the Exchequer, he could get nothing out of the tenant farmers. He was told to take 500 merks out of another account while the farmers would be detained pending payment.

2nd July

William Eliot, born in Hawick, appeared before the magistrates, charged with stealing ten sheep from Sir Robert Cockburn of Clerkington and the tenants of Letham, then transporting them to the west of Edinburgh to be sold. He was caught red-handed and confessed. In reaching a verdict the magistrates offered William Eliot the choice of being the Burgh's locksmith and executioner for the rest of his life. He accepted willingly.

19th July

George Hepburn (elder), Bailey, who was chosen as Commissioner to go to the Convention of Burghs at Edinburgh on 12th July, reported on what had transpired, especially in relation to shipping goods out of the country. An Act had been passed that no Scotsman was to trade with four Flemings, named Bartholomew, Martin de Ovine, Maximiliano and Jacob de Klein, for reasons stated within the Act itself.

11th October

Sir Richard Cockburn of Clerkington, Lord Privy Seal, was made a burgess.

12th October

Certain persons had neglected their duties as Councillors in the past, and had therefore been 'put to the Horn' by Our Sovereign Lord. Therefore, it was ordered that anyone denounced as a rebel as 'called to the Horn' would not be allowed to serve in any office in the Burgh.

22nd October

All hides for sale, either by freemen or otherwise, which were found to be like tar leather, would be forfeited. Similarly, sheepskins which were either 'pulled' or 'clipped in the womb', unless they were blooded, would be confiscated; under penalty of a 11s fine per offence.

4th November

James Kirkwood, Treasurer, was instructed to give Thomas Paton, Schoolmaster, 10 merks. He had declared that he could not remain in the Burgh to teach and was therefore allowed to go.

10th November

The Act of 11th October 1605, referring to the building of dykes, was ratified, whereby all citizens owning dykes should maintain in a good state of repair, thus denying access to swine ; under penalty of a £5 fine. Any person, whose corn was eaten, or whose swine were killed because of trespass, would be answerable for the damage caused and vice versa.

17th December

Thomas Maislet, ringer of the Kirk bells, was told not to ring the bells at funerals etc., without the permission of the Provost or one of the Baileys.

1620

7th January

Twenty new firlots were ready for use for measuring quantities of beer, oats or malt, with one level available for all buyers and sellers. A public pronouncement was to be made from the Cross on 8th January whereby no other measure was to be allowed.

A complaint was heard from the townsfolk that the freemen would not allow meat to be cut by 'unfreemen' on a Saturday. Therefore, it was ordered, and made known to Thomas Simpson, Deacon of the Fleshmongers, that, in future, all meat was to be cut up as requested by whomsoever, it being entirely legal for fleshmongers, outwith the Burgh, to do so.

Thomas Maislet was instructed to ring the bells in the Tolbooth to announce prayers, and at all other times as necessary. He was also to maintain the clock in good condition – at a fee of 16 merks p.a. with 8 merks for William Sinclair for ringing the hand bell, plus 11s for making proclamations throughout the Burgh.

The Treasurer was instructed to pay the following sums:

To Janet Russell, Thomas Devine's wife, who was sick	11s
To Nathaniel Weir, long sick and on his deathbed	£3/6s

| To Bernard Brown, sick | 11s |
| To Margaret Douglas, widow of John Kerr | 11s |

William Blake, Deacon of the bakers, was told to produce, before the Council, the gift of their freedom. He produced an Act of Court, drawn up by the late Nicholas Swinton, Notary Public, Common Clerk of the Burgh, dated 3rd December 1550, outlining the rights and duties of bakers as freemen of the Burgh.

2nd February

John Ayton was accused of slandering the Provost, Baileys and Council. He was also a councillor and a burgess who, quite openly, called them all traitors, scoundrels and participants in the murder of the late James Ayton, his uncle. In point of fact, they were all innocent, and he duly confessed his guilt, saying he was drunk at the time. He was ordered to be detained in the Tolbooth, and removed from the Council for the current year.

24th March

The whole Burgh suffered from a lack of bread baked by the craft of bakers, despite them having been publicly admonished for the same fault. William Black, Deacon of the bakers, together with David Kyle, councillor and freeman baker, were told to redress the situation, which they agreed to do.

Nicol Brown, drummer, was accused of not carrying out his duties, by not going through the Burgh daily, and also for allowing the drums to fall into a state of disrepair. He was ordered to be detained until he could find a guarantor for his good behaviour in future, and was given until 4th June to return the drums, whereupon the Treasurer would have them repaired at the Burgh's expense, and the bill passed to Nicol Brown for payment.

19th June

The military review and general muster of the Burgh were to be held on 7th July. All burgesses, freemen and townsfolk were to be warned by the beat of the drum through all the streets. James Kyle was to carry the banner.

The Treasurer was instructed to have Myldsburn cleared of rubbish between the bridge at Thomas Veitch's house to the Water of Tyne beneath Gymmers Mill.

1st July

George Hepburn, Bailey, was chosen as Commissioner to go to the Convention of Burghs at Stirling on 6th August, and to make a contribution towards the repair of Linton bridge.

27th October

On a day in September James Anderson lost all his possessions due to a fire at his house. John Cockburn, Treasurer, was instructed to give him 100 merks, to go towards repairing his house, by using timber from the Burgh.

The Treasurer was instructed to deliver £20 to Christine Veitch, widow of the late David Thomson, candlemaker, as rent for life on his property, which stood adjacent to James Anderson's, which had been burnt down.

10th November

John Cockburn, Treasurer, was instructed to build the pend at the West Port to match that at the East Port as quickly as possible.

Discussion took place about the £20 paid to James Carmichael, Minister, each year for house rent, since he had stopped visiting the sick.

1st December

The danger posed by stacks of heather, broom, whins etc., which was used for fuel, not only to the immediate neighbours but to the whole Burgh should they go on fire, was the subject of discussion. It was decided that, as from 2nd February, there would be no more stacks kept in any vennel, wind or close, or set to stand against any property. It was to be removed and placed in a safe part of the Burgh; under penalty of a £5 fine. Every property owner was to have a stout, long ladder ready for use in case of an emergency; under penalty of a £5 fine.

1621

8th January

The Treasurer produced a Commission document referring to the taxing of wine, dated 20th July 1620, granted by the Earl of Mar, Treasurer of the Realm, Sir Gideon Murray of Elybank, deputy knight, giving full powers to the authorities in the Burgh to impose a £4 tax on each tun of wine sold in Haddington for five years.

Richard Spottiswood was accused of showing contempt towards James Kirkwood (elder) and John Vallance, Baileys, by first disobeying them by running away to his own house after being arrested for a disturbance between himself and Thomas Hastie on 5th January. On being taken to the Tolbooth, he again swore at the Provost , and avowed he was as good a man as James Kirkwood, or any other Kirkwood in Scotland, and that the Secret Council should hear of his arrest. He also assisted his son Robert Spottiswood to avoid capture the same night. He finally confessed he had done wrong, but swore his innocence of any other offence of which he was accused. He was found guilty on all counts, ordered to be held in custody, his son to be returned to custody, and to pay a fine of 20 merks. Any further offence would result in a fine of £11.

14th March

The bell, announcing the start of the horse-racing, was to be rung on Saturday, 15th March, with a race due to be held on 16th April. The Treasurer was instructed to have a velvet saddle made, with a silk, golden fringe, which was to be the prize at stake.

20th March

The Treasurer was instructed to pay the fee of John Purves, surgeon, for mending the broken leg of John Ramsay, son of James Ramsay.

The Treasurer was instructed to give Henrietta Geddes, his wife, £3 in support, since she was a poor thing, feeble and bedridden.

Discussion arose on the poor returns from the two Common Corn

Mills, and the low prices fetched for victuals generally, plus the extra support which had been given to various cases, leaving the Burgh in debt. It was ordered that no more support would be given to anyone, without the full consent of the whole Council.

Nicol Brown, drummer, was granted £3.

26th September

John Cockburn, Treasurer, was instructed to find eight men to guard the cornfields day and night, to prevent the theft or destruction of corn, until Michaelmas Fair on 29th September. Six other men would mount guard on the highway during the Fair with halberds, together with three officers.

9th November

William Brown, legal son of Nicol Brown, saddler, was appointed as drummer to the Burgh for one year, under similar conditions of work to his father, and a fee of 40 merks. The Treasurer was instructed to provide him with sufficient gray cloth for an outfit.

1622

8th May

James Lowrie, musician, was appointed to teach men and children to sing, to take up the alms in the Kirk on a Sunday, with other prayers before and after the sermon, and each morning and evening.

The Treasurer was instructed to pay him 100 merks, and the Kirk Session 50 merks, payable at the two usual terms, WhitSunday and Martinmas, in equal portions. He was also charged to keep the Session books etc.. of the Reader of the Kirk as Richard Wilson used to do. He was also allowed to teach children from outwith the Burgh at whatever charge, and Burgh children free of charge. The Treasurer was instructed to pay him £10.

26th July

Patrick Brown, Commissioner to the Convention of Burghs at Dumfries, reported back. Considering the drought and scarcities on the way to Dumfries, James Kirkwood, Treasurer, was told to pay him £6/10s as extra expenses.

Patrick Skowgll was appointed as Burgh drummer, from Lammas night 1622, until the same day in 1623, on similar terms and conditions as Richard Skowgill, his son.

16th August

James Carmichael, Minister, produce a document in French, written by Basuage, Deputy of the General Assembly of the Reformed Kirk of France and the Sovereignty of Bearne, containing £2305, collected for the French Kirk, which came from all the Presbytery Kirks of Haddington, requesting that this be placed in the Common Chest for safekeeping.

11th October

Since the Burgh was in debt to the King to the tune of £316/13/4d, powers were granted to William Cockburn, Robert Learmonth, Andrew Gray, John Cockburn, James Dawson and Patrick Hogg, representing the merchants, builders, craftsmen and citizens of the Burgh, to accept the burden of the taxes owed.

16th October

James Cockburn, Provost. Patrick Brown, James Barns, Baileys. Andrew Gray, John Cockburn, Harry Cockburn, Robert Learmonth, Francis Lyle, James Dawson, Robert Trotter, James White, James Kirkwood, William Cockburn, John Forrest, John Wilson, George Makanell, Gilbert Ayton, Patrick Hogg, John Barns, James Ayton and Thomas Simpson.

James Cockburn, Provost, produced a levy roll for taxation purposes.

22nd December

David MacCulloch, servant to Thomas, Earl of Melrose, appeared before the Council, to read out a missive. It claimed to represent a reasonable proposition in relation to joint rights to the Moor of Gladsmuir. A response was delayed pending further consultation.

A 12d loaf was to weigh 10 ounces. Bread from outside was to weigh 13 ounces. Wheat was to be sold for £11 per boll.

1623

30th January

James Cockburn. Provost, had been chosen as Commissioner to attend the Convention of Burghs at Edinburgh, earlier this month, to consider the export of wool to England. To the agreement of all, it was felt that he had discharged his duties well.

James Barns, Bailey, laid a complaint against George Fraser, officer, for disobedience in a) refusing to erect the ladder at the bridge for the execution of John Thomson, common thief, and b) in forewarning John Cockburn, son of Thomas Cockburn of Newhall, allowing him to escape from the Burgh and avoid arrest for certain riotous behaviour and demonstrations of contempt. George Fraser was ordered to be detained in the Tolbooth while they considered sentence, He was stripped of his Sergeant's rank and office.

All officers and sergeants were ordered to carry their halberds when walking the streets; under penalty of an 11s fine.

13th February

In view of the remorse expressed by George Fraser, ex-official and Sergeant of the Burgh, and of his punishment for former offences, plus pleas from divers persons, he was pardoned and restored to his former position of Sergeant.

28th February

The Treasurer was instructed to give £10 in support to James Lawrie, reader and musician, to help him move to Montrose.

28th March

All mealmakers, both burgesses and citizens of the Burgh, were told to grind their corn at the Common Mills in future; under penalties instituted by the Courts of Shillinghill, unless prior agreement had been reached with the tenant farmers of the Mills to grind their corn elsewhere.

The Treasurer was instructed to pay £3/6/8d expenses to Lawrence Sadler for a trip to Ireland.

25th April

It was proclaimed throughout the Burgh, at the sound of a drum roll, that a Silver Cup was to be raced for on Market day, 20th May, by noblemen, barons and gentlemen. The horse race was usually run from Nisbet Lane End to the West Port, under the normal rules for horse racing which require each rider to donate a gold piece, called a Rose Noble, or 16 merks, to the Treasurer, and that there should be more than two or three horses taking part.

The Treasurer was instructed to have the common highway repaired, which leads to and from the Burgh, making it safe for horses, carts and wagons.

2nd June

Ludovic Fuller, son of William Fuller, Secretary to the Queen, and Peter Arbuthnot, were made burgesses.

7th July

Walter Seton, Treasurer, was instructed to pay £26/13/4d to William Main, potter, that being the price of a handbell which he had made.

The Treasurer was instructed to give Helen Henderson, widow of George Geddes, £10 to assist her passage to Poland, and 10 merks to her fellow traveller, John Ramsay, son of the late James Ramsay, for clothing.

To John Purves, for healing the poisoned hand of Francis Yule, the sum of £5.

13th August

Andrew Gray was accused and convicted immediately for showing contempt to the entire Council and magistrates and for calling Walter Seton a false rascal and knave, not fit to sit on the Council – all without provocation. Also for his obstinate and wilful refusal to take the office of Commissioner, along with the Provost, James Cockburn, they having been elected by the Council, that they might confer with Richard Douglas of Brookhill and George Butler of the Kirkland of Bolton, Commissioners appointed by Thomas, Earl of Melrose, to assess His Lordship's right to the Moor of Gladsmuir. His refusal was in breach of the burgess oath; therefore he was fined the sum of £100 and detained in custody until he paid, nor would he be allowed to serve in public office again.

10th November

Agreement was reached between the Council and Alexander Seton, eldest son of the late Alexander Seton, burgess, for his appointment as Master of the Grammar School for one year. He accepted and agreed to work diligently, and to teach the children put in his charge Greek and Latin and grammar, for which purpose he was to appoint a man qualified in these tongues to serve under him. He agreed not to have more than four days off without the special permission of the magistrates, nor would he seek or accept any other post e.g. from Ministers. He was to be paid 200 merks per year at the two usual terms in equal portions, with £20 for his assistant. He would also receive 2s per head per student. No other person would be allowed to have a school, but children from outside the Burgh were welcome to come to the Grammar School. He was given a house in the school grounds.

The said Alexander, having sworn a solemn oath, was made a burgess.

11th November

The dispute, between the Earl of Melrose and the Burgh about the rights to the Moor of Gladsmuir, was to be taken to the law for settlement. The Burgh feared that the Earl would prevail because of his position, and because no advocate could be found to stand against him. It was feared that the whole freedom of the Burgh was at risk. Therefore, James

Cockburn, Provost, George Hepburn, Bailey, James Ayton, Deacon of bakers, John Barns, Deacon of skinners and James Gray, Clerk, were appointed as Commissioners to go to the Earl and allow him as little of the Moor as they could.

14th November

James Cockburn, Provost. Robert Learmonth and James Barns, Baileys. George Hepburn, John Cockburn, Harry Cockburn, William Wood, Patrick Brown, Richard Chaplin, Patrick Campbell, James Ayton, James Kirkwood, William Cockburn, William Edgar, John Forrest, George Mackonnell, William Spottiswood, David Kyle, John Barns, James White and John Trotter – present.

Agreement with the Earl of Melrose was reached viz : that part of the Moor was assigned to him which lay at the west end, called the little 'mott' or little 'mount', leading directly from the north part of the Moor to the south, plus the part of the Moor stretching from the east of the said 'mount' to that part of the Market gate leading to the Burgh, which lies before the head of Samuelston lane. The Burgh officers were instructed to ride to Edinburgh to draw up the contract legally.

10th December

Having found the contract (see above) to be satisfactory, it was decided to have it signed by the Provost, Baileys, Deacons, the Clerk and a Notary Public who would sign on behalf of those who could not write.

Considering that the Moor at Gladsmuir had proved to be unprofitable in the past, it was agreed to have it sold off in portions, in feu, to burgesses, freemen and citizens of the Burgh, in return for payment of a reasonable feu duty.

1624

9th January

A charter, relinquishing the Burgh's right to that part of The Moor of

Gladsmuir assigned to the Earl of Melrose, was drawn up. James Cockburn, Provost, was instructed to go to Edinburgh on Tuesday night to deliver it into His Highness' hands.

The Treasurer was instructed to pay Thomas Coutts, Writer to the Signet, 100 merks for drawing up the charter.

Thomas Rae and George Thomson, fish salesmen, were accused of false trading at the Fishmarket. They were found guilty and fined £5.

16th January

The Treasurer was instructed to send to Hester Quentin, widow of Wiliam Bowie, former Schoolmaster, in return for good and faithful service rendered by him in the teaching of the Burgh children, and for the repair and building of a house on Grammar School ground etc., the sum of £100.

James Cockburn, Provost, was chosen to go to Edinburgh to defend the action brought against the Burgh by the Laird of Lamington.

6th March

The Treasurer was instructed to send ten merks to Robert Short, N.P. for drawing up sasine papers.

The Treasurer was instructed to send £10 to George Johnston, traveller, to help him buy a horse.

7th May

French wine was not to be sold for more than 9s per pint; under penalty of a £10 fine.

Wheat bread was to be of good quality. A 12d loaf was to weigh 12 ounces; under penalty of an 11s fine.

Bread from outside the Burgh was to weigh 15 ounces for a 12d loaf.

Malt was not to be dearer than £10 per boll.

Ale was not to be sold for more than 20d per pint; under penalty of a £5 fine.

29th June

The Request of James Lawrie, Reader in the Parish Kirk of Haddington, to have his stipend increased to 50 merks, was refused by the whole Council, who said that he did not make enough use of what he already had.

20th September

A petition was lodged by the Kirk Session to receive 400 merks from the Gentlemen of the Parish which they could offer to the Council as annual rent, provided that a slater and glassworker could mend the broken windows of the Kirk. The Council refused the offer.

24th September

John Stevenson was elected as Deacon for the woodworkers. After of his suitability for the position, the Council refused to accept him and ordered John Barns, Bailey, to make the Convenor of Deacons convene the craftsmen to choose another qualified man as Deacon for one year. If they refused to do so, their choice of Deacon would not be allowed to vote or sit in the Council.

Spanish wine, known as dry wine, was to be sold for 18s per pint; under penalty of a £10 fine.

17th November

The plague, having broken out in Edinburgh, brought fears that the constant to and fro of people from the Burgh thence would cause the infection to spread. The Ports were ordered to be kept shut night and day. James Kirkwood was chosen to go to Edinburgh to inform them of this decision and prevent any misunderstanding.

4th December

The Burgh was to be quartered, with two men on duty night and day at each Port. No one was allowed to travel to Edinburgh without special permission.

John Douglas, eldest son and heir of Andrew Douglas, burgess, having sworn a solemn oath, was made burgess for spice and wine.

Haddington House (View from rear)

Chapter 5

The Reign of Charles I
1625 to 1649

Charles married Henrietta Maria of Spain, a Roman Catholic, which came as a great disappointment to his subjects in England and Scotland. It added to his problems with the English Parliament over financial and political issues. Throughout his reign, Charles seemed unwilling to recognise that society was changing its attitudes to fundamental issues, and that the old ways of ruling were under challenge. His first forays into war with France and Spain brought huge debts which were never satisfactorily resolved. His attempts to clear these debts brought no help from Parliament. The Petition of Rights, which was laid before him, brought no response. Instead he asserted the old Divine Right of Kings, as though he was still living in a bygone age. Seeing that he and Parliament were at loggerheads, he dissolved it in 1629, deciding instead to impose an old-fashioned, personal rule, lasting 11 years till 1640. He turned next to religion, and, in an early attempt to insert a general, all-embracing code of practice on the three countries which formed his kingdom, England, Scotland and Ireland, he tried to impose an English-style Prayer Book on the Scots without even seeking consultation. In 1637. the first use of the Prayer Book in St Giles, Edinburgh, resulted in a riot, leading to demonstrations throughout Scotland. A National Covenant was drawn up in protest, which, nevertheless, pledged allegiance to the Crown as well as Reformation. It sought an end to bishops and the re-establishment of a free Parliament in Scotland.

Charles had waited until 1633 to visit Scotland. In the intervening eight years, the Scottish economy had suffered. Grain prices were rising and overseas trade was falling, while, all the time, the Crown was making increasing fiscal demands. Burgesses complained bitterly about the level of taxation. Edinburgh paid more tax in the first two years of Charles' reign than in the final 22 years of James's. Grumbling over higher taxes, anxiety over the economy, and fears of interference in the Church, dominated the thoughts of Scottish nobles, lairds and the rising middle classes. Ultimately, the British State Church issue boiled over and led to the series of 'Bishops' Wars' which took place in the period 1638 to 1640. There followed the more intense Wars of the Covenant, lasting to 1651.

Charles never understood the problems besetting his three Kingdoms.

Whether it was because he was poorly advised, (in England, especially, his advisers were regarded with suspicion from the outset), or because he clung desperately to the belief in the Divine Right of Kings, we shall never know. His attempts to make one religion suffice throughout England, Scotland and Ireland, were guaranteed to fail, given that Ireland was strongly Roman Catholic, and that the seeds of Protestantism had already taken a firm root in both England and Scotland. Wherever he turned he misread the mood of his countrymen, until eventually, he found himself at war in all three of the home countries. He never accepted, until it was too late, that the new ideas in religion and politics had progressed too far for him to ever hope that there could be any reversion to old ideas of the supreme leader, unquestioned in all he did. Charles was a King too late.

In Scotland this period saw the rise of the 'middling sort,' i.e. lawyers and lairds. The Covenant itself had been signed by Henderson, a minister, and Johnson, an advocate, although it is fair to say that nobles did play a leading part in the Covenanting revolution. They led most of the regiments which fought the 'Bishops War.' The Clergy were not amused by this sudden rise of the nobility to power. In June, 1638, Charles acquiesced to growing demands for a free Assembly. It met in Glasgow Cathedral and moved to abolish bishops and episcopacy, which was not what Charles had anticipated. By January 1639, both Charles and the Covenanters were forming armies. The 'Bishops Wars' which followed did not end until the Treaty of Ripon in October 1640. An agreement was reached between the Committee of Estates in Scotland and the English Commission on religion as practiced on both sides of the border.

General George Monck

The English Civil War which followed, between Parliamentarians and Charles saw, on the one hand, Sir David Leslie and his 20,000 strong army, help defeat the Royalists at Marston Moor, while, on the other hand, Montrose was winning six battles on Charles' behalf in a year, only to be defeated by Leslie at Selkirk in 1645.

Charles was captured, tried and executed in 1649.

His son, Charles II, signed the Covenant in 1650 and formed an army to fight the Parliamentarians. Cromwell marched north, and, after a brief campaign, defeated Leslie at Dunbar.

Scotland was incorporated into a Commonwealth with England, having been granted 30 seats at Westminster. General Monck effectively governed Scotland.

CROMWELL: 1649–1660

From July 1650 Cromwell was actively engaged with the Scottish army under Leslie in and around East Lothian, fighting short, sharp engagements near Haddington. Ultimately he retired to Dunbar where he was victorious on 3rd September 1650. He appointed General Monck to be Commander-in-Chief in Scotland. Monck pursued his task actively, regulating civil affairs and seeing that the Parliamentary elections of the burghs were carried out correctly. His brother-in-law, Dr Thomas Clairgis, was chosen to represent the Burgh of Haddington in Parliament. From Haddington, Monck marched south to London, at the head of his troops, in time to welcome the new King, Charles II.

Haddington Burgh Council Records 1656 to 1660

1656

10th November

John Cockburn, Provost. Wiliam Seton, Richard Chaplin, David Wilson, John Sleich, John McCall, Patrick Brown, James Forrest, James Edington, John Trotter, David Kydd, Robert Dawson, George Forrest, John Ayton, John Brown, George Cockburn, George Paterson, Thomas Spottiswood, James Kirkwood, Archibald Gulland, John Hastie – present.

In order to increase revenue, The Council ordered tax changes in the Fleshmarket: Each sheep and lamb to pay 4d; each ox, cow or calf, young and old, 18d; each pig 18d. The tax collector would collect this money. Each trader would pay 6d each market day once he was given a stall for his beasts, unless they were worth less than 10 merks, in which case he paid 2d. This revenue would compensate for that formerly paid by the Shoemakers in the Crossgate.

The use of the wooden dish and ladle would continue at the Corn-market until it came up for discussion at the next Council meeting. William Seton, Commissioner to the next Convention of Burghs at Edinburgh on 12th November, would seek advice on the matter.

Because the number of schoolchildren, who attended Grammar School, was dwindling, due to the 12s charge, it was decided to reduce this to 2s per quarter. The Master was given 100 merks increase on his 300 merks salary, payable at WhitSunday and Martinmas in equal portions, commencing 11th November.

1st December

The Council ordered every merchant burgess, who had a stall at the market, to pay 3d every market day. Shoemakers and bakers would pay the same as before. Archibald Forrest was to return the poinding (seizure of goods for debt) taken from William Johnstone and James Anderson last Friday, since they had settled their debts.

8th December

James Brown was chosen to go to Lauder to meet representatives of Jedburgh, Selkirk, Peebles, Lauder, Dunbar and North Berwick, to select a Parliamentary Commissioner.

1657

12th January

John Vincent of Warnsworth was elected to replace John Douglas as Parliamentary Commissioner. James Brown was paid £9/5/4d expenses.

31st January

The Treasurer was instructed to pay Pittenweem £40 since it was in a bad way.

21st March

The Council ordered the undermanagers to be removed from the Council pew in the Kirk. Any unauthorised person was forbidden to occupy a Council pew, these being reserved for the Council and magistrates.

Agreement was reached and approved between Lord Lothian and Alexander Jaffray about the payment of £27 which constituted the Burgh's portion of expenses due to the Lord and his company for their trip to Holland to bring back Charles Stewart. Richard Chaplin promised to pay the agreed sum to James Cockburn, Collector, before 2nd May. Patrick Young, David Kyle, William Seton, David Wilson and James Edington were appointed to meet on 29th March to tax the Burgh's inhabitants for the £27, with a further £3 going to Robert Carmichael, the appointed Collector.

The Treasurer was instructed to mend the drumhead which was broken when the drummer had a fall at the Tolbooth at 4 a.m. this morning.

27th May

The Treasurer was instructed to buy linen for a tablecloth, and one dozen napkins for Captain Legg, plus a bed without curtains. He had taken over Lady Bearford's house.

11th June

William Seton, George Forrest and James Forrest, were appointed to compile a roll of those who had troops quartered on them last year, how many troops there were, and to pay 'coal and candle' to those who were due payment. The tax roll was ordered for collection for May, June and the four months preceding.

The Council ordered the Deacons of the Tailors and Hammermen (smiths) to attend the next Council meeting, in order that they might hear the Act which refers the sale of cushions, similar to that which is used by the Saddlers and Skinners. If they failed to appear, the Skinners would be the only ones allowed to sell cushions.

The Council ordered a full enquiry into complaints about who took the Burgh's money rather than pay taxes.

25th June

The Tax Roll was calculated at £386/17s. Robert Carmichael was appointed to distribute this amount among those due payment for their 'coal and candle', following the quartering of troops.

It was decided that, in future, only Skinners would have the right to sell cushions, as was previously the case.

Andrew Gray denied that he had slandered Patrick Young and William Seton. It was claimed that he had said Patrick Young would use the taxes collected to build a house. After witnesses were called, Andrew Gray was found guilty of slander, detained in custody, and fined £100. Thereafter he was required to seek the pardon of the magistrates. He was told never to repeat the offence or he would forfeit his burgess-ship as well as be fined.

The New Port was to be taken down and enlarged. The trellis on top of the East Port at the school, was to be removed so that fully loaded carts would not be impeded as they passed underneath.

18th July

Andrew Gray confessed his guilt in slandering Patrick Young and William Seton and craved their pardon, having been detained in custody for 29 days and fined £100. He vowed never to repeat the offence, whereupon he was set free.

22nd July

A letter was received from General Monck, via the Sheriff, desiring that the proclamation about the return of His Majesty be made public. A copy was to go to the magistrates of Dunbar. The following Friday was chosen as the day for proclamation. The Council, Deacons and Magistrates would assemble dressed in full regalia. Captain Legg would supply trumpeters. The Clerk would write to the Sheriff, asking him to be present.

10th August

William Seton reported that landowners on the Aberlady road were content to have any damage, incurred during roadworks, repaired afterwards. The Council calculated the damage at £3/10s per landowner.

The Deacon of Skinners would visit the Fleshmarket to seek out damaged skins and have the offenders punished.

22nd September

The Treasurer was instructed to pay James Douglas 20s per day, with 10s for each of his workmen, for repairing the Town House at Aberlady.

7th October

John Sleich and David Wilson were appointed to meet James Ayton and prepare accounts for those who travelled as cavalry dragoons to Leith.

10th October

The Crafts were granted leave to vote on the leet for Provost.

It was unanimously agreed that, in future, a person would be appointed as Provost for no more than two years.

14th October

William Seton, Provost, was appointed as Commissioner to the Convention of Burghs at Glasgow on 20th October. He would be accompanied by David Kyle, appointed as Assessor, and the Clerk who would take along the Burgh's Charters.

2nd November

William Seton protested, at the Convention, about the creation of a special body of Guild members, and appealed to His Majesty.

9th November

Because of the damage caused by huge loads on foreigners' carts passing through the Burgh, it was ordered that they should each pay 6d to the Customs Officer at the Port of exit, and 2d per horse load, except for loads which were sold to the townsfolk.

William Brown, agent for the Burgh, was given £27 for his efforts, and Robert Forrest was authorised to employ him as a replacement for Craig.

The Provost, Patrick Young, David Wilson, John Sleich (elder) and George Forrest were appointed to listen to the proposal made by Richard Chaplin and James Spottiswood, that exporters of skins and hides would be free from paying Customs dues. This would be heard together with a proposal to pay rebates, and a consideration of whether wool exports would be also liable.

19th November

The Tax Roll was to be compiled and payment set at 5s per head.

Richard Chaplin, former Treasurer, was to advance £400 towards defraying the Burgh arrears, before Candlemas.

A document was to be sent to Dunbar, complaining about their use of weights, which did not conform to those of the Burgh for weighing goods. If not rectified, a complaint would be made to the Convention of Burghs.

William Seton was allowed £27/6s for attending the Proclamation of My Lord Protector.

One key for the Master Chest was sent to Richard Chaplin, one to James Forrest, and one to Alexander Swinton. The door key was sent to the Treasurer.

The solemn oaths of Captain Roger Legg, Regiment of Horse of General George Monck, and Daniel Dalton, his Quartermaster, were received, whereupon they were each made burgesses.

21st November

The Treasurer would meet half of the charge in making burgesses of Captain Legg and his Quartermaster, and the Magistrates the other half.

23rd November

The Provost and Patrick Young were summoned before the Commissioners for the Administration of Justice, at the request of Robert McConnell, for payment of the tax due for August and September, 1650.

The Clerk was chosen to go to Edinburgh to hire Longformacus (lawyer) in actions against Craig and the above Commissioners.

The Treasurer was instructed to repair the Mill dam and race.

10th December

All landowners, adjoining Mylnburn and Lothburn, were asked to clean their 'runs'; under penalty of a £5 fine.

28th December

Having heard from Longformacus that the case against the Laird of Craig has come to his notice, he asked that Robert Forrest, Commissioner, go to Edinburgh to consult other advocates. George Hume and Andrew Gilmour were also appointed, along with Longformacus.

The Provost was granted £15/18/8d as expenses for attending the recent Convention.

A bowling green was to be laid in the Sands, with an enclosing wall. The Treasurer and Richard Chaplin, David Wilson and John Ayton were to settle details with the tradesmen. The Treasurer would buy bowls, hire a greenkeeper and agree terms with the masons.

1658

18th January

The Treasurer was to open a lane between St. Lawrence House and Letham, and try to open a stone quarry.

The Provost was to go to Edinburgh to seek advice on what to do about Margaret Anderson, confined at the time in the Tolbooth, and, if possible, to get a warrant transferring her to Edinburgh.

15th February

The Clerk was to go to Edinburgh to speak to the Town Advocate about the summons taken out against the Burgh by Hugh Kennedy, on behalf of the Government, seeking higher taxes. A letter would be sent to neighbouring burghs seeking their agreement to share in any future expense.

The four men, who escorted Margaret Anderson to Edinburgh, were to be paid two merks each.

27th February

The Clerk reported that he had spoken to Longformacus, and shown him Hugh Kennedy's summons. Provost Glen of Linlithgow was prepared to join the defence, and had also spoken to the Provost of Edinburgh, who advised that it should be entered into the missive, which the Council accepted.

All those owning waste ground were to report to the Council within twenty days, to show their certification of ownership.

The Treasurer was instructed to strengthen the New Port, and continue with the building of the candle houses there.

10th March

Captain Bryson offered to sell salt in the Burgh for 3/6d per peck, as well as sell it to the market stallholders for the same price. Robert Gray, John Sleich (elder), George Forrest and George Cockburn were appointed to hold a meeting to report on the matter.

3rd April

Since the Gentlemen of the Shire were about to claim the excise therefrom, William Seton, Provost, was ordered to go to Leith with them, that he might represent the Burgh's interest. He was allowed £22/10s for transferring Margaret Anderson to Edinburgh, but nothing for her husband, Thomas.

17th April

The Provost reported that the rate to be set for excise from the Shire was not acceptable, therefore he refused to be a party to it.

He was chosen to go to Edinburgh to attend a Convention of Burghs on 20th April.

The Council of State was to be petitioned about the taxing of Nungate.

24th May

A letter from General George Monck, in the name of the Highness Council of Scotland, and addressed to the Convenor of Assessment for the Burgh, dated 11th May, was read out. The Convenor was required to assess the Burgh for six months, this being the ordinary tax for a quarter payable on the 6th July, plus the following quarter payable on the 6th October. The Council ordered that the Burgh be taxed for the said six months, and the Provost be exempted.

The Provost and Clerk were to ask the Exchequer about the dismissal of the suspended dues, and the Hugh Kennedy summons.

The Treasurer was instructed to continue the work at St. Lawrence for a further eight days.

The Provost's expenses, for the Leith and Edinburgh excursions, amounted to £16/12s.

26th May

Having formed a high opinion of the abilities of Robert Sinclair of Longformacus, advocate, the Council appointed him to be their Assessor, and instructed the Treasurer to pay him 20 merks p.a. from WhitSunday, and allow his servant 50s p.a.

10th July

Mr Forrest, apothecary, was granted a licence to practice within the Burgh, provided he obtained a testimonial from doctors, certifying his worthiness to practice.

12th July

The Treasurer was instructed to have the rail outside the Court House removed, and to repair the east face of the chimney. He was also to have the Tolbooth drawbridge and the Great Drum repaired.

The Treasurer reported that he had received £10 from Robert Naysmith for Captain Legg's bed.

9th August

The Exchequer had fixed the rate of exchange at £10 (Scots) to £1 (Sterling).

The Council were to protest in Glasgow against the decision to start a guild organisation in Haddington.

John Trotter was found guilty of contempt, saying that he would not give a "fart of his erse" for the Provost. He was fined £100, deprived of his burgess-ship, and detained in custody until he had paid up. He was also told to kneel and ask the Provost's pardon.

The Treasurer was instructed to buy a pair of shoes for Edward Dickson.

The Treasurer was instructed to give Margaret, widow of John Vow, £3 to transport her and her two children to Edinburgh, on condition that she asked for no more.

The Treasurer was instructed to give George Todd £6 for expenses incurred in burying Gavin Mathie, Writer to the Earl of Lauderdale.

23rd August

James Forrest, Bailey, George Forrest, Thomas Spottiswood and the Treasurer were told to find the memorandum they had prepared about the payment of 1,000 merks, paid in either 1650 or 1651, and to report back.

The Treasurer was instructed to advance 500 merks towards the settlement of the Burgh's Exchequer dues. The Provost was to go to Edinburgh to pay it.

The Provost was allowed his expenses of £65/ 2s, incurred during the visit of the Edinburgh Commissioners on 10th August, to consider the guild organisation issue.

9th October

Five craft representatives were to be included on the leet for the election of Magistrates, along with ordinary Councillors, totalling 11 in all.

6th November

The Burgh's income, which came from the Mills, customs dues taken at the Ports, and the anchorage at Aberlady, the Tron, stalls in the Crossgate, firlots and pecks from the Wheatmarket, Peasmarket, Beer, Malt and Oat markets, Meal and Salt markets, Flesh and Fishmarkets, and the two Common haughs, were all to be collected on Wednesday , 10th November at 3 p.m. following the ringing of the West bell. All burgesses and freemen were to be warned by the ringing of the handbell through all the streets.

The Council was perturbed about the selling of loads of grass to a buyer by the haugh tax collectors. It was ordered that this be restricted to one-to-one. No ponies, over six months old, were to be allowed to pasture on the haughs.

13th November

The procedure for electing Burgh officials was revised as follows: conforming to the Acts of Burghs dated 10th July 1655 at Edinburgh, the Council aws to comprise 25 persons, i.e. 16 merchants, qualified as drawn up by David Wilkie, Dean of Guild in Edinburgh, and John Mylne, burgess of Haddington in their Act of Distinction, 9th October, 1655, and ratified by the Convention of Burghs, Haddington, July 1656, and 9 tradesmen from among whom the Treasurer and Magistrates were to be chosen. The leet for the Magistrates should comprise 20 Councillors, I.e. 116 old Councillors as chosen annually by the Provost and Baileys, and 11 tradesmen, I.e. 7 Deacons, 2 old Councillors and 2 new Councillors. The representative body for the Crafts was to continue so long as agreement prevailed, with 7 Deacons, one Bailey and one Councillor the Council representing the Crafts. The 31 persons on the Council at the time would lose four at the next election plus two Craft Councillors.

William Seton, Provost.

Councillors: John Vallance, George Paterson, John Douglas, Robert Gray, Robert Wallace, George Cockburn (elder), George Bathgate, Thomas Spottiswood, Robert Forrest, James Spottiswood, George Learmonth, Alexander Swinton, James Simpson, James Edington, John Thomson, Richard Chaplin, Bailey, John Bower, James Forrest, Bailey, Patrick Cockburn, Richard Kyle, Bailey, Thomas Kyle, David Wilson, Treasurer, John Cockburn, George Cockburn, Patrick Young, John Sleich, George Brown, George Forrest, John Ayton. James Gray, Notary, signed on behalf of John Warrender and William Kirk, who could not write.

6th December

The Provost, James Forrest, Bailey, Patrick Young , David Kyle and Alexander Swinton were chosen to represent the Burgh in a meeting with Archibald Sydserf, merchant burgess from Edinburgh and arbiter for their magistrates and Council, together with William Thomson, Town Clerk of Edinburgh and arbiter for the merchants, who were both promoters of the organisation of guilds within Haddington. The purpose of the meeting was to establish the number and qualifications of the persons who would constitute the Council for such a guild, plus the rules and regulations, powers and administration thereof.

29th December

The Provost was appointed to go to Lauder on Tuesday, 4th January, to meet the Commissioners for Dunbar, North Berwick, Jedburgh, Selkirk, Peebles and Lauder. The purpose was to decide who would serve as Commissioner for the Westminster Parliament on 27th January 1659 – according to the writ issued to Alexander Don of Newton, Sheriff of Berwick, by the Commissioners of the Great Seal of England.

John Summer, formerly a Burgh soldier, was made a burgess for £8. Similarly David Young, formerly a soldier and street cleaner during the plague of 1645, for £6.

1659

24th January

Dr. Thomas Clairgis, brother-in-law to General Monck, was unanimously chosen to serve as Commissioner to Westminster.

The Provost, Patrick Young and David Wilson, Baileys, plus the Clerk, were to decide on Robert Kerr's stipend, based on the acreage bought by the Burgh from the Earl of Haddington.

The Treasurer was instructed to repair both the Port at the Horsemarket and the New Port.

The Provost's expenses were allowed for a) the night the Tolbooth door was broken, b) when the Council came from Edinburgh, c) the State Commission visit to the markets, d) the agreement between the Council and the Crafts. Total £62/5s. Also for when Archibald Sydserf and William Thomson came to settle the question of the Dean of Guild – £35/13s.

14th February

The Council, in order to improve the manufacture of malt in the Burgh, and to punish the transgressors and spillers of malt etc., ordered that an inspector be appointed from amongst the maltster burgesses, who would have no vote in the Council.

19th February

The Provost was allowed expenses for going to see General Monck to seek advice on who should be the Westminster Commissioner, and also for the Lauder meeting.

The Treasurer was instructed to pay Robert Murdo, one of the under-millers, £12 who had had his leg broken at the East Mill while trying to free the waterwheel from ice.

James Heriot was created a burgess. He had been twice thwarted in this endeavour, while serving as a soldier. He paid £6.

12th March

A letter from Archibald Sydserf and William Thomson, noting the agreement between the Council and the Magistrates on the one hand, and the promoters of the Organisation of Guilds on the other, was read out. The powers, rules, regulations and administration procedures were laid out in the letter. Signatures had yet to be appended.

21st March

The signatures for the agreement for Guilds were delayed until the 26th March.

The Treasurer was to give George Cockburn £12 to buy a horse.

7th May

The Treasurer was to give William Dudgeon £16 to buy a horse and care for his children.

The Treasurer was instructed to give David Walker one pair of shoes and hose.

Patrick Young, former Treasurer, was to give James Barns £16 to relieve his poverty.

25th May

The Provost's expenses were granted for the submission, prepared by a group of Councillors, craftsmen and merchants, plus William Thomson, Clerk of Edinburgh, with regard to the Guild system, due to be started in the Burgh.

28th May

The Treasurer was instructed to give Alexander Thomson, fishmonger, £18 to help him buy a horse, on condition he sold fish in the market and not elsewhere.

The proclamation about the Guilds was to be made at the Cross.

John Sleich (elder) and James Spottiswood were put on the leet for Dean of Guild. James Spottiswood was elected.

John Sleich, George Forrest, George Cockburn, Alexander Swinton, John Douglas and John Bowes were to form the Council for the Guild.

George Guthrie, tailor, was chosen to be the Officer for the Dean of Guild.

James Edington, cooper, and John Vallance, tailor, were appointed as office administration to the said George.

James Gray, Common Clerk, was to be the Clerk of the Dean of Guild.

4th June

Tuesday was chosen as the day on which the Dean of Guild would hold his Council, but other days were to be allowed in the case of an emergency.

The Treasurer allowed expenses of 16 'Rex dollars' to be paid to William Thomson, which were incurred in the preparation of the submission for the Dean of Guild.

Four officials were given £18 among them, for the great pains they took in the preparation.

13th June

A discussion took place on the problem of seeking new quarters for soldiers, whose horses were supposed to graze outwith the Burgh, or else to agree on a sum of money to be paid to the landlords, in the hope that it would be repaid by the soldiers.

The Treasurer was instructed to give James Home, son of George Home, burgess, who was now at college in Edinburgh, 50 merks to help him pay for board and books.

With regard to those who seek help to pay their rent, or buy horses, and who, instead, misuse the money given, it was decided to refuse such applications in future. Any Councillor who proposed otherwise, would be fined 40s.

9th July

Provost, Baileys, Dean of Guild, Treasurer, Patrick Young and John Sleich, were chosen to go and see the Earl of Haddington, Lord Elibank and the Laird of Alderston, through whose land lies the road to Aberlady, and seek ways to have the road repaired.

31st August

The Convention of Burghs, held at Edinburgh in July, approved that a correspondence be maintained between the Deans of Guild at Edinburgh, Linlithgow, Glasgow, Stirling , Haddington, Culross and Dunfermline. They were to meet at Linlithgow on the first Tuesday of August, to decide on such matters as the restrictions to be placed on 'unfree' traders. David Wilkie, Dean of Guild at Edinburgh, gave notice of the above in his letter of 20th July, whereupon Thomas Spottiswood was ordered to attend the meeting.

The Deacon and brethren of the Skinners and Fleshmongers sought the right to search the market for holed, scored and 'pulled' hides and skins.

In order to free the Burgh from having to pay tax or 'coal and candle', it was suggested that a plaque be placed on a pint pot of ale, which had been brewed in the Burgh and sold there.

5th September

At 12 midnight a great flood swept in from the Tyne up to Robert Duncanson's stair, and then on to the crest of the highway, near the Tron, and then into the gutters at the Cross.

8th September

The dam wall collapsed after the flood, and all of the sluices, except one at the east end of the water gate, were swept away. The Treasurer was instructed to have them repaired as soon as possible, and to dig out the fords. The bridge end, which had collapsed, would also have to be repaired.

The Provost, James Forrest and David Kyle, were chosen to pay a visit to General Monck, to see if a quarter of the troops, stationed in Haddington, could be moved elsewhere.

5th September

It was decided that as many stones as were needed should be taken from the Old Kirk to repair the bridge etc..

The Treasurer was instructed to give John Vaughan, who was sick and destitute, 10s.

7th November

General George Monck, by his letter of 27th October to the Burgh, instructed them to appoint someone to meet him at Edinburgh on 15th November. This was passed on to Dunbar, who sent a Commissioner to meet the Provost on the Wednesday. North Berwick were also invited to attend.

Wheat was sold for £13/10s per boll. A 12d loaf was to weigh 8 ounces.

One pound of candles was to be sold for 4/8d for a year.

One pint of ale was to be sold for 2s.

House in Nungate

Chapter 6

The Reign of Charles II
1660 to 1685

Religion and bankruptcy were to prove the dominant issues of the period 1662–1680 in Scotland. Parliament and the Privy Council were both full of bankrupt nobles. Loans and debts proliferated at a scale never seen before, including, for the first time, Highland chieftains. There were two uprisings, 1666 and 1679, which demonstrated the gulf between Government and the important areas of Scottish opinion. Lauderdale and Argyle, an unlikely duo, dominated Scottish politics. Both were Presbyterian believers. Lauderdale, himself, held an unrivalled position at the head of affairs, having been given the position of Commissioner to Parliament. Towards the end of the 1670s, with Lauderdale in poor health, the Government was losing control. An uprising, in support of the Covenant in 1666, was brought to an end at Rullion Green, on the slopes of the Pentland Hills, by a Government force led by Tam Dalyell of the Binns. Thereafter, a policy of limited tolerance of non-conformity was practised. The First Indulgence, 1669, restored 42 dissident Presbyterian ministers to their parishes, and a second, in 1672, allowed a further 90. Another uprising, in 1679, merely served to highlight the different groups with the dissenting Covenanters. Bothwell Bridge (July 1679) saw the decline of the dissenters.

Life in Haddington was changing. The Restoration of the Monarchy was welcomed and increasingly good relations between town and King were pursued quite vigorously. Invitations were issued to anyone who was passing by who had a connection with the Court. Burgesses were created gratis for those who had a noble background, and lavish entertainment was laid on for those who represented the King in any way.

The other side of the coin saw Edinburgh exert greater pressure on internal matters. Visits by the Provost to consult on regulations relating to market activity were a regular event. Summonses to answer questions on similar affairs were frequent. It seemed that the Burgh, in common with other Royal Burgh was to be drawn into the control of the King's Officers.

Pressure was definitely laid on Haddington officers. One of the side effects was to see an increasing number of internal disputes among these same men.

Nevertheless, life was getting better for the townsfolk. There was time to relax and pay more attention to enjoyment. This period saw the development of horse-racing, with large amounts spent on prizes, not always to everyone's satisfaction. Meanwhile the eternal problems of beggars, idlers and opportunists persisted, and the Tolbooth prison was kept busy.

To everyone's relief, the plague had gone – at least for the time being.

The climate itself, may have had a part to play in this. There were many storms, floods and devastation to endure. Harvests were not always as good as had been hoped. Overall, though, life was improving for the citizens of the Burgh.

Haddington Burgh Council Records 1660 to 1685

1660

7th January

John Trotter, tailor, craved forgiveness for previous offences for which he had been punished. The Council agreed to restore his burgess-ship on payment of £100, and on condition that there would be no repetition of his crimes.

The Treasurer was instructed to pay Henry Cockburn, wright, for the old chests belonging to the late George Dickson, Beatrix Maislet and Helen Richardson, and to fix a price as low as possible, not exceeding 40s per item.

The Provost was granted expenses of £25/15s for attending the Edinburgh meeting of the Burghs to consider General Monck's letter.

The Provost was granted expenses of £60 for going to Berwick on the 12th December to meet General Monck.

The Treasurer was instructed to keep enough aside to pay the letter tax.

23rd January

William Seton, Provost, was ordered to go to Edinburgh on 31st January to meet those from other burghs to consider applications and petitions to be made to the Parliament in England, and to discuss General Monck's letter.

11th February

James Forrest, Dean of Guild, was to go to Edinburgh to meet other Deans to discuss punishment for 'unfree' traders. He was also to meet the Commissioners of Edinburgh, Linlithgow, Dunfermline and Burntisland, and receive William Thomson's report to General Monck.

James Aitken was exempt from paying tax because of his old age, infirmity and poor sight.

The Treasurer was instructed to pay Elspeth Gray, spouse of John Hart, a soldier in England, £3 to help her and her bairns.

He was also to pay Edward Dickson 12s to assist him in his removal out of the Burgh.

17th March

The Dean of Guild reported on his meeting in Edinburgh.

It was ordered that the Burgh executioner should put his knife to use.

The Treasurer was instructed to give George Cockburn £6 to help him place his infant child with a wet nurse, since the mother had no milk.

9th April

Robert Naysmith, tax collector for the Haughs, was relieved of collecting taxes because the Haughs were still flooded.

The Treasurer was instructed to go to Edinburgh to have a silver cup made, bearing the Haddington coat-of-arms, to be run for on the 29th May (the King's birthday) from Winton Graystone to the West Port. Also a saddle was to be made, to be run for on the 30th May, from Nisbet Loan Head to the West Port.

23rd May

29th May being Coronation Day, bonfires were to be lit by all citizens. The three Baileys, the Dean of Guild, John Cockburn, David Wilson, John Sleich, Robert Chaplin, James Thomson and Thomas Sydserf were appointed to see to it.

Three Baileys and the Clerk were to meet the Laird of Niddrie, factor to the Earl of Lauderdale, and Charles Maitland of Saltoun, his brother, to agree on the placing of stones on the south side of the Haughs, on his Lordship's ground, in a bid to repair the dam.

29th May

A £9 entry fee per horse was required for the horse race on 30th May. John Hay of Baro and Gavin Jameson of Calder, paid their fees and cast the die to see who would go first and who should have the right hand. John Hay won both times.

This day was the King's birthday. The Council ordered all citizens to light a bonfire at night, and to follow the Magistrates and Council in a procession through the Burgh, in testimony of their joy. This event would be repeated annually. Three troops of Colonel Saunders' regiment joined in the dancing.

18th July

Forty able men and women were to be put every day to dig out the sand bed, above and beneath the bridge, with two supervisors in charge. If anyone was not able to work, the overseer would send them away and fine them. Someone else would be set to work at their expense. This work to begin on Wednesday.

13th August

The Treasurer was to give the four officials £20 to be divided equally amongst them, for the service they had shown in warning the Burgh to clear the Haughs and the water at the bridge.

10th September

The Treasurer was to meet those to whom money was owed for wine, sweetmeats, glasses etc., used on the three solemn occasions, 9th May, 29th May and 19th June, and he would settle the account.

6th November

The Treasurer was instructed to give 11s to one of the Dunfermline Baileys, John Hutton.

A bonfire was ordered for each household in commemoration of the Gunpowder Plot, 5th November 1605; under penalty of a £5 fine. This was to be proclaimed following the beat of the drum through all the streets, and would be observed annually.

19th November

George Pringle, who had been unable to find surety for the 4,500 merks he had borrowed for the Mills, was declared unfit for public office in the Burgh.

The Treasurer was instructed to repair the Burley Walls as soon as possible.

1st December

The Earl of Middleton, His Majesty's Commissioner to Parliament, was due to arrive in Edinburgh. The Provost, Dean of Guilds, Treasurer and Baileys would ride out to meet him, dressed in their regalia, to invite him into the Burgh, and to provide him and his train of followers with spice and wine.

The Dean of Guilds was ordered to admit John, Earl of Crawford, and Lindsay, High Treasurer of Scotland, Lieutenant Colonel George Stewart, Sir John Whiteford of Milton, Andrew Forrester and Thomas Moncur, servants to the said noble Earl, to be burgesses.

1661

14th January

William Seton, Provost, was appointed Commissioner to Parliament, that he might raise the problem of having the Burgh Charter changed from sterling to Scots money.

The Council announced that they were willing to pay half of the maintenance costs of John Thomson, son of Mr Thomson and Sibilla Arnot, who have gone to live in England. The Kirk Session would pay the other half.

28th January

The bill for confections, sweetmeats and spices, provided for the Lord Commissioner's meal by Robert Naysmith, came to £75, plus £8 for his fee and hire of horses.

12th February

The Provost's expenses, incurred while entertaining the Earl of Middleton and the Earl of Crawford and their train of followers, totalled £203/4s. This was paid.

The Treasurer was instructed to give George Guthrie, Dean of Guild, £10 towards the expenses incurred in burying his wife.

15th April

On 8th April, William Seton, Provost, James Spottiswood, George Forrest and James Edington, Baileys, James Forrest, Dean of Guild, Richard Chaplin, John Sleich, David Wilson, David Kyle, William Allan, Robert Gray and Robert Naysmith, met to decide what arrangements to make for horse-racing. It was resolved that the Cup would be run for on the usual course on 21st May. One saddle, worth £40, would be the prize awarded on the following day. Because the previous year's race was postponed when the riders failed to put up the 200 merks required, it was agreed that each rider would, in future, put up 20 merks in gold, plus £4 for the saddle.

20th May

An Act of Parliament, passed at Edinburgh, decreed that a solemn anniversary of His Majesty's Restoration would be observed annually. 29th May would be set aside for this purpose. John Sleich, David Wilson, David Kyle and John Lyle. Magistrates, were appointed to see to this, and to place their instructions as a reference in the Council Book.

21st May

James Cockburn, Captain, John Sleich, Lieutenant, John Ayton, Ensign, Robert Wallace, William Swinton, John Thomson, all Sergeants, would have a company of 100/120 under their command. They would march with the Magistrates and Council on Restoration Day.

25th May

A stage was ordered to be erected at the Market Cross on 29th May, and, attached to it, for the persons who were to sit at the tables to be set on. Tables, stools and forms would be provided by the Treasurer and the seats necessary for accommodating the Magistrates. Sweetmeats etc., would be made ready on plates viz: 20 pounds of sweetmeats, plus figs and raisins and one whole puncheon of wine. Ten dozen wine and beer glasses would be needed, plus one dozen blue and white taffeta napkins bearing the Burgh coat-of-arms and the word 'Haddington'. Gunpowder and matches would be provided for the soldiers. The Treasurer would supervise proceedings.

20th July

The Treasurer was ordered to pay Marion Forrest £10 compensation for the medicines etc., used by wounded soldiers from Doonhill, plus the fees owed to the late Alexander Hepburn, her husband, surgeon to the Burgh.

29th August

James Forrest, Dean of Guild, was allowed £19/3s expenses incurred while making Mr Murray of Alderston a burgess, together with Colston, James Dundas etc..

14th September

The Provost's expenses while making burgesses, plus some public meetings – £299/19/6d.

No Councillor or Dean of Guild was to be arrested in the Tolbooth during the Council meeting.

The entire Council took the oath of allegiance.

8th October

William Seton was elected as Provost.

The Dean of Guild admitted the following as burgesses: Sir Robert Sinclair of Stenton, Robert Sinclair of Longformacus, advocate, John Veitch (younger) of Daik. William Douglas, son of Sir Robert Douglas of Blaikerston, William Boig, son of the late Alexander Boig of Burnhouse, John Pollock, Minister of Stenton, Alexander Turnbull and James Couston, servants to the said Robert Sinclair, Henry Sinclair, John Drummond of Lenoch, Robert Lauder, servant to John, Earl of Haddington – all free of charge.

18th November

The sum of 25 merks was awarded to James Home, son of George Home, a student of philosophy at Edinburgh University.

1662

5th January

James Forrest, Bailey, was granted expenses of £10/17/6d for making William Liddell (younger) a burgess and Guild brother, and for going to Edinburgh to speak to Mr Thomson about excise duties. For staying there for two days, a further £8 was granted.

The Treasurer was instructed to give £6 to help Alison Brown and her four children.

8th February

The Treasurer was instructed gauges for one peck, a half peck and a quarter peck, which would be used by all the linseed sellers. It would match the Linlithgow gauge.

The same pension awarded to James Home was to be awarded to David Anderson, son of the late George Anderson, from 1st February, instant.

Mr James the Clerk, was granted £100 for providing parchment and wax to sundry gentlemen and nobles, in order to complete their burgess tickets. They were entered gratis on the burgess roll.

9th April

A cup, worth £120, was to be raced for on 20th Mayh. The Saddle would be raced for on the following day.

The Treasurer was instructed to buy 40 flintlock guns and 40 pikes before 29th May – to be kept in the Council House.

30th April

Robert Lindsay was re-appointed as the Burgh drummer.

John Reid of North Berwick was appointed as the Burgh piper for the same fee as the drummer, plus livery.

Two men were hired to get rid of the vagabonds and beggars, for a fee fixed by the Magistrates.

7th May

The horse-race, which was to be run between West Port and Gladsmuir, would be run around the posts.

Entry fee was set at 40 merks per rider, since only three riders entered, and ten merks for the Saddle race.

28th May

The Colours were to be run up, and the militia called to arms. They would assemble after sermon on Sunday; under the usual penalty for non-attendance.

21st July

The Treasurer was instructed to give Henry Cockburn, wright, £18 as travel expenses for him and his son to go to Holland.

Prince Charles, Duke of Lennox and Richmond, the Earl of Darnley, March and Lichfield, Lord Tarbolton, Methven, Aboyne and St. Andrews, Chamberlain and Admiral of Scotland, were all to be made burgesses and Guild brothers. This was also granted to William, Lord Witherington, Colonel William Struthers, Sir John Fletcher, His Majesty's Advocate, Alexander Cunningham, Governor of Dumbarton, John Stewart of Kettlestone, the Earl of Dundee, the Viscount of Dundee, and Lord Scrimgeour.

4th August

The Dean of Guild was to create Robert Millar, apothecary, a burgess and Guild brother, and grant him £20 p.a. for visiting and helping the poor, with medicines paid for by the patient, except when he chose to give them for nothing.

Marion Forrest, widow of the late Alexander Hepburn, Surgeon, was allowed £10 in full settlement of what was owed to her husband for medicines etc., given by him to the wounded soldiers from the Dunbar battle.

18th August

William Allan, merchant burgess and former Treasurer to the Kirk Session, gave Patrick Young £160, previously collected for the building of a bridge at Saltoun, to be used instead for the laying of a bowling green at the Sands.

The Treasurer was instructed to provide financial support to William Anderson, son of Farquhar Anderson, who lost an eye to a gunshot wound on 29th May.

1st September

Having received an invitation from the Baileys of Jedburgh to attend a meeting there of the Burghs of Glasgow, Dumfries, Haddington, Dunbar, Lauder, Selkirk and Peebles on the first Wednesday in September, Jame Forrest, Bailey, was ordered to attend.

Markets, having been changed from Saturday to Friday, in contradiction of the Burgh's Charter, the Council decided to revert to Saturday in the future. This would be proclaimed publicly at the Cross and through the streets at the next Michaelmas Fair.

24th September

James Forrest, Bailey, announced that a report of the Jedburgh meeting would be made at the next Convention of Burghs.

1st October

John Sleich (elder), Bailey, complained that John Ayton had told his son "You are the son of a traitor", confirmed later by the Provost and two

Baileys. John Ayton was deprived of his burgesship and fined £100. He was detained in custody until he paid his fine.

27th October

The excise rate for Haddington was set at 40 bolls per week.

One pound of cotton was to be sold for 4/4d. One pint of ale was to be sold for 20d.

1663

23rd February

The Provost and Commissioners of the Shire were told to go to Edinburgh on 24th February to meet Mr McConnell to discuss the action brought against them for the cornmeal supplied to the King's army in 1650.

13th March

The above case was settled for 4,500 merks. The Burgh tax was set at £36 Sterling.

The Treasurer was instructed to buy a long coat for George Learmonth, postman, in blue cloth with a white piping, providing that he bought a silver badge bearing the Burgh arms and name.

The Treasurer was instructed to pay Patrick Aikman £8/14s in settlement of the bill incurred by the Magistrates and Councillors at the funeral of Patrick, Lord Elibank, at Aberlady.

Marion Forrest was allowed 10 merks for all fees due to her late husband Alexander Hepburn, Burgh Surgeon.

19th May

The Silver Cup was announced. The horses entered were as follows: a chestnut, belonging to the Earl of Morton, ridden by Thomas Kerr; a light bay gelding with a snip on his forehead, belonging to the Laird of Ayton, rider John Purves; a bay gelding with a snip on his forehead belonging to John Hay of Baro, rider John Colvill. Baro had the right hand. The stakes were placed in the Treasurer's hands.

19th June

The Earl of Rothes, His Majesty's Commissioner to Parliament, and the Earl of Lauderdale, plus an attendant company who visited Tyninghame recently, were all invited to the Burgh. Sweetmeats, confections and wine were ordered, to be offered to His Grace et al.

9th November

The Burgh excise rate was fixed at 40 bolls per week.

Hearing of and Act of Parliament which altered all the days of the Burgh markets, the Council sent for it, that it might be examined before a response was given.

A complaint against George Forrest was made, and all witnesses were warned to be ready for the Hearing on 18th November.

One pound of candles was to be sold for 4/4d. A 12d loaf was to weigh twelve and a quarter ounces and two drops.

10th November

Fishmarket stall leases were awarded to John Hastie, burgess weaver, for one year for £29.

Two Common Haugh leases were awarded to James Edington for one year for £60.

Tron and Tron weights leases were awarded to John Hastie for one year for £300.

Customs of the Ports and Aberlady anchorage lease to William Gladstone for one year for £659.

Fleshmarket stalls lease to James Heriot for one year for £120.

Crossgate stalls lease to John Coupland for one year for £77.

Firlots and pecks of Meal and Saltmarket leases to John Hastie for one year for £78.

Firlots and pecks of Wheat and Peamarket leases to Alexander Burnett for one year for £109.

Firlots and pecks of Beer, Malt and Oatmarket leases to Walter Veitch for one year for £83.

A Common Mills lease to James Edington for one year for 3000 merks.

All payable to the Treasurer.

18th November

George Forrest, James Sleich (younger), William Swinton and Robert Naysmith laid a series of complaints against the Provost and Council. They were found to be not proven.

1. It was found that William Seton, Provost, had fully discharged his duties.

2. To the charge that he was not legally elected as Provost, it was answered that he was elected quite legally from a leet.

3. To the charge that the Provost charged £6 per day as a Commissioner fee even when he was at home, it was answered that the Council, at the time, had allowed the Provost his fees, as shown, quite properly, in the accounts kept by the Treasurer, following which the citizens of the Burgh were thrice advised, following the sound of the handbell, to hear the accounts. None questioned the accounts at the time. The auditors had declared the accounts to be an accurate record.

4. To the charge that 10,000 merks was owed to the Burgh, it was answered that, at the time of the Provost taking office, the Burgh's debt was 11,000 merks plus, whereas it was now only 7,500 merks. For seven years the Burgh Mills, millraces, dam heads and sluices had proved to be more costly than previously; the Burgh's debt was not down to one man but to the whole Council. The present debt was incurred long before William Seton was a Magistrate, and the debt had not increased in his time of office, but had diminished.

5. To the charge that Councils were not called for five months, it was answered that the Council record showed that the greatest interval between Council days was ten weeks, during which time the Provost was attending Parliament at Edinburgh.

6. To the question of what fee the Provost received for attending Parliament, it was answered that, as yet, he had submitted no claim.

7. To the charge that the Provost freed prisoners arbitrarily and imprisoned two persons unjustly, it was answered that John Hastie, weaver, was imprisoned by John Sleich, Bailey, then freed by the Provost on appeal. As for the two witches who dwelt in the back streets of Samuelston and were imprisoned by George Forrest, Bailey, they were freed, on appeal, by the Provost. William Swinton, who was imprisoned by the Provost on 28th May, was later freed, on appeal, by the Provost. Whoever sent prisoners to the Tolbooth had to find surety, in the presence of a Magistrate, before committal to trial. In the case of the witches this was not done, therefore the Provost ordered them to be freed. As for William Swinton, he was due to appear as a Sergeant in the Anniversary parade for the King's Restoration. He had flatly refused to appear in the parade, claiming that, as a Convenor, he ought not to appear as a mere Sergeant. When reminded that he should therefore have referred the matter back to the Council, that another might be chosen in his place, he again demurred, claiming he was as much a Magistrate as the Provost. The Council almost unanimously decreed that all of the complainants had broken their burgess oaths, and should be deprived thereof, and fined £100.

4th December

The Declaration of the above to be signed the following Monday by the Council.

7th December

The Declaration was duly signed.

14th December

A letter was received from the Chancellor, asking for the shops of George Forrest, John Sleich, William Swinton and Robert Naysmith, which were closed by order of the Council, to be re-opened. The Provost, James Cockburn, Bailey, and the Clerk were ordered to go to Edinburgh to find the Act of Parliament referring to the alteration of the market days in Royal Burghs, and have the day changed from Monday and Saturday to any other day they chose.

30th December

Saturday's market was changed to a Friday.

The Earl of Roxburgh, The Earl of Haddington, The Earl of Tweeddale, Lord Belhaven, the Laird of Gosford and Alexander Cockburn in Letham assembled to hear charges brought by George Forrest, John Sleich, William Swinton and Robert Naysmith against the Provost, Baileys and Council, previously heard on 27th November at His Majesty's Privy Council. The entire Council was told to attend.

1664

10th November

2d per day was charged to each burgess with a stall in the Crossgate, payable to the taxman.

The Treasurer was instructed to give £6 to Patrick Cockburn, cooper, who had become blind in old age.

12th December

Ten merks p.a. was allowed to Robert Millar, Burgh apothecary and surgeon, on top of the £20 he received as well, in recognition of the medicines and plasters he provided for the poor and sick, starting from Martinmas.

1665

25th January

The Council unanimously approved the appointment of Robert Watson, Precentor of the Tron Kirk in Edinburgh, to be Precentor of the Parish Kirk in Haddington, following the death of William Brown, at the same fees, duties and housing allowances. This was to be confirmed following his appearance at the Council.

4th February

Robert Watson was also appointed Master of the Music School, to teach men and children to sing and play instruments. It would be open to those outwith the Burgh as well as residents. He was to take up Psalms on Sunday, as well as before and after sermons, to read prayers every weekday morning and on Sunday before the sermon. He was to read the Scripture before the sermon, a.m. and p.m. He was provided with a house, rent-free, and paid £100, plus a further fee from the Kirk Session.

The Treasurer was instructed to pay the hangman £3 for parading four thieves through the Burgh.

27th February

A £100 Silver Cup was to be made and run for at Gladsmuir around the posts erected on 23rd May. A £48 Saddle was to be made and run for from Nisbet Loan Head to the West Port on 24th May.

22nd March

The Treasurer was instructed to repay George Cockburn, Bailey, £6, who had previously given this sum to Nicholas Kerr, a distressed Gentleman, who was robbed by Highlanders.

3rd April

A dispute arose between Robert Forrest and John Ayton about two furrows taken from the latter's land. The ploughman, who did this, was ordered to replace the two furrows until such time as a decision was reached in law.

The Cup or Plate was to be displayed along with the Saddle, and a proclamation made concerning entry fees.

Robert Lindsay was restored to his position as Burgh drummer, following his dispute with James Cockburn, Bailey, on condition that, if he re-offended, he would be punished by the Magistrates and then banished.

25th November

The Magistrates, plus James Cockburn, John Sleich, Patrick Young, David Kyle and John Lyle, were to discuss ways to raise money to defray the Burgh's debts, and also to discover whether the 1650 levy in the Charter Chest had been all spent.

6th December

The above group reported that every brewer would be charged 13/4d on their bill.

9th December

One merk was to be levied on every boll of malt, whether sold or not, commencing from 7th January 1666.

The Magistrates, Treasurer, John Sleich, David Kyle, Thomas Spottiswood and George Learmonth, were to meet James Marr, wright, James Spavin and Mr Millar, to hear their conclusions on the building of a Walk Mill next to the West Mill.

23rd December

The Treasurer was instructed to give William Brown, agent for the Burghs, £60 for his efforts.

1666

31st January

William Brown was allowed expenses for missive dues and for stopping the £960 charge on the Burgh, which represented its share of the 80,000 merks levy imposed on the Royal Burghs in 1650, and also for purchasing a commission for John Hay of Baro to take action, at the instance of James Somervell, against the alleged transgressors of the Act of Parliament made concerning pecks and bolls, which altogether totals £156/1/10d.

10th March

Magistrates Patrick Young, John Sleich and David Kyle were appointed to consider the problems that might arise from the building of the Walk Mill and the Corn Mill.

James Marr was allowed his expenses for travelling to buy timber for the Walk Mill, amounting to £40, i.e. 40s per day each day for 20 days.

The Provost was allowed his expenses for attending the Privy Council on the matter of the Act for 12d ale, which amounted to £17/6s.

9th April

James Marr, wright, was paid £48 for improving the West Mill, working with servants, James Spavin and his son, who all had their wages paid on top of what was paid to James.

James Marr built the Walk Mill house loft and the masonry wings plus other items to do with accommodation, as well as blocking off the south close at the east end of the dam head with stakes, flagstones and clay underneath the water, with stone and lime above.

James Edington, Bailey, complained that John Hastie, burgess weaver, had vilified him in contemptuous terms. When John Hastie was summoned he flatly refused to respond to the Baileys' call to come downstairs, whereupon he was seized. He was stripped of his burgess-ship, fined £100, and ordered to confess his offence in public, seek forgiveness and agree never to repeat the offence, to all of which he agreed.

18th April

Because of the fine work of James Marr at the Walk Mill and the West Mill, the Dean of Guild made him a burgess and a Guild brother, gratis.

Because the Treasurer refused to pay James Marr £40 to complete the work, the tax collectors for the Mills were told to share the amount between them. The Treasurer was to be censured for saying that he would not pay because he didn't have the revenue.

2nd June

The Provost was chosen to go to Edinburgh to transact a continuation of the payment of the Burgh's due taxes for the first term.

William Allen, former Treasurer, produced his statement of accounts for the period Martinmas 1664 to Martinmas 1665, amounting to £4,461 of which £4,371 was spent, leaving £90 for the current Treasurer.

David Kyle was allowed expenses for making James Marr and William Nisbet into burgesses, amounting to £24/9s.

30th June

William Allen, former Treasurer, produced discharge papers from Alexander Maitland, Chamberlain to the Earl of Lauderdale, for the £4 payable annually for the Burgh Mills to the said Earl, together with the sum of 40s, previously payable to the Abbot and Convent of Dunfermline, and to the Earl.

The Provost was chosen to go to Edinburgh to discuss the payment of the Burgh's taxes. He reported that he had received an extension until mid July. He asked for expenses of £12, plus £5 for going to Pencaitland Wood on four occasions.

The Provost's expenses were granted for 29th May, when news was received of the victory against the Dutch, and at the rendering of the Treasurer's accounts, amounting to £133/11s.

18th July

James Douglas, mason, was ordered to take all the Burgh masons to the Walk Mill on Monday; under penalty of forfeiture of their burgess-ships.

The Marches were ordered to be ridden on 1st August. All burgesses, Magistrates and Councillors were required to attend.

The Provost's expenses were granted for attending the Convention of Burghs, in company with the Clerk and tax collectors, in order to achieve an extension for paying the Burgh taxes.

25th July

Absent Councillors were ordered to pay 6s for not attending Council meetings.

Because the Treasurer had placed Magistrates in a hazardous position of being denounced for not paying Burgh dues to the Exchequer, censure was accordingly postponed until the following evening, allowing James Forrest, Dean of Guild, John Sleich, Patrick Young and David Kyle to talk to him.

21st August

Alexander Ogilvie, one of the deputy collectors serving under the Duke of Hamilton's General Collector of Taxes, produced an invoice, dated August 1665, to the Burgh for £400, being the taxes due for the first term. It was given to James Cockburn.

£26/4s was due as payment for tax out of the aforesaid £4,000, therefore two months tax, as per tax register, was to be collected as soon as possible.

David Kyle's bill for wine etc., at meetings with James Marr, and James Shaw's bill for providing ale, meat etc., for the company that marched on Aberlady, amounted to a total of £67/12s.

1667

2nd February

William Seton, Provost, Commissioner to the Convention of Burghs, reported that the Burgh owed £1,000 sterling out of £6,000 to be levied every month for a year.

9th February

James Cockburn, David Wilson, James Edington and John Douglas,

Magistrates, were appointed too calculate the tax due to be paid by burgesses and citizens per month at £300, starting from 1st January, for 12 months.

30th April

Lieutenant General Dalziel wrote to the Earl of Winton advising him of the need for forces of the Shire to join him at Musselburgh straightaway, in order to oppose one part of the enemy's navy, numbering thirty sail at least, at present in the Forth. Drums were to be beaten through the streets, so that all militiamen, plus their weapons, would be ready immediately with their officers to await further orders. William Gladstone, William Brown, Richard Cockburn and John Wilson were chosen to go to the coast to spy on the enemy's movements until the following morning, from Cockburn beside Aberlady, to Gullane Head. One of them was to report any movement to the Magistrates and officers in the Burgh.

28th May.

The Treasurer was instructed to send the foot post to Edinburgh to buy five dozen ordinary mortar vessels @ 2s each, to be used at the solemn celebration of the King's birthday on the 29th.

15th June

The Treasurer was instructed to give the soldiers of the three companies 15 pounds of gunpowder to fire a volley for the Lord Commissioner at the rendezvous at Cockenzie on Monday.

25th June

James Cockburn and John Brown were appointed to walk through the Burgh and Nungate with officers to take note of 'quarters', how many soldiers each person has in the house, and how long they have been there, so that when money arrives for payment there would be no argument.

Robert Millar was ordered to brick up his window which was broken at the south gable end of his house, which lay adjacent to the Minister's house on the west side of the Sidegate.

12th July

James Forrest and James Edington, Magistrates, acting on the Minister's advice, were to select a Schoolmaster now that the previous one had died.

The Treasurer was instructed to give Patrick Young (younger) £6 for writing the petition to the King for remittance of £960, being the Burgh's portion of the greater sum imposed on all the Royal Burghs.

16th July

The Provost, Treasurer and Clerk were to go to Jedburgh to see if Andrew Rutherford, Schoolmaster, would consider a transfer to the Burgh Schoolmastership.

7th August

Andrew Rutherford having flatly refused to move to Haddington, it was the turn of David Skeoch to be approached.

24th August

David Skeoch accepted the position of Schoolmaster on condition that he would not be asked to do anything else.

13th September

George Sinclair was to be approached to be the Schoolmaster.

The Provost's expenses of £103/3/6d were allowed.

The Treasurer was instructed to give William Brown, agent, 26 tholers (dollars) as a gratuity for his painstaking efforts on behalf of the Burgh.

8th October

James Cockburn was elected Provost for the following year.

10th October

George Cockburn, former Treasurer, was appointed to collect payment from the workers in the Walk Mill for the clothes they wore. He was to be accompanied by David Chaplin who had the account details, and was told to pay the second term's taxes, for August 1665, from the proceeds.

The Treasurer was instructed to give Janet Morrison £3 for the entertainment she provided during John Sibbald's little diversion.

23rd December

James Cockburn, Provost, James Forrest, John Sleich (younger), William Swinton, Baileys. George Cockburn, Dean of Guild. William Lamb, John Sleich (elder), George Forrest, Patrick Young, William Seton, John Kirkwood, Henry Cockburn, Robert Chaplin, Patrick Cockburn, William Brown, James Douglas, Robert Naysmith, James Holden, Robert Skirving, Walter Veitch, James Lindsay and John Taes.

Skinners were deemed to be a free craft with the associated freedoms for as long as can be remembered, therefore, since arguments were likely to break out between them and the merchants of Markets and Fairs, it was decided that one box penny, worth 2d per hide, will be paid by such merchants on Market day and Fairs day, over and above the box penny charged on each of the smiths and weavers. No more would be charged on any trader. The Deacons of the Skinners craft would be empowered to search the hides on any Market or Fairs day, for insufficient wear. No gloves would be sold that were worth less than 30s per dozen. Fines would be decided by Magistrates. Otherwise merchants would enjoy the privileges awarded to them.

1668

10th November

Firlots and pecks of the Meal and Salt markets were freshly set by John Archer, burgess weaver for £94, which he promised to pay to the Treasurer.

The bowling green was leased to Robert Millar, burgess apothecary, for £15.

The Fishmarket was leased to James Edington, burgess cooper, for £27.

The East haugh was leased to Robert Millar for £30.

The Common Walk Mill and West haugh was leased to Hannibal Seton for 540 merks.

The Crossgate was leased to Robert Smith for £101.

The Fleshmarket was leased to John Sleich for £105.

The Tron and Tron weights were leased to James Barns, skinner, for £244.

The Wheat and Peas market were leased to Alexander Barnett for £96.

The Beer, Ale, Malt and Bag markets were leased to Robert Smyth for £120.

Customs of the Ports and the anchorage of Aberlady were leased to John Sleich (younger) and James Douglas, baker, for 860 merks.

Two Common Mills and the Kyle at the West Mill were leased to Hannibal Seton, principal, and James Edington, adviser and co-partner, for 3200 merks.

Each sum was said to be binding on the purchasers, their executors and heirs, conjointly.

1669

September

John Hay of Baro, Robert Forrest (elder), Robert Robertson and George Wilson, were to be new Councillors.

2nd October

The militia regiment was to muster soon. Each soldier was to have a hat, therefore, William Lamb, Treasurer, was instructed to buy 58 hats.

5th October

John Hay was chosen as Commissioner to attend the Convention of

Burghs at Edinburgh on 14th October, and the Parliament in Edinburgh on 19th October. He would be allowed £4 per day for expenses. Two commissions were to be drawn up for him for theses events, signed by Andrew Young, Notary Public and Burgh Clerk.

23rd October

Henry Sleich produce the Burgh handbell which had been sent to him from Rotterdam where it was cast, plus a bill for £18/11/8d, which the Council instructed the Treasurer to pay.

William Seton, former Provost, produced an Act granted by the Commissioners for Excise, dated February 17th, 1661, at Edinburgh, and signed by Sir Archibald Primrose, Clerk of Registry, which stated that mouldy malt should be ground at the Common Mills free of duty, thus freeing farmers and collectors from collecting any duty. Asked why he had kept the said Act secret, he professed he did not know. The Council referred the Act to the magistrates to see what should be done.

The bowling green was leased to Robert Millar, apothecary, for £15.

29th November

Considering that Acts had been passed dealing with the absence of Councillors from meetings, together with the fact that such Acts were not enforced or penalties exacted, these Acts were now ratified, and a Council meeting was called for on 4th December. Each Councillor who was absent without permission would pay 30s.

27th December

John Hay, Commissioner to Parliament, reported that duty was taken off exports and put on imports. All corn was freed of tax and duty.

George Forrest and William Lamb, Baileys, presented a bill against William Wilson, fleshmonger, who controlled the Burgh's meat stocks, to determine whether he was fit to do so. The matter was referred to the Magistrates.

1670

7th January

The tax assessors were to meet at 2 p.m. Those who had not paid for the months of January, February and March, 1669, were to be warned, by the sound of the handbell, to pay the taxes due.

Soldiers were to be quartered on any who failed to pay.

Hearing that John, Earl of Lauderdale, H.M. Commissioner, was due to arrive en route from Edinburgh to London, the Council ordered George Forrest and William Lamb, Baileys, to go to Edinburgh on Monday and salute His Grace in the Burgh's name, and then invite him to the Burgh to accept a gift.

5th February

John Hay, former gardener of Tyninghame, agreed to take over the maintenance of the Bowling Green. The Magistrates were to meet him and come to an agreement.

2nd April

Since Robert Millar was likely to have to go to great pains and expense in laying the Bowling Green, the Treasurer was instructed to pay him £40.

It was also agreed that, since it was necessary to build a house next to the Bowling Green, John Douglas and Patrick Spavin, wrights, would be hired to decide how best to build it.

19th April

Robert Millar, surgeon, was prepared to take on the building of a house next to the Bowling Green, on condition that he was paid 200 merks, plus any further expenses incurred, or else to be allowed the rent which would accrue from the Green. The Treasurer was instructed to advance him 200 merks.

The Gentlemen of the Shire proposed to send beer, which they brewed from malt for home use, to the Burgh, provided that it was free from duty, otherwise they would take it elsewhere. The Provost agreed to admit it into the Burgh free of duty for all time to come.

James Smyth, the proprietor of a small feu in Dirleton, and Clerk of Tranent, was to be the next Clerk of Haddington. George Forrest and William Lamb were to go to Tranent to finally convince him.

13th June

The meeting between Robert Millar and the Magistrates to agree on the completion of the building of a house adjacent to the Bowling Green, took place this day. The Magistrates agreed the sum of 800 merks to Robert Millar, bringing the total expenditure to 1000 merks. The house was to be three storeys high with a slate roof. The rent from the house and Green was to be waived for three years. Title was awarded to Robert Millar and his heirs for 19 years. For the remaining 16 years of the title, rent would be set at £20 for the house and Green. Robert Millar signed on behalf of himself, his heirs and his successors.

4th July

The Treasurer was instructed to hire and consult Robert Sinclair of Longformacus, advocate, about the action pursued by Mr Cunningham of Cambuskenneth against the Burgh for a cup he alleged he won at the horse racing.

24th August

The Provost and his attendants would greet H.M. Commissioner when he arrived from Edinburgh and give him a gift.

30th November

An inventory of the Court Books, Council Books and protocol records, scroll papers and three seals, was produced by Andrew Young, former servant to the late James Gray, Clerk. They were handed to James Smyth, the present Clerk, who transferred them to Robert Robertson, Treasurer, to put in the Charter Chest. Similarly, one black box containing the Burgh Charters, including the lease of Gladsmuir, and decrees and submissions about the Guild System, plus another lease between the late Earl of Haddington and the Burgh which refers to the upkeep of the acreage belonging to the Burgh, were also placed in the Charter Chest.

1671

13th September

His Majesty, having seen fit to grant the Burgh freedom to hold a Michaelmas Fair on 29th September, which, being a Friday, is Market Day, it was re-scheduled for Tuesday, 3rd October .

Henry Cockburn, Provost, was chosen as Commissioner to meet the Committee of the Shire to discuss the burden laid on the Burgh.

The lie-days at the Mills seemed to operate detrimentally to the Burgh, therefore no further lie-days would be allowed, except when the dam heads broke down, following violent storms.

James Spavin, wright, presented a bill for 100 merks for the extraordinary efforts he had made in restoring and repairing the East Mill, now in full working order.

Edward Dickson, cripple, was awarded 24s to buy a new pair of shoes.

2nd December

William Young, the son of Patrick Young, Bailey, was chosen as lieutenant, and John Sleich, son of Harry Sleich, merchant, was chosen as adjutant to the Burgh militia, to replace Harry Cockburn and William McCall.

30th December

It was alleged that the hammermen used their pallcloth for those other than their own members, to the detriment of the poor. It was therefore ordered that such be used only by their own, otherwise the cloth would be seized, and the delinquent parties punished.

1672

26th February

Grissell Seton was awarded £9/11/6d for services performed during the ceremony of the creation of burgesses at Borthwick and Carfrae.

Five shillings was allowed to the Tax Master for collecting the tax roll at Mr. Lamb's house.

3rd April

An order was produced from the Committee of the Shire, which ordered the Burgh to place three men at the service of His Majesty. Magistrates were chosen to find two men, one having already been selected.

Nobody was allowed at the little common bridge at the haugh, or to make fires there in future; under penalty to be set by the Magistrates.

No more money was to be spent on clearing molehills on the haughs.

11th April

Considering that, in the past, the Burgh has borne the full cost of raising a company of militia, it was decided that, in future, every fourth man chosen would himself find a fifth, as was the practice in the rest of the Shire.

6th June

The Treasurer was instructed to pay Charles Jacobson 10s for healing a soldier on HM service.

18th June

It was agreed to draw up instructions for the Sterling Imposition etc., as the Magistrates wished, as following:

1) that the Commissioner to the Parliament shall take such measures as the Magistrates think most convenient for imposing one merk of tax on each boll of malt to conform with a previously ratified Act.

2) that the Commissioner make supplication to His Grace My Lord

Commissioner to procure a gift of £24 for each tun of wine sold within the Burgh.

3) that the Convention of Burghs in Edinburgh be asked to assist the Burgh in resisting the heavy burden of dues imposed by the Committee of the Shire.

4) that the Commissioner makes supplication to His Grace for the relief of the Sterling Imposition.

5) that the Commissioner makes supplication to the Burghs with regard to the imposition by the Burgh of Edinburgh for the previous years of one merk on each ton of goods brought from Leith which was not in bulk, with another 6d on each cartful of goods.

23rd July

Henry Cockburn, Provost.

Edward Jamieson, Schoolmaster, who had the trust of the public, and had sworn an oath of allegiance, was required to acknowledge and sign for the same, by Act of Parliament. If he refused, he would be stripped of the office of Schoolmaster. He duly refused, and was removed from his post, which was then declared vacant.

27th August

With regard to the pair of stocks which stood at the bridge end, they were ordered to be removed, and a stone plinth erected on the same spot, bearing the Burgh's name and coat-of-arms.

The Provost informed the Council that he had been notified by John Yeaman of a construction which was concave and dangerous insofar as it allowed water to flood into the Burgh. The Magistrates were told to inspect it and report back.

Robert Smyth was told to appear before the Council for his disobedience and display of contempt for authority in not going with officials to pay the patrimony at the Provost's instruction.

The Treasurer was instructed to provide a ring and beacon for the Aberlady anchorage.

17th September

St Peter's Fair, held annually and scheduled for 29th June, was not shown in the Almanac. Therefore, it was decided to announce the date to all concerned, and for it then to be put in the Almanac.

Robert Smyth was detained in custody at the will of the Magistrates.

21st September

The piper and drummer were to be paid 20s.p.a. to purchase livery and stockings.

It was agreed that an Act be restored which dealt with the abuse in Council of everyone speaking at the same time, by insisting that they address their remarks to the Provost only; under a considerable penalty.

30th October

Patrick Young, Bailey, John Sleich (elder), John Sleich (younger), and John Brown representing the merchants, James Douglas, Bailey, and James Edington for the crafts, were to meet and regulate all of the customs dues of the Tron, Meal and Salt markets, Ports, Fishmarket and Cornmarket before the leases of the patrimony were due.

An account was to be settled from Grissell Seton, on behalf of Catherine Baird, at the time of her entertainment, amounting to £3/10s.

9th November

The Act of 30th October 1672, showing the result of the customs dues regulations, was presented to the Council.

7th November

Patrick Dawson, Robert Smyth (younger), Thomas Hastie, burgesses, appeared before the group who regulated the customs dues, and gave their opinion as former tax collectors as follows:

> Tron – every peck of wool of 9 stones weight, should pay one fleece of wool.

Every half peck should pay half a fleece of wool, and any lesser quantity should pay a lesser amount.

Every stone weight would pay 12d over and above these charges,

Every stone of cheese, butter, lint and tow would pay 12d; unfreemen to pay half.

Every stone of tallow to pay 4d – unfreemen to pay 8d.

Every stone sold to outsiders pay 3 to 4d.

Every stone bought from outsiders pay 4d for weighing.

Meal/Salt markets – every peck of linseed sold by unfreemen in a public market to pay 2s.

Every peck of hempseed "   "   "   " 1/4d.

The above revised to 1s. For linseed and 8d for hemp seed.

Ports – every bag of corn to pay 4d.

    – every peck of linseed to pay 4d.

    – every peck of hemp seed to pay 2d.

    – every back burden to pay 4d.

    – everything carried by hand, or under the oxter, to pay 2d.

The Council approved all of the above.

11th November

A review of the agreement between James Smyth and the Council, concerning Master Millership of the two Common Corn Mills and the conditions, payment and duties of the Mill grinders, as applied to the late James Spavin, was carried out as follows:

1 for each two bolls of wheat – one dishful of flour allowed. For each one boll of wheat, one heaped bottom allowed (to the Master Miller).

2 To the Undermiller – per bag, one dishful of husk grain; per 7 firlots, 2 dishfuls.

3   for each bag of ground corn, one heaped dishful to the Master Miller; for 7 firlots, 2 dishfuls.

4   To the Undermiller, for each 7 firlots, 2 dishfuls; for every boll one dishful.

5   For every quarter-boll of husk grain, one dishful of meal; for 3 bolls, one peck; for one firlot one bottom (to the Master Miller).

6   To the Undermiller, for every 7 firlots, 2 dishfuls; for every boll, one dishful.

7   For one half boll of husk grain, one dishful of meal; for three bolls, one peck; for one firlot one bottom (To the Master Miller).

8   To the Under Miller, for each keelful of oats (7 bolls) , 6 dishfuls of meal: for 6 bolls. 5 dishfuls.

9   To the Mill boy – for each keelful of oats, one dishful of meal.

10   To the Master Miller, for each 6 firlots of malt, one dishful; for each 7 firlots, 2 dishfuls.

3rd December

A document from the Bishop of Edinburgh to the Council, ordered them to accept Edward Jamieson as Schoolmaster. A civil answer was prepared and returned to him.

28th December

William Skein, a qualified teacher, was asked to be the Schoolmaster.

1673

27th January

A proclamation was to be fixed to the Market Cross, and to the doors of the School, on Friday, allowing eight days for a reply.

17th February

A Schoolmaster was to appear for interview on the Thursday.

George Cockburn, Bailey, and William Lamb, Dean of Guild, were to meet to consider hiring light horsemen for service within the Burgh at a reasonable rate, as was the custom in other Burghs.

22nd February

William Skein was appointed as Schoolmaster at 400 merks p.a. plus children's fees.

2,000 merks were borrowed from Margaret Kirkwood the previous Candlemas, to pay Isobel Yeaman, spouse to Robert Robertson, merchant burgess.

Two dollars were given to Harry Cockburn, wright, to settle his bill.

William Skein, Schoolmaster, was to teach Greek, Latin and Grammar. He was to have an assistant who was qualified in these languages. He was not to be absent for more than four days without special permission. He was not to accept any other office, either from the Ministry or elsewhere. He was to be paid 350 merks at the usual terms, with 50 merks to his assistant, on condition that no one else would teach within the Burgh. A house was granted to the Schoolmaster.

22nd March

Ale was sold for 20d per pint, with the dearest at 2s.; under penalty of a 30s. Fine. Wheat was sold for £7 per boll; a 12d loaf had to weigh 16 ounces; under penalty of a 40s. Fine.

Wheat bread from outside the Burgh, which was sold in the Market, had ro weigh 18 ounces for a 12d loaf; under the usual penalty.

Candles were sold for 4s.per pound; weighed at the Tron with brass weights; under penalty of a 40s. Fine.

31st March

Magistrates were appointed to review the Burgh's patrimony, the Minister's stipend (paid out of the proceeds from the acreages left by the Earl of Haddington), plus taxation rolls, taxes etc..

No one was to leave rubbish on the public roads.

James Bennett, herdsman, was to be deprived of his patrimony after WhitSunday. Instead, in return for information of those who left rubbish on public roads, or pastured their beasts illegally on Gladsmuir, he would be granted a proportion of the fines levied by the Judges.

The Collector, William Gibson, was to raise three months taxes, amounting to £231/10/4d.

George Wallace was to be made a drummer since he was formerly a soldier.

The Convenor and nine Deacons were to make a request in writing for a pall cloth. It would be considered by the Council.

Alexander Thomson, on his deathbed, was granted 5s. Sterling.

12th April

James Calderwood requested the letter sent by the Bishop to the Council about Edward Jameson, but this was refused.

The Charter Chest was to be searched or a contract between the Earl of Haddington and the Burgh about the disposition of the Tithes, the Parsonage and the Vicarage in the Burgh acreage, and all other papers relating thereto, and of payment of an annuity or taxes therefrom.

13th May

Having read the document sent by the Earl of Roxburgh about the burial of his Lady, the Magistrates were chosen to go to the Lady's funeral at Kelso; under penalty of a fine of £30.

Thomas Hastie, Deacon of the weaver craft, place a petition before the Council, showing the gift of the Council to the weavers within the Burgh. It was ordered that no one should remove, from the Burgh, any yarn made by the freemen weavers. Nevertheless, several had done so, to the general discredit of their craft, thereby causing a reduction in the tax they paid. Thomas Hastie asked that the Council reassure him and his colleagues that the original Act was still in operation, and to punish the delinquent weavers. The Council forbade all burgesses and citizens to export any kind of yarn, either linen or wool, for any 'unfreeman' to use, nor any person to import such. The Deacon, with the assistance of an official of the Burgh, was empowered to arrest transgressors, and take them before a Magistrate to be censured and punished. The aforesaid Act was again ratified and approved, provided that the weavers gave good service to burgesses and citizens in doing their work as well as previously, and at the same price as any weavers in other Royal Burghs. This Act was to be proclaimed publicly at the Cross, so that no one could proclaim ignorance thereof.

31st May

Harry Cockburn, Provost, was chosen to go to Perth as Commissioner to the General Convention of Burghs on the first Thursday in July, and to present a supplication to the Burghs for procuring a case of missive dues.

A discharge from the Earl of Haddington for £10/13s. for the first term's taxes of the Burgh of Haddington was received.

7th June

An Act was passed about the right granted by the Earl of Haddington to the Burgh, for the Tithes for the Parsonage and the Vicarage.

16th June

George Sinclair's bond for 1,000 merks was received. The Treasurer was instructed to pay Robert Kerr, Minister, his proportion of the Tithes for the Burgh acreage.

19th July

The Treasurer was instructed to give 10 merks to My Lord Lyon to 'matriculate' the arms of every Burgh, and also commissions for George Cockburn and John Sleich (younger) to collect the said arms. He was also to speak to the Provost of Edinburgh about the imposition of 6s. for every cartful of goods brought from Leith in bulk.

The Treasurer was instructed to advance 100 merks to William Skein, Schoolmaster.

The Council instructed the Treasurer to have the School thoroughly cleaned, since it was in a sorry state after the last flood, and to provide rushes of hay for the children to sit on.

Alexander Maitland was to be made a burgess.

29th July

Magistrates were obliged to seek the disposition granted by the Earl of Lothian to the Burgh of the annuity from the Charter Chest, so that it may be made clear to all concerned.

15th August

A pursuit by the tax collectors of the excise due from the family of Robert Naysmith, was approved by the Council.

The Bishop of Edinburgh, and the brethren of the Presbytery, were all made burgesses during a visit to the Kirk.

1st September

The Kirk tax contract, dated 1589, was produced, showing that the Burgh agreed to pay a sixth part.

Burgesses were instructed to appear clad in armour, following their appointment made on oath, according to the custom practised in Edinburgh.

6th September

Members of the Court Circuit were all made burgesses, gratis.

The Treasurer was instructed to pay Jean Blair £23/25/8d for dry wine, consumed when the Bishop of Edinburgh etc., were made burgesses.

26th September

The Council ordered the action, raised against the Treasurer by John Sydserf about a box of sweetmeats, be defended at the Burgh's expense.

27th October

John Hay of Baro was chosen to be Commissioner to Parliament.

Samuel Colville paid five dollars for his book.

The Council awarded George Cockburn £54/2s which he had spent in the action against him for imprisoning the two surveyors of excise.

10th November

A list of the Magistrates and Councillors elected for 1674:

Harry Sleich, Provost.

William Lamb, Patrick Kerr and John Brown, Baileys.

John Lessells, Treasurer.

Harry Cockburn, Richard Chaplin, William McCall, Alexander Syme, George Sleich, George Wilson, Robert Millar, George Chaplin, Thomas Millar, John Cowden, Patrick Young, John Sleich (elder), George Cockburn, Patrick Wood, Francis Edington, Patrick Cothill, John Taes, James Nisbet, George Young, John McGall and John Paterson – all Councillors.

THE NEXT EIGHT AND A HALF YEARS ARE NOT REPRESENTED IN THE COUNCIL RECORDS, POSSIBLY BECAUSE OF THE DEATH OF THE CLERK.

THE RECORD RESUMES IN 1682.

1682

6th May

Henry Cockburn, Provost. John Brown, John Robertson, John Douglas, Baileys. William McCall, Dean of Guild. Thomas Ayton, Treasurer. Harry Cockburn, John Lessells, John Sleich (younger), William Scott, Robert Brown, John Toderick, Thomas Hastie, Robert Gray, William Archer and Robert Anderson, Councillors.

£182/3/4d given to John Thomson, tailor burgess from Edinburgh, in settlement of a sum due to him from Patrick Hepburn of Nunraw, who was imprisoned in the Tolbooth at the said John Thomson's insistence, and who subsequently escaped but had until Martinmas to settle his debt to the Burgh, with interest added thereafter. Whereof John Thomson was to give an assignation of Nunraw's bond to the Burgh.

Because of the incompetence of the Tolbooth jailers, who had often allowed prisoners to escape, thereby leaving the Burgh to pay debts they owed, the Council recommended that a young, fit, able man be sought to be the Keeper of the Prison, being someone who could find surety so as to relieve the Burgh of this burden. The Council would promise him all satisfaction, profit and benefit to the same extent as other prison keepers.

William McCall, Dean of Guild, was instructed to remove all the Burgh's armoury to the Burgh magazine.

20th May

Archibald Trent, Councillor, who was absent from the previous meeting of the Council, was ordered to pay one merk by the Provost, but refused. He left immediately, refusing to obey the Provost's command to stay. It was ordered that he be brought back and put in prison, and to remain there, at the Provost's pleasure, until he had confessed.

24th May

A Commissioner from Inverness sought help to build a bridge there. This was granted and the Treasurer instructed to contribute 50 merks.

The Treasurer was instructed to provide coal, glasses and wine for the solemn celebration of the King's Birthday, as heretofore.

22nd July

The Treasurer was instructed to have a door from the Bowling Green house removed, so as to effect an entry and allow a stair to be put there for a play which was going to be performed there by the Noblemen's and Gentlemen's schoolchildren on Friday, 28th July.

No one in the Burgh was allowed to keep stacks of whins, either within the Burgh, on the streets or near property, except in yards which were at a distance from houses; under penalty £20 plus forfeit of the whins and liability for damages. Alexander Borthwick was ordered to remove his stack of whins before 5th August; under penalty of a fine of £20 and confiscation of the stack.

11th September

Notwithstanding the many Acts regulating the holding of Public Fairs on Saturdays or Mondays, the Michaelmas Fair was due to be held on a Friday. Therefore, the Council ordered that it be moved to Tuesday, 3rd October 1682. This was to be broadcast throughout the Burgh on Market day, so that none could plead ignorance.

Magistrates and Council were asked to consider how best to reward John Adair for drawing the map of the Burgh of Haddington.

6th November

John Sleich (younger), expressed his desire and willingness to become a Councillor, but said that he was unable to take the test as yet.

11th December

John Smyth, Commissioner, was to go to Edinburgh with the Great Charter, and deliver it to the Laird of Moncrieff, one of the Clerks of the Exchequer. Agents were appointed to attend.

John Smyth delivered the Act of Exchequer, on behalf of the Magistrates, referring to the 80,000 merks imposed on the Burgh in 1650, which was placed in the Charter Chest, and exonerated the Provost from all such Acts. John Smyth produced his account of spending and charges amounting to £54/12/8d plus £5/7/4d for a man and horses. The Council approved the Treasurer to pay with thanks for his pains and diligence.

The Council chose William Kennedy, tailor burgess, to be the Keeper of the Tolbooth during their pleasure, and gave him £60 as a fee.

The Council were handed a note of debt incurred by the Laird of Nunraw, on behalf of Henry Rankin, Edinburgh merchant. The Laird was imprisoned in the Tolbooth but escaped, therefore the Council ordered John Smyth to settle with Henry Rankin.

A petition was presented to the Council by the Tanners and Dyers of Haddington against Alexander Burnett, tax collector of the Wake Mill, for allowing 'unfreemen' to work at the Mill, shears and presses, to their great prejudice. The Council forbade anyone to dye or dress cloth, or any other job, who was not a burgess. John Eveling and his assistants, who had taken over the Wake Mill, were forbidden to work in the Burgh.

1683

4th January

Four officials were ordered to arrest John Brown and put him in gaol, until he paid his debt to the Burgh.

William McGall, wright, was given 5 merks for a coffin, which was made for George Hume, trader

Margaret Neill was allowed 24 merks for a jacket and halberd for her husband, George Guthrie, to be given to Robert Wolf and paid for at Candlemas.

£3/6s was allowed to Henry Cockburn, which had been spent by him with the Ministers.

20th January

The Council employed William Kennedy as Jailer and Keeper of the Tolbooth. He gave his oath of fidelity and his bond of surety, which was ordered to be recorded in the Council Books together with his instructions. The Magistrates were empowered to give him the keys of the Tolbooth, with a record of those imprisoned.

Henry Cockburn, Provost. Thomas Ayton and John Douglas, Baileys, handed the keys of the Tolbooth to William Kennedy. The list of prisoners was as follows: Richard Chaplin, Haddington merchant, John Anderson, baker, Margaret Cockburn, widow of James Cockburn, former

Provost, William Weddell, John Richardson of Panston, Margaret Buchan, spouse of James Liddell, baker. Thomas Ayton, Bailey, signed the instruments and gave them to John Swinton, Notary Public, one of the Clerks of the Burgh.

Instructions to William Kennedy, Jailer and Keeper of the Tolbooth :

1 That the Keeper and Jailer provide sufficient surety to relieve the Burgh from damages incurred as a result of prisoners escaping. The Burgh agreed to provide enough doord, locks and keys, and ensured that they would be strong and firm.

2 An able-bodied, capable servant would be kept by the Jailer, for whom he would be responsible. One or the other should be on duty at all times, from 6 a.m. when doors opened to 10 p.m. when doors were closed and locked. No one was to have entry except in case of emergency, or when the Provost or Baileys visited. The Bellman and Keeper of the bells and clock would have access to the parapet. The Courthouse and loft doors, as well as the prison doors, would always be kept locked and closed. It was not in the Jailer's power to hinder the Bellman, therefore keys would be kept at the foot of the spiral staircase , and the door at the head thereof, for access to the parapet and the Bell and Clocktower.

3 The Jailer would act as doorman for the Burgh Council and the Courts, Guild Councils, meetings of the Deacon and his craft, several crafts in the Burgh, Sheriff Courts, meetings and Conventions of Commissioners of Assessment, Excise and militia, JPs, Shiremen, plus other lawful meetings. He would receive prisoners and keep them in custody until ordered to release them, plus all of the things his predecessor was wont to do.

4 The Jailer would receive all prisoners into the Tolbooth having informed the Magistrates. All prisoners must first be booked into the Burghs' Court books, kept by the Common Clerk, who would receive such booking money from the prisoners as the Council decreed. He would charge 4s per day for each prisoner,

except for burgesses of the Burgh who would pay 2s. Craftsmen freed before 10p.m. would pay no fee. Thereafter they would pay 2s. plus a further 2s. per day.

5   No prisoner would be allowed to buy or bring any ale, wine, beer or other drink, except as provided by the Jailer.

6   The Jailer and his servant must wear sword and scabbard at all times.

7   The Jailer and his servant must assist the Burgh officers when commanded by the Magistrates to arrest and imprison.

8   The Jailer must not allow anyone to carry arms into the Tolbooth or anything else which could be used by the prisoners in helping them to escape.

9   The Jailer must allow no one to drink too much, or otherwise be incapable in the Tolbooth.

10 All prisoners were to be detained after their sentence, until they had paid the Jailer's fee.

11 No one was allowed to leave prison without a warrant from the Magistrate.

12 The Jailer must obey the occasional orders and instructions of the Council.

31st March

The Council and Magistrates considered how best to prepare the West and East Ports, in order to receive the funeral cortege of the Duke of Lauderdale on Thursday, 5th April.

The Dean of Guild was ordered to clean up the Clartiburn in the Burgh.

5th April

The Provost reported that Thomas Bell, a common beggar, born in Musselburgh, killed another beggar at 6 p.m. at the South Port by stabbing him with a dagger. The corpse was still lying in Alderston's Aisle in the Kirkyard. After consideration, it was agreed to ask the Fiscal to commence proceedings against the perpetrator of the crime.

14th April

A letter was received from the Marquis of Queensberry, Lord High Treasurer of Scotland, and James Drummond of Lundie, Depute, requiring the Council to prepare a list of fines for ecclesiastical offences before 26th April, plus a statement of account of the fines themselves, so that it could be decided how much belonged to the King. Henry Cockburn, Provost, and John Smyth, Clerk, were to present a list of persons fined since 1679.

William McCall, Dean of Guild, complained that George Sleich had called him a liar, cheat and rascal, and the son of a liar, during the previous Council meeting. On that same day, John Douglas, Bailey, complained that George Sleich called him an ignorant person.

George Sleich confessed that, during the last Council meeting, while debating the Act of Regulation, he had said that the Act should not be given to such an ignorant person as John Douglas to be explained.

Archibald Trent, Thomas Barns, Alexander Thomson, James Reid and others, confirmed that they had heard George Sleich call William McCall a liar and the son of a liar.

George Sleich was found guilty of slandering William McCall and John Douglas. His punishment was referred to the Magistrates, and he was ordered to be retained in custody until they had reached their decision.

19th May

Thomas Hogg, tailor, owed the Burgh £20 for his burgess-ship. He had recently lost everything in a fire, therefore the Burgh agreed to wait for payment.

The Provost and John Smyth completed the list of fines and offenders of Ecclesiastical disorders, and produced receipts for the same.

John Smyth produced the Great Charter of the Exchequer, which was then place in the Charter Chest.

Herbert Kennedy, Schoolmaster, asserted that he was owed a full quarter's salary of 100 merks, which he claimed on behalf of himself and his assistant, John Black. The Council allowed the claim.

John Douglas was allowed payment for a bill of £11/14s. for wine and ale drunk by the Magistrates in his house, together with Magistrates from Edinburgh, and others who were present at the Duke of Lauderdale's funeral.

The Treasurer produced an account of money spent on behalf of the Burgh on several occasions I.e. burial of James Sinclair of Drem – £9/7s.

funeral of the Earl of Lauderdale at Inveresk and Haddington – £10/13s.

execution of Thomas Bell, murderer – £13/5/2d.

The Council approved the accounts.

28th May

The Treasurer was instructed to provide two cartloads of coal for the bonfire on the following day, as well as wine and glasses.

The Treasurer was to pay the Burgh's cheque at the usual time.

2nd June

The Council ordered the purchase of a Silver Cup or Plate, to the value of £7 sterling, to be raced for on 4th June from the West Port to Samuelston Loan Head, around the post erected there, and thence back to West Port. The cost of the Cup would be split among the riders. The horses would go on show before the Magistrates fourteen days before the race. Proclamation would be made throughout the Burgh market and also in Edinburgh.

Thomas Ayton, Bailey, protested that the Cup acted to the detriment of the Burgh. William McCall, Archibald Trent and Robert Gordon were in agreement with him and refrained from voting.

14th June

The Council ordered the Silver Cup Tankard, or Plate, worth £10 sterling. It would be run for from West Port to the Two Mile Cross, thence to the Samuelston road, and then back to West Port. Posts would be set up along the route. Riders must weigh eight stones. The cost would be borne by the Burgh. The first horse past the post would win the Cup. The last horse would get the oatmeal.

Henry Cockburn, Commissioner, was granted his expenses of £50. John Smyth was allowed 50 merks for his efforts. Robert Gray, Fiscal, was allowed £6 while serving as Fiscal to the Court of the Justiciary, when Thomas Bell, the murderer, was found guilty and condemned to death.

Henry Cockburn, Provost, Robert Robertson, Bailey, Robert Brown, Treasurer and John Smyth, Clerk, were to go to Edinburgh on 10th July to attend the Lords of the Justiciary at the Circuit Court of Edinburgh. The Treasurer was to make out the Burgh's cheque, and John Smyth was to pay the Burgh's tax for the two terms of 1682 with as much of the tax as he had received so far. The Council sent the Charter to be ratified. An official was also sent to attend the Magistrates in Edinburgh.

13th August

Burgesses, living outwith the Burgh, were advised to move into it before Martinmas, or else forfeit their 'freedom'. This action was to be made known following the beat of the drum.

The Fleshmongers, who were granted their 'freedom' in 1680, despite the fact that there were only a few of them, were still low in number. Therefore the Council removed their 'freedom' until such time as their numbers had increased. Their dues would still continue to be paid until three Councillors and the Convenor had considered the matter further.

£7/10s. was given to James Spence as charity on his release from the Tolbooth.

John Douglas's bill of £20, for repairing the West and East Ports, was paid.

Henry Cockburn's bill for going to Edinburgh in July 1683, which amounted to £15/6/8d, was ordered to be paid by the Treasurer.

25th August

John Smyth produced the Great Charter which was placed in the Charter Chest.

Information about the marches around Gladsmuir was sought in the Charter Chest to establish the difference between there and Clerkington. The information was found to be inaccurate, so a further search of the Chest was ordered.

The Mill Dam banks were to be strengthened, following the damage done to them in the last great rainstorm.

John Smyth, tax collector, presented his account of the Burgh's taxes imposed by the Convention of Estates in 1678, payable on WhitSunday and Martinmas 1682, including what he had already paid to the General Collector, plus £86/0/10d. paid by him to cover the shortfall in the tax roll.

Robert Brown, Treasurer, was ordered to pay him his dues.

Robert Kay was given £4. He was sick and close to death.

Janet Tait, servant to John Sleich, was granted settlement of a bill for wine drunk at his house on several public occasions, amounting to £4/17s. The Treasurer was instructed to pay.

Robert Wallace, smith, was awarded £30 for mending the Burgh clock.

Thomas Warrender, painter, was given £9 for painting the Burgh arms on the drum.

11th September

Patrick Hepburn of Nunraw, was detained in prison in the Tolbooth, at the request of Thomas Somervell, tailor, of Edinburgh, by virtue of Our Lord's letters of arrest, for a debt of £116. Patrick Hepburn escaped, whereupon issued a summons against the Burgh for payment of the said debt. The Treasurer was instructed to pay him £130 in satisfaction of the total sum due to him, provided that, in return, Thomas Somervell gave an assignation of the settlement of the debt.

Magistrates were ordered to meet William Dinnson, Second Minister of Haddington, about the Burgh's share of the cost of building his Manse.

Margaret Richardson, widow of Robert Kay, was awarded £12 to defray the cost of his funeral.

1st October

Thomas Ayton, former Treasurer, presented his accounts for the period Martinmas, 1681 to Martinmas, 1682 wich amounted to £4614/9/10d. of which £4138/17s. was expenditure, leaving £475/12/10d. to the Treasurer, Robert Brown.

a 12d. Loaf, made from wheat selling for £7/10s. per boll, had to weigh 14 ounces, three quarters and three drops.

COUNCIL RECORD FOR HADDINGTON FOR THE YEARS 1684 and 1685 ARE MISSING FOR UNKNOWN REASONS.

Chapter 7

James VII and II
1685 to 1688

In Scotland it was the 'killing time.' Covenanters were ruthlessly hunted down. In the Highlands, Argyll led an uprising in 1685 which was violently dealt with. Charles' son, James, Duke of York, like his forbears before him, misunderstood the strength of religious extremism in both England and Scotland. Although it was in the Highlands that most of the repression occurred it became obvious that this draconian policy simply did not work.

The 1680s saw the rise of the Stuart influence in Scottish politics. James withdrew the 3rd 'Indulgence', which allowed for a multi-religious framework, in May 1686. He persuaded Parliament to pass legislation which required all office-holders, in the Church and State, to acknowledge the superiority of the Crown in 'all matters temporal and ecclesiastical.' James, as Duke of York, left Scotland in 1681, which allowed for a resumption of a bitter struggle for power. By 1686, the Earl of Perth and Melfort, Secretary of State, were in control. Both were Catholics. James saw to it that he had many 'puppets' in place, in important positions, well before he finally became King in 1685.

Argyll briefly attempted revolution in 1685, but his bid ended in failure, noit even managing to secure the help of most of his kinsmen. By 1688 the Highlands were as lawless as ever. However, James popularity in England was even lower than in Scotland, leading to William of Orange, summoned by English nobles who were hostile to James, landing in Torbay in late 1688, and the hurried departure of James to France.

In Scotland, two 'indulgences,' in February and June 1687, granted 'unlimited toleration' to all shades of religious opinion. This gave the

Edinburgh 'mob' encouragement to rise in protest against all manifestations of Catholicism. Holyrood Abbey was sacked.

Nevertheless, on the domestic front, things were improving. There were signs of progression in overseas trade and home manufacture. Glasgow became a 'boom' town, with soap works and woollen manufactories springing up. Fife and Lothian witnessed improvements in the use of land, with crop rotation, partial enclosure and the liming of soil. This was achieved, however, at the price of farms being consolidated into larger units and rising rents for tenants.

Haddington Burgh Council Records 1686 to 1688

1686

30th November

William McCall, Provost. Robert Robertson, John Lessells, John Taes, Baileys. Archibald Trent, Dean of Guild. Thomas Ayton, Treasurer, John Sleich, Robert Brown, William Rye, James Smyth, Robert Kay, Thomas Hodge, Alexander Maitland, Alexander Edgar, James Lauder, Alexander Millar, Alexander Smyth, Robert Gordon, William Begbie, Thomas Borthwick, William Burnett, Robert Anderson and John Thomson – Councillors.

John, Earl of Tweeddale, appeared before the Council as one of the members of the Privy Council, and produced a document signifying His Majesty's pleasure at the election of Magistrates, Council and Deacons, which the Clerk read out:

"Edinburgh, 25th November, 1686.

For as much as it has pleased the King's Most Excellent Majesty by a letter written under his Royal Hand, dates at Whitehall, the 19th November. To the Privy Council of this ancient Kingdom, signified that he is now resolved to nominate and appoint the Magistrates, Council and Deacons for the Burgh of Haddington, as being such as His Majesty judges to be most loyal and ready to promote his service, and most forward to support the good and interest of the said Burgh. And therefore authorises his Privy Council to that effect. Therefore, the Lords of His Majesty's Privy Council, for pursuance of His Majesty's commands, do hereby nominate and appoint Sir William Paterson, Knight Clerk to His Majesty's Privy Council, to be Provost of the said Burgh of Haddington, Alexander Maitland, Merchant Bailey, Robert Robertson, Merchant Bailey, James Douglas,

Trades Bailey, John Lessells, Dean of Guild, and Alexander Millar, Treasurer. And the Merchant Councillors to be William McCall, Charles Maitland, Archibald Trent, James Lauder, Alexander Edgar, Thomas Ayton, Robert Brown, William Rye, Alexander Smyth, Robert Gordon, Richard Millar, and William Lilley, Craft Councillor and Convenor. Trades Councillor to be John Jack, Deacon of the masons. Richard Carraill, Deacon of wrights. John Hay, Deacon of hammermen. Robert Byres, Deacon of tailors. John Main, Deacon of shoemakers. Bartholomew Byers, Deacon of weavers. James Outtersyde, Deacon of fleshmongers and James Carmichael, Deacon of glovers. James and John Smyth to be conjointly Clerks.

All of which persons are hereby authorised to continue in their respective offices in the said Burgh until next Michaelmas. The said Lords admit them to their offices on Tuesday, 30th November, and recommends the Earl of Tweeddale, one of their own number, to be present so that he could see that His Royal Majesty's Pleasure was put into execution."

After the reading, all of the above named, except James Outtersyde, accepted their respective offices and gave their oaths.

1st December

The Treasurer was instructed to pay the Secretary's dues for HM letter about the election of Magistrates and Council, amounting to £7.

Convenor and Deacons, named by the King, were to be Convenor and Deacons of their respective trades. The old Convenor and Deacons were ordered to give up their books to them. The Council authorised the oldest Bailey, or, in his absence, the second oldest, to summon Council in the absence of the Provost in an emergency.

7th December

James Outtersyde, Deacon of Fleshmongers, accepted the office he was given by the Privy Council, and swore his loyalty.

1687

10th January

The Council allowed an amount of money, spent by Alexander Smyth while making the Clavers' cornet a burgess, which amounted to £12/4/6d. The Treasurer was instructed to pay.

Ale was to be sold for 16d per pint. A 12d loaf was to weigh 14 ounces, threequarters and three drops. Bread from outwith the Burgh was to weigh 16 ounces, threequarters and three drops.

7th April

William McCall, former Provost, explained that John Elliott, former surgeon and apothecary, had left 800 merks to buy a good, large clock for the Tolbooth, bearing the inscription "Ex done Joannis Elliott." He sought the Council's advice on how best to acquire such a clock. He was asked to accompany Magistrates to inspect clocks in Edinburgh or Leith or elsewhere, and either buy one in Scotland, or have one made, or send abroad for one.

Robert Robertson bailey, John Lessells, Dean of Guild, and William McCall, reported that William Moore, Clockmaker in Musselburgh, had been commissioned to make the said clock, similar to the one in the Steeple of the Tron Kirk in Edinburgh, matching its dimensions at all points. He would install the clock in the steeple. The clock to have three faces, with one at the west side of the Tolbooth. He was to maintain the clock for ten years, with the Burgh paying all expenses. It was agreed that he be paid £20, with the promise of a further £5 if the Council was pleased with the result, on condition that the clock was ready by the middle of August.

The Dean of Guild was ordered to make Roderick Urquhart, servant to George Dunbar, Second Minister, a burgess and Guild brother-gratis.

20th June

George Gowans was appointed as agent for the Burgh in the action against Thomas Fender. The Treasurer was instructed to pay him six dollars and his man one dollar.

John Smyth, Clerk, was instructed to go to Edinburgh to consult Sir John Lauder, advocate.

The Treasurer was instructed to advance whatever money was necessary, especially to the jailer, for Patrick Fleming's fees.

The Council ordered a saddle worth 15s. to be raced for on the second day of St. Peter's Fair, from the West Port to the post on Gladsmuir and back again.

It would be made known throughout the Burgh, following the beat of the drum. Entry fees would not exceed £5.

The widow of Robert Millar, apothecary burgess, and her three children, were awarded £6 to relieve distress.

15th July

Sir William Paterson, Provost, was elected as Commissioner, and Alexander Maitland, Bailey, as Assessor, for the Convention of Royal Burghs held in Edinburgh on the following Tuesday.

The Council ordered letters of restraint to be raised against all of the tenants who lived near Gladsmuir, to stop it from being destroyed by the pasturing of their cattle.

The Burgh's cheque for 1686, representing the Burgh's portion of the £2,871 due, was given to Bailey Maitland to take to the Convention of Burghs.

The Treasurer was instructed to buy a bolt of broad white ribbon and one of blue ribbon, to be attached to burgess tickets, plus a dozen parchment skins.

The Clerk was allowed £24, with £6 for his man.

12th August

The moor of Gladsmuir, being of no further use because of the damage caused by neighbours, and considering that it might be improved by tillage and enclosure, it was agreed that 200 acres, lying adjacent to Robswalls, be leased to burgesses of the Burgh for terms of 19, or thrice 19, years, at whatever rates could be arranged. The Magistrates, William McCall and James Lauder, representing the merchants, plus William Lilley, Deacon, Convenor of Trades, were appointed as Commissioners, empowered to use whatever methods they chose, to improve the moor, and to write down the taxes to be levied.

Recognising that there was only one Fleshmarket in the Burgh on Friday, which was not enough to supply all the citizens with fresh meat, it was decided that all Fleshmongers should hold a market every Tuesday as well. Beef would be cut up for sale before 9 a.m. Outside suppliers were also given permission to operate on both market days. This would be made known following the beat of the drum.

The Council deprived Thomas Nielsen, fleshmonger, of his burgess-ship for leaving the Burgh and living elsewhere, and setting up business outwith the Burgh, to the prejudice of the Burgh markets.

Patrick Wylie was made a burgess for 20 merks and a stand of arms.

22nd September

Alexander Maitland, Bailey, showed a letter addressed to the Council from the Duke of Hamilton and signed by him, under the warrant of HM Privy Council, signifying the Royal Will and Pleasure that the election of Magistrates and Council be suspended, pending HM further pleasure as follows:

> "Whereas His Most Sacred Majesty hath by His Royal letter, dated at the Court of Bath 8th September, signified that all elections on Royal Burghs be suspended until HM pleasure be known. You are hereby expressly prohibited and discharged, as you will answer at your peril, to elect any new Magistrates or Council within your Burgh this year. And you and the present Magistrates and Council are, by HM authority, hereby authorised to continue until HM shall signify his further pleasure."

Signed in the name and by the warrant of HM Privy Council by your affectionate friend "Hamilton GPD" and dated Edinburgh, 16th September, 1687.

Directed on the back "For the Right Honourable The Provost and remaining Magistrates of the Burgh of Haddington.

To be communicated to the Burgh Council.

The Council instructed the Treasurer to recruit sixteen men to mount guard during the Michaelmas Fair, commencing on the following Thursday. Robert Byres was appointed as Captain. The Fair was to be proclaimed on Friday next.

The Treasurer was instructed to give 100 merks to Henry Cockburn to buy clothes, since he was in a destitute state.

Following the 6th Act of the 3rd Session of Parliament, 1663, referring to ruined houses in Royal Burghs, and finding that several houses in the Burgh have lain ruined for several years, to the great shame of the Burgh, and in order to lessen the danger to citizens, the Council ordered officials and Sergeants to warn the owners of such properties that hey should have them repaired within one year and a day, failing which the Council would act within the powers granted to them by the said Act.

22nd October

The young Laird of Nunraw was arrested, having previously escaped twice from prison in the Burgh. He was incarcerated in the Canongate Tolbooth, for which James Mitchell and Thomas Reid were awarded 7 dollars. The hire of their horses, as well as that of Nunraw, was to be paid for by the Treasurer. Three officers, who assisted in the arrest, were awarded two dollars.

Because the streets and highways of the Burgh were in a poor condition, all property owners were ordered to repair the roadway adjacent to their property, as far as the painted line, and to lay stones and sand to repair the High Street and the King's Highway from the painted line to the crown of the road as soon as possible. The Burgh would provide the stones.

19th December

James Douglas, Bailey, was ordered to recover the arms from those who fought on the Burgh's behalf in the West country, and to keep those people in prison until they had done so. A charge of 10 merks per musket and bandolier, £3 per pike and £3 per sword would be made.

Patrick Fleming, jailer, was awarded £30/15s. for 'coal and candle' provided by him for the guard during March, October and November 1687. A deduction was made for mending the door which the guard broke when he did not receive his 'coal and candle'.

26th December

William McCall and John Sleich, Magistrates, the Treasurer and the Clerk, were to meet property owners and scour records in order to raise taxes with which to repair the Parish Kirk and build the Second Minister's Manse.

1688

28th January

Patrick Fleming, jailer, was awarded £5/19/6d for providing 'coal and candle' during December to Claverhouse and his troops when they kept guard.

Margaret Cockburn, widow of the late Robert Wolfe, Burgh official, was given £18 to care for her children.

28th January

Alexander Maitland, Bailey, declared that he held a charge of 'outlaw', raised on behalf of the Ministers of the Parish and their Collector, for a quarter of the taxes due to be paid by the Burgh, to repair the Kirk and build a Manse for the Second Minister. In fact, he had ascertained that the Burgh was liable for only one sixth of such taxes. Therefore, the Council ordered that the charge be suspended pending further discussion. Sir William Paterson, Provost, and Alexander Maitland, Bailey, were to go to Edinburgh to seek on the matter.

Alexander Maitland had a letter read out in Council which was addressed to him from Sir William Paterson, Provost, stating that the Privy Council had ordered the Magistrates of Edinburgh to have the bells rung on Sunday next after sermon, and to build bonfires and use all other demonstrations of joy with which to celebrate the Queen's conception with child. The same would take place in the Burgh.

17th April

Alexander Maitland's expenses were allowed for consulting advocates about the tax levy for repairing the Kirk, and building a Manse for the Second Minister, which amounted to £23/11s.

Robert Robertson's expenses, amounting to £33/19/4d. for wine, glasses, iron and rope for use by the Burgh, were allowed.

John Smyth, Clerk, was allowed expenses of £20 for wine and for travelling to Edinburgh on the Burgh's business.

The Treasurer was instructed to revise Patrick Fleming's expenses for 'coal and candle' provided for the guard, and to pay him what he thought fair.

29th April

William Lilley, wright, was allowed expenses for his work on the Tolbooth steeple, amounting to £23.

Agnes Black was paid £4/16s. for ale and wine supplied to the tradesmen who mended the steeple.

The Council ordered everyone to remove middens of muck from the High Street within eight days, even if if was to be for their own use. The Dean of Guild was to ensure that this was carried out.

20th June

Patrick Hepburn (younger) of Nunraw, a prisoner in the Canongate Tolbooth, made supplication that he would not be able to repay his debt as long as he remained in prison. His plea was granted, provided that he gave a bond of corroboration for the sum due, which the Burgh took into their possession, plus the annual rents due. The Clerk was told to draw on the bond, and to instruct the Keeper of the Tolbooth to free Patrick Hepburn.

Sir William Paterson, Provost, was elected Commissioner. Alexander Maitland, Bailey, was elected as Assessor. They were to meet the other Commissioners of the Royal Burghs at the first General Convention at Edinburgh on 3rd July.

John Smyth, Clerk, was allowed expenses of £47/3/6d. for wine etc., used while entertaining several Nobles and Gentlemen when they were made burgesses. Also for when the Burgh was meeting the Earl of Perth, Lord High Chancellor, when he passed through the Burgh en route to Edinburgh.

Agnes Black was paid £14 for this same occasion.

John Smyth, Clerk, produced a bond of corroboration given by Patrick Hepburn of Nunraw for £600, following which he was fined

Wheat was to be sold for £6/10s. per boll.

William Brown, Burgh cattleherd, received 40 merks at Candlemas for keeping Gladsmuir free of stray cattle etc.. He was told to impound all such, and to take the spades from strangers who attempted to dig on the Moor. This fee was over and above what he was paid by burgesses for looking after their cattle.

Robert Robertson, Bailey, was allowed expenses of £31/5s. for wine and glasses used at the birth celebrations of the Prince. Agnes Black was paid £6 for wine drunk when the Earl of Home was made a burgess.

John Smyth was allowed expenses of £17/10s. for conducting the Burgh's affairs with Sir Adam Blair and the owners of property in the Parish of Haddington.

13th September

With St. Michaelmas Fair due to fall on a Saturday, 29th September, it was agreed to postpone it until 2nd October. This was to be announced at the Cross on market day, and through the Burgh following the beat of the drum. A guard of 16 men with one Commander would be appointed by the Magistrates to keep guard in the Tolbooth.

Following HM proclamation on 15th August, all persons making Scots cloth worth more than £7, should have the seal of the town affixed thereto. The Treasurer was instructed to have a seal made for the Burgh, bearing it's name and arms.

James Lauder, Sheriff Clerk of Haddington, was awarded £7 for entertaining the Provost of Glasgow.

22nd September

Alexander Maitland, Bailey, presented to the Council an Act of HM Privy Council, Dated 13th September at Edinburgh, suspending the election of Magistrates of Royal Burghs, which was to be recorded in the Council books as follows:

"Edinburgh, September 13th, 1688.

Whereas His Majesty hath, by a letter directed under his Royal Hand, dated at the Court of Windsor 29th August, signified to His Privy Council here, that he hath thought fit to suspend the election of Magistrates and Councils of Royal Burghs within this Kingdom. In pursuance of HM Royal Commands, the Privy Council does hereby authorise and allow the Magistrates and Councils of the Royal Burghs of the Kingdom, to continue until His further pleasure was intimated to them."

The Council ordered the Treasurer to take in all of the Burgh's arms, stock them in the magazine, and have them inspected and restored to good order. Receipts would be given. All burgesses and other defaulters who did not comply would be imprisoned, and their goods impounded to the value of £8 per musket, bandolier, pike and sword.

Because the Shire militia was due to leave on Tuesday next, 25th September, the Council recommended to the Magistrates to name those who went out and those who did not.

Agnes Black was paid £5/18s. for purchases made by Josiah Paterson and other Gentlemen burgesses.

13th October

A bonfire was to be built at the Market Cross, and the bells rung on 14th October, to celebrate the birthday of Our Present Sovereign Lord James VII, King of Scotland, England, France and Ireland.

James Lauder was awarded £4 which he had spent while making the Convenor and Deacons of Edinburgh burgesses.

Agnes Black was paid £8 for wine drunk while making the Provost and Baileys of Edinburgh burgesses.

27th October

The Treasurer was instructed to pay £14, representing 40 days pay, to 14 soldiers who formed the Burgh's quarter part of the militia ordered by HM Privy Council. If the Treasurer had no money to spare, the Council instructed him to borrow the same on credit. The Magistrates were to name the soldiers who were to go from the Burgh, and give them such encouragement as they thought fit.

Agnes Black was paid £3/4s. for four gallons of ale, given to the militia on 14th October, which was the King's Birthday.

6th November

Each landowner, Master and head of family, was ordered to pay 12s. and each servant one merk as tax. The Magistrates were told to take a roll of those due to pay. The usual action was to be taken against those who did not pay. Any deficit would be made up by the Burgh out of the Common Good. Masters were ordered to advance the payment of their servants.

Robert Wallace, gunsmith, was granted a pension of £8 for dressing the Burgh's muskets and pikes.

The Treasurer was instructed to pay Patrick Hepburn, Lieutenant to Sir James Hay of Linplum and the company of militia, 16s. for bandoliers for the soldiers.

The Treasurer was instructed to pay for the powder and match bought by the Magistrates and stored in the Magazine.

31st December

Alexander Maitland, Bailey, presented to the Council an Act of HM Privy Council, sent to him by Sir William Paterson of Granton, Provost, whereby the Lords of HM Council granted a warrant to the Magistrates and Council of the Burgh to elect an choose a new Provost, Baileys and Council, which Act was ordered to be recorded in the Council Books as follows:

"At Edinburgh, 27th December, 1688. The Lords of HM Privy Council, having considered an address presented to them by Sir William Paterson of Granton, desiring that the Council would be pleased to grant warrants to the Magistrates of Haddington and the Town Council thereof, who were in office for the year immediately preceding the said Sir William, his being appointed by His Majesty to be Provost thereof, to meet and make a free and regular election of a Provost, Magistrates and Town Council of the said Burgh. To succeed them in their respective offices, and that those now to be named might be allowed to practise as Magistrates and Town Council of the said Burgh until the Feast of Michaelmas, at which time they might also be allowed to make a new election conforming to the use and want of the said Burgh. The Lords of HM Privy Council do grant the aforesaid desire, and order theses presents to take effect and to be put into execution every manner of way accordingly."

Following the above, the Council granted the crafts the freedom to elect Deacons and Trades Councillors.

John Maitland

Chapter 8

The Reign of William and Mary
1689 to 1702

Once again Scotland found itself with an absentee monarch, William being primarily engaged in fighting foreign foes. He was content, and obliged, to rely on Hamilton as Commissioner to the Scottish Parliament, and Sir John Campbell of Glenorchy, Earl of Breadalbane. The exiled James VII was supported, in his bid to re-establish himself on the throne, by John Graham of Claverhouse, Viscount Dundee. The battle of Killiecrankie, in July 1689, brought a heavy defeat for the Government forces, led by Hugh Mackay of Scourie, albeit Dundee, himself, was killed. The Jacobites raised a force of between 3,000 and 5,000 to meet 800 Cameronians at Dunkeld on the 21st August 1689. The outcome was indecisive and the uprising lost momentum, being finally crushed at Cromdale on 1st May 1690. The Edinburgh Convention acted decisively in voting to deprive James of his Crown, following up with the Claim of Right and the Articles of Grievances. These edicts established key principles, in that no Catholic could be Monarch or hold high office; the royal prerogative could never override the law. Parliament would meet regularly and frequently. There would be free debate. Parliament would decide what resources to award the King, and episcopacy was condemned. William accepted, with some reservations, and was offered the Crown of Scotland. Thereafter the politics of Scotland were dominated by the contrasting efforts of Presbyterians and Episcopalians to succeed – not least in political affairs.

Events took a bewildering, ever-twisting course in the latter years of the seventeenth century. In the Highlands, clan chiefs were required to swear an oath of allegiance to the King. Alistair Macian, chief of the

Macdonalds of Glencoe, delayed in doing so. It was not necessarily his fault, but it resulted in a fierce retribution when 38 members of the clan were massacred by troops belonging to Glenlyon of the Campbell clan.

In 1695 a Company of Scotland, trading in Africa and the Indies, was formed. A Scottish colony was founded at Darien, in Panama, in 1697. Investment in the scheme poured in from all over Scotland. Two expeditions to Darien were made but both ended in disaster. The Company of Scotland collapsed, causing a grave political, as well as financial, crisis. In addition, harvests throughout the period 1695–98 were very poor, causing a serious subsistence problem. Some starved. The social and political impact was grave. The path to Union with England was opened.

During this time, Haddington was of a mind to pursue the Protestant line, and their delegate to the Edinburgh of Estates was instructed to do so. At the same time he was to swear allegiance to William and Mary. Thereafter, on 6th August 1690, the Council prepared a lengthy document asserting their loyalty to the new King and Queen. Once they were safely registered as loyal subjects. The Council turned its attention to local matters. Alert to a financial opportunity, the Council invested £400 in the newSouth Africa Company. Alas, a series of poor harvests , added to an increase in outlays, notably in investments and providing lodging for a succession of regiments of troops led to a complete downturn in the fortunes of the Burgh. A petition was drawn up in May 1701, which was ordered to be raised in the Scottish Parliament asking for help. The Act of Union could not come quickly enough for Haddington.

Haddington Burgh Council Records 1689 to 1702

1689

1st January

Sir William Paterson, Provost, was given hearty thanks for his good service. The Council sought both an occasion and opportunity to show their appreciation. A letter of thanks was to be written to the said Sir William for his good service to the Burgh.

8th February

George Cockburn was restored to his former burgess-ship because of his good behaviour, following previous misdemeanours for which he had been fined £100.

5th March

James Lauder, Alexander Smyth and James Douglas, Baileys. Archibald Trent, Dean of Guild. Alexander Millar, Treasurer. William McCall, Alexander Maitland, Robert Robertson, John Lessells, Robert Brown, John Sleich, Alexander Edgar, Robert Gordon, John Lamb, William Rye, William Begbie, James Smyth, John Ayton, James Robertson, Richard Millar, John Taes, Robert Gray, James Lindsay, William Archer, Alexander Burnett, James Leckie, Thomas Hastie, Robert Anderson, John Kyle, John Todrick – Councillors.

Merchant Burgesses: James Hunter, James Dagleish, James Home, John Dickson, Alexander Dalgleish (elder) John Moffatt, James Denholm, John Cockburn, George Hunter, George Porteous, John Smyth, William Young, Walter Ayton, John Edgar, William Ross, Alexander Sinclair, R.Shortswood, R. Murdoch, Thomas Reid, John Simpson, George Sleich, William Gibson, David Bail, Andrew Malloch, Patrick Fleming, William Bell, Patrick Sinclair, Richard Cockburn, Henry Cockburn.

Tailors: Robert Byres, George Kelly, John Aitchison, Thomas Hogg, John Bower, George Young, Walter Ayton, Robert Wood, James Lilley, William Vallance, Richard Vallance, John Wood, William Christin, James Moody.

Skinners: Thomas Barns, James Kerr, George Yeaman, Andrew Cockburn, James Carmichael, John Reid, George Barnes, John Murgeon, Robert Sleich, John Howieson, Patrick Cockburn.

Hammermen: Robert Wallace, John Kemp, William Hay, Simon Sawers, Robert Kay.

Fleshmongers: John Neilson, Charles Heriot, William Burnett, John Veitch.

Bakers: James Anderson, James Borthwick, Patrick Sinclair, Richard Cockburn, John Anderson, William Smythe, Thomas Borthwick, William Jack.

Masons and Wrights: John Anderson, James Hogg, Patrick Thomson, William McCall, James Brown, Richard Carroll, Robert Hogg, William Lilley, Robin Hadden, George Wilson, John Cochran, John Douglas, John Thomson, William Vallance, George Edington, James Cathie, James Lilley.

Shoemakers: James Caldoun, John Baird, George Caldoun, John Main, Thomas Wilson, William Main.

Weavers: Bartholomew Bower, John Heriot, George Stevenson, Richard Scott, Robert Paterson, John Campbell, James Paterson, John Lister, Alexander Knight, John Watherston, William Tait, Alexander Robertson, Adam Coach, George Young, Robert Wilson, James Hogg, John Sampson, David Todrick, Alexander Steel.

A letter to the Town Clerk from His Highness, William Henry, Prince of Orange, was read out, referring to a summons to a meeting of the Estates of the Kingdom, to be held at Edinburgh on 14th March, and requesting that a Commissioner attend. Following which, John Sleich, Provost, was chosen as Commissioner, with power to sit, vote and conclude upon all matters therein proposed.

9th March

John Sleich was enjoined to vote for the preserving of the Protestant religion, and, if any other issue at the Convention, to inform the Council so that they might decide what to do.

Archibald Hadden, wright, an old man, was granted £6 because he was not able to work.

The widow and daughter of David Allen, messenger, who were both poor and in a distressed condition, were allowed half a boll of oatmeal.

The Treasurer was instructed to pay Andrew Gray, merchant, £40/2s. for the ribbons for burgess tickets. William Ray, merchant, was given £12/4/8d. for the same item.

17th March

In order to repair the damage caused by two regiments of foot soldiers (Colonel Hastings and Colonel Leslie), all persons wishing to make a claim were instructed to inform the Clerk.

Those who served as militia in 1688/9 were exempted from paying tax for those years.

19th June

St. Peter's Fair, which was due to fall on Saturday, 29th June, was altered to Tuesday, 2nd July. This to be intimated following the beat of the drum on the next two market days.

The Council ordered a saddle, worth 20s., to be raced for on the second day of the Fair, from the West Port to the post at Gladsmuir and back again. Horses entered for the race were not to be worth more than £5. First past the post would win the saddle, the second the entry fees, which were half a crown per horse, and the last to finish would get the oatmeal. At least three horses would have to be entered. If there were more then the Magistrates would reduce the entry fees.

The Treasurer was instructed to pay Robert Robertson, former Bailey, £6/13s. for glasses and a tar barrel, which were in use at the Cross on the occasion of the Accession of King William and Queen Mary.

The Treasurer was instructed to pay John Sleich, Provost, his Commissioner fee for attending the meeting of the Estates in March and April, and for his man's livery, amounting to £179/ 0/8d.

10th September

The Treasurer was instructed to repair the stonework at the hidden-pond sluice with stone and lime. He was also to repair the bridge at the North Port, as well as the Golden Bridge stair at the Choir leader's house, and to roughcast the south wall. The sluice at the East haugh also had to be repaired.

The Treasurer was instructed to pay Robert Wallace and John Kay, gunsmiths, £10/18s. for mending and dressing the Burgh's muskets and pikes.

George Home, a very old man, was allowed £6 as charity.

23rd September

John Sleich, Provost, swore allegiance to King William and Queen Mary, and wished it to be recorded in the Council Book.

Baileys and Councillors also swore allegiance, and wished the fact to be recorded in the same book.

1690

10th May

Fleshmongers were in short supply, so the Council allowed those from outwith the Burgh to come in on Market day, or any other day, to slay, cut, and sell meat with the same freedom that was extended to freemen of the Burgh, who, however, were still allowed to charge their box-penny and dues from fleshmongers from outside as previously.

The Treasurer was instructed to pay John Smyth, Clerk, £172/4s. for prosecuting the debate before the Lords between the Burgh and country landowners about their proportion of the Kirk Tax – the money to go to advocates and agents' fees.

The Treasurer was instructed to pay John Lamb and Andrew Gray £46/14/6d. For matches for the Burgh guards and ribbons for burgess tickets.

6th August

The Treasurer was instructed to pay John Smyth £10, spent in his house and Bailey Smyth's, while preparing the Treasurer's accounts. Plus two pints of dry wine and four pints of ale, at the proclamation of St. Peter's Fair.

The Magistrates, Council etc., prepared a document asserting their loyalty to their Majesties as follows:

> "We do, in the sincerity of our hearts, assent ,acknowledge and declare that their Majesties King William and Queen Mary are the only lawful, undoubted Sovereigns, King and Queen of Scotland, in law and in fact, in the exercise of Government . And therefore, we do faithfully and sincerely promise and engage that we will, with heart and hand, life and goods, maintain and defend their Majesties' title and Government against the late King James and all other enemies, who, either by open or secret attempts, shall disturb and disquiet their Majesties in the exercise thereof."

Agnes Black's bill for dry wine and glasses, used on the 29th May, and amounting to £6/18s. was ordered to be paid by Robert Brown, Treasurer.

The Earl of Melville, HM High Commissioner, was to travel through the Burgh on his way to London. The Magistrates and Council were to pay their respects.

10th November

John Lessells, Provost.

The Council ordered that the Burgh's patrimony be publicly announced at 4 p.m. on this day at the Tolbooth as formerly, then through all the streets by bellman and Town Crier.

James Robertson, Miller, having inspected the two Corn Mills, announced that the Malt Mill was a going concern, and that the Corn Mill had a potential for growth, but needed a bridge and two cloaves (the division between two flues in a chimney) although the old ones would serve for a while yet.

The Magistrates, Robert Robertson, Archibald Trent for the Merchants, Alexander Burnett and James Brown for the trades, met to approve the accounts of James Lauder and John Smyth, which had been spent making the officers of the battalion from Lieutenant-General Douglas's regiment, all burgesses. Agnes Black's bill, for items used during the meeting between the Magistrates and the Earl of Melville, HM High Commissioner, was also to be considered.

1691

5th February

John Smyth, Clerk and Collector of the Burgh's taxes, revealed his four-monthly account, payable on 1st July, 1690, and collected by him. Income amounted to £781/16s. and expenditure £861/18s., therefore the Burgh owed £80/2s. which the Treasurer was instructed to pay.

The Magistrates and Committee for the scrutiny of the accounts allowed the following:

1 An account due to John Smyth, Clerk, amounting to £133/19/10d. for money spent in entertaining the officers of the battalion of Lieutenant -General Douglas's regiment.

2 An account due to John Smyth for wine etc., of £15/7s. spent in making the major of the above battalion a burgess. Robert Brown, Treasurer, was instructed to pay the same.

3 The Council allowed an account fo £60/1s. for coal provided for the Guards regiment by Patrick Fleming.

4 An account due to Richard Millar, Bailey, for wine etc., consumed when the hearths were taken up, and when the Laird of Buchanstown was made a burgess, amounting to £12/7s.

5   An account due to Alexander Smyth, Dean of Guild, for wine drunk when Andrew Kerr, adjutant to the battalion of HM footguards, and George Fenwick, Edinburgh merchant, were made burgesses, amounting to £10. Robert Brown, Treasurer, was instructed to pay.

23rd February

All burgesses and Guild brethren were required to dwell within the Burgh within one year and a day from this date, otherwise they would be deprived of their offices.

Alexander Millar, former Treasurer, was instructed to pay Robert Brown, Treasurer, the money he owed to the Burgh, before Saturday, under threat of imprisonment. Robert Brown was instructed to be diligent in collecting money to pay off the Burgh's debt.

An account due for money spent by John Sleich, Bailey, including the Burgh agent's fee, consultation with the advocate, in the debate between the Burgh and outside landowners, amounting to £47/13s. was to be paid by the Treasurer.

A bill from George Gollan, agent, amounting to £34/3s. was to be paid by the Treasurer, together with one of £26/18/4d. for John Smyth, Clerk, going to Edinburgh.

An account was due, to be paid to Robert Brown, Treasurer, for cart and horse hire, carriage of baggage and ammunition belonging to the battalion of Scots footguards, quartered from here in the Burgh to Musselburgh, amounting to £25/6s. In the meanwhile, it was to be placed in the Burgh's Common Good, following an order written by the Provost.

19th March

The Council, having assessed the burgh's expenses in defending the action pursued by Thomas Fender against the Burgh for the escape of John Cowan from the Tolbooth, found them to amount to £188. Patrick Fleming, jailer, had served from Martinmas 1685 to Martinmas 1690, without receiving any fee, other than £100, so that he was owed £200, which, after expenses, left him with only £12. The Treasurer was instructed to pay him his fee.

18th May

The Council convened, along with several landowners of the Parish, before the Lords Mersington, Fountainhall and Pressmennan, to decide the levels of payment to repair the Kirk. It was agreed that the Burgh would pay one fifth and he landowners the rest. This agreement served only to restore the present exigency, and was not to be regarded as binding in future years.

20th June

An account was due to be paid for ale and wine, drunk in John Smyth's house, on the occasion when several Gentlemen were made burgesses, amounting to £27/16s. which the Treasurer was instructed to pay.

An account was due to John Smyth, Clerk, for consulting advocates on the matter of William Smyth's suspension against the Burgh, and about the process of choosing the Kirk Commission, at the instance of the Presbytery of Haddington, Dunbar and the Kirk agent, who sought a disjunction of part of the Parish of Haddington to agents. His own fee of £53/9s. was also due, and the Treasurer was instructed to pay.

John Smyth, Clerk, was allowed £24 for his extraordinary service, with £6 to Patrick Sleich, his servant. The Treasurer was instructed to pay.

Robert Gordon, delegate, was granted £18 for keeping the Burgh's stock of corn and straw safe, when the Edinburgh regiment were quartered in the Burgh. The Treasurer was instructed to pay.

Robert Brown submitted his accounts for the period Martinmas 1689 to Martinmas 1690. Expenditure was £5293/10s. and income £5784/13s. leaving a balance of £491/3s. which was retained by him and would be shown in the following year's accounts. Witnessed by John Smyth, Clerk, and Robert Sleich, servant.

John Smyth, Collector of the Burgh's taxes, presented his two monthly accounts for the previous Martinmas, and two and a half months' taxes collected at Candlemas amounting to £996/12/6d., leaving a deficit of £26/6/6d. which the Treasurer was instructed to pay.

3rd August

The Treasurer was instructed to repair the steeple of the Tolbooth where the clock and Great Bell were housed. Workmen's advice was sought on the task involved, I.e. whether to cover the roof with timber or lead slates, and how best to repair the Tolbooth windows in stone, timber and ironwork.

The Hammermen presented a petition desiring further privileges as follows :

Act in favour of the Hammermen: Baileys, Dean of Guild, Council and Deacons of crafts of the Burgh, representing the community thereof. Wherefore appeared before them William Hay, Deacon of the Hammermen, for himself and in the name of the remaining members and freemen of the said craft, who, on 3rd August, did present a supplication and petition. Making mention that where your petitioners are incorporated in one free incorporation and craft and none of our trade has liberty to work within this Burgh but such as are incorporated with us. As freemen of our craft and trade neither ought any of the inhabitants within this Burgh employ any unfreeman of our said trade to work any work, either house work or work belonging to their labouring and horses, or to mend any old work. But ought only to employ their Lordships' and Council's petitioners to work the same. Otherwise the design of our being incorporated in a free trade and craft will fall, and the said petitioners neither be able to live, nor pay any public burden within this Burgh. Which burdens are very heavy upon the said petitioners, and laid on them for their trade. Nevertheless, it is that the most part of the inhabitants of this Burgh employs smiths, saddlers, pewter-workers and others who live not within this Burgh, and who are not members of the said craft and incorporation, not only to work their new work (such as shoeing their horses, making plough irons, harrows, shoeing of wheels, making house work or labouring work, but employs them to mend their old work of these and other kinds. And take out the iron and other materials for making the said new work and mending the said old work out of this Burgh, to workmen living outwith the same, and inbrings them again to the shame of this Burgh and Your Lordships and Councillors' petitioners great prejudice and damage. And if not remedy be not speedily provided, the said petitioners will be necessitated to leave this Burgh altogether. And, therefore, craved the said Provost, Baileys and Council to take the premises to their serious consideration. And to act and ordain that none of the inhabitants employ any smiths, saddlers or pewter-workers from outside the Burgh, and that the petitioners be granted leave to seize iron, pewter, timber, leather etc., from unfreemen and fine them.

On 22nd August, the petition was granted.

6th October

Baileys, Dean of Guild, Council and Deacons of crafts, convened in the Tolbooth and unanimously elected James Lauder to be Provost, John Sleich and Richard Millar to be Baileys, Alexander Smyth to be Dean of Guild, and William Begbie to be Treasurer. All chosen gave their oaths of fidelity and allegiance.

Guild brethren were to pay £4 to the Guild box on being admitted.

7th November

The practice of selling muck and dung to outsiders was frowned upon, since it could be used by those who worked in the Burgh on the land. Therefore the Council ordered that no one in the Burgh should sell any muck or dung to outsiders, but exclusively to Inhabitants. All former Acts on this matter were rescinded. Any transgressor would pay 6s. to the Magistrates for each cartful.

The practice of leasing houses to strangers and vagrants, with no obvious means of support, was considered. In future, no landlord was to lease any house to strangers, or vagrants, who lacked testimonials from former dwelling places, and were without visible means of support. Such landlords would be obliged to relieve the Burgh of the maintenance of such people, and also to pay a year's rent to the Burgh. Robert Tweedie, Robert Millar and William Lilley were to prepare a list of such folk in the Burgh. This Act was to be made known at the Market Cross.

A meeting between landlords, Baileys and Councillors, held before Lords Mersington, Fountainhall and Pressmennan, about the proportion of the tax payable by the Burgh for the repair of the Parish Kirk and the Minister's Manse, took place. The Council agreed to pay the first instalment, but argued that this was not to be seen as an indication of future action on their part.

10th November

Leases of the Patrimony of the Burgh of Haddington from Martinmas 1691 to Martinmas 1692:

> Two Corn Mills, with the kiln at the West Mill, leased for one year to James Lauder, Provost, for 2,500 merks, payable at the usual terms; under threat of arrestment. poinding and appropriation of goods, plus imprisonment of the lessee for non-payment.

Custom of the Ports and Anchorage of Aberlady leased to William McCall, Adam Steel, John Howieson and William Richardson, for the sum of 1,010 merks.

Tron and Tron weights leased to William Smyth, Nungate, for £262.

Stands of the Crossgate leased to William Young and William Archer, for £112.

Firlots and pecks of the Beer, Oats, Malt and Bag Market leased to William Smyth, Nungate, for £142.

Firlots and pecks of the Wheat and Peas Markets leased to George Forrest and George Stevenson for £142.

Fishmarket leased to Alexander Sinclair for £28.

Fleshmarket leased to Alexander Jack, dyer, for £82.

Firlots and pecks of the Meal and Salt Markets leased to Alexander Sinclair for £116.

Easter haugh leased to John Sleich, Bailey, for £37.

Bowling green house (without the yard) leased to Richard Millar, Bailey, for £22.

Naveship of the two Corn Mills leased to William Smyth, Nungate, for 400 merks.

Magistrates were instructed to put he Acts of Parliament, relating to the breadth of linen cloth, into execution.

23rd November

Those houses in the High Street which were in a poor state of repair, were to be valued and appraised, according to the terms of the relevant Act of Parliament.

The Council allowed James Lauder's expenses, incurred when action was brought against him by the Privy Council for the escape of James and John Seton, who were brought to the Burgh by the Sheriff for robbing the King's Packet of £142/16/8d. The Treasurer was instructed to pay.

23rd December

The street leading from the Crossgate to the Tolbooth, which was the busiest street in the Burgh, was very narrow, whereas it should be the broadest street. The houses on the west side were in a ruinous state. Therefore the Council deemed it necessary to buy those houses and demolish them so that the street might be widened. Magistrates were to agree prices with the householders.

1692

7th March

The Treasurer was instructed to pay £12/12s. to Christine Chaplin for four and a half stones of candles supplied to the guard in the Tolbooth belonging to Colonel Beveridge's Regiment of Foot, who had been quartered there from 12th December 1691 until 27th February 1692.

A bill was accepted to be paid for coal provided to the same guard which amounted to £13/2s. The Treasurer was instructed to pay.

6th August

The Treasurer was instructed to pay neighbours of the Burgh their cart and horse hire, for removing HM baggage and ammunition last winter and summer.

John Cockburn, official, was removed from office after being uncivil to the provost in his language and for other misdemeanours. His office was declared vacant.

The council allowed an account for coals supplied to the Tolbooth, when Captain Hay and Lord Elphinstone's Dragoons kept guard there from 2nd May until 2nd June 1692, amounting to £7/14s. The Treasurer was also instructed to pay Christine Chaplin £23/12/6d. for the candles she supplied to the same guards.

4th September

The Treasurer's accounts for the year ended Martinmas 1692 – Income £4802/6/8d. Expenditure – £5030/11/8d.

20th October

Richard Millar, Dean of Guild, William McCall, Alexander Maitland, William Lilley and Thomas Hastie were to prepare lists of the poor, categorise them, then award the appropriate week's maintenance. The total to be spread among landowners and householders in the Burgh.

9th November

The Ports were to be sold off by public auction, together with the West Mill haugh and the Walk Mill: West Port and the anchorage at Aberlady, North and North East ports, South and South East Ports.

The West haugh was to be planted with trees on the edges to stop them being washed away.

1693

30th January

A saddle, worth 20s. was to be raced for on Thursday, 6th July, from the West Port to the foot of Hugeton Rig and back again.

24th February

An account of £54/12s. was allowed to John Smyth, Clerk, for wine and ale, parchment and wax. The Treasurer was instructed to pay.

An account of £7/4s. was allowed to George Wood and Henry Turnbull, gardeners, for digging out trees at Tyninghame and replanting them in the Burgh haughs.

The Council formed a Committee to consider how best to repair the Market Cross.

11th September

Five guineas was awarded to the Clerk. And one guinea to his servant, for writing out burgess tickets etc..

An account was allowed to James Sherwood for laying the roadway on the bridges at the West Port, plus the gathering of stones, totalling £36/14s.

An account for £54/17s. was allowed to William Rye for supplying ribbons and wax. The Treasurer was instructed to pay.

The Committee heard the account of John Jack, mason, for rebuilding the Market Cross with a long stone and some smaller ones, amounting to £40. The Treasurer was instructed to pay.

Expenses were granted to James Douglas, for travelling to Edinburgh to consult John Robertson, prisoner, accused of denouncing Their Majesties, amounting to £16/10/8d. The Treasurer was instructed to pay.

10th October

William McCall was elected as Provost

1694

3rd February

Eight volunteers were sought to serve in HM Forces, representing the Burgh's share of the conscript levy. Inducements to serve were to be distributed among the townsfolk. A list of militia was to be prepared and divided into eight parts in case the volunteers could not be found.

23rd April

A lane between Peachdales and Lawrence Land, between the King's highway leading northwards and the street leading from the West Port to Letham Burn, was to be laid out during the year. A dyke was to be built at either end, plus a gate for entry.

The Council allowed an account to John Turnbull for ale drunk when some Gentlemen were made burgesses, along with several of Major-General Livingstone's officers and Colonel Buchan's officers, plus money given to some fiddlers. The total amounted to £23/3/4d. The Treasurer was instructed to pay.

11th September

James Wallace, Clock-Keeper, was given £18 representing six month's fee from WhitSunday to Martinmas. The Treasurer was instructed to pay.

5th November

The Council approved and vouched for James Forman, Minister, against whom an action for libel had been raised by the united Presbyteries of Haddington and Dunbar. He was cited to appear before the Synod at Edinburgh to answer the charge. William McCall, Provost, Richard Millar and John Robertson, Baileys, were to accompany him in a show of solidarity, and to read out the address given previously by the Presbytery in his support.

1st December

John Smyth, Clerk, was allowed £60/18/8d. for wine and ale drunk when making several Gentlemen burgesses. The Treasurer was instructed to pay.

The Council allowed payment of an account, due to several people, amounting to £80/14/6d. for transporting the regimental baggage of Colonels Buchan, Cunningham and Douglas, plus Major-General Livingstone and Lord Jedburgh, from the Burgh to a variety of destinations. The Treasurer was instructed to pay.

1695

17th June

William Ray was allowed £19/15s for ribbons for burgess tickets.

Richard Millar, Bailey, was allowed £9/10s. expenses, incurred when visiting the Magistrates of Musselburgh.

William Johnston, Postmaster, was allowed £39.14s. spent on wine and ale when making Doctor Pitcairn and Sir Walter Seton burgesses.

8th November

Magistrates ordered the collection of the rent of the Sheriff's gloves at Michaelmas Fair – to be sold at auction and leased together with the custom of the Ports.

Alexander Edgar was elected as Provost.

1696

8th January

William Begbie, former Provost, was to pay John Ayton, Kirk Treasurer, what the Burgh owed to the Kirk Session for the timber that grew in the Kirk yard, and which was put to the Burgh's use.

The Treasurer was instructed to give Margaret Mitchell, widow of the late Andrew Malloch, Procurator Fiscal, and her children, 10s. per week as aliment.

15th February

Walter Gray, Minister of Garvald, was allowed 20s. for his gown, for the two years that he was the Precentor, and for Pardons granted in the Burgh during King James's reign. The Treasurer was instructed to pay.

10th March

HM Proclamation dated 6th March, ordering half of the militia of East Lothian to be mustered on Beanston Moor on 12th March, with their arms and ten days' pay. Advice was sought as to the position of the Burgh militia. Magistrates were to meet William McCall, Robert Brown, Robert Gray, Robert Byres and James Brown, to make up the militia roll, and list every person they thought fit.

25th March

The Provost sought the Council's advice on what to do about the Burgh's portion of the thousand men needed to serve His Majesty in the war. The Council agreed that the burgh would be split into four quarters, and the young men listed who were eligible for service, thus conforming to the Acts of Parliament. The list would be ready by 9 a.m. on the following day. The Council empowered the Magistrates to see the persons listed throw the dice or draw lots.

26th March

Richard Cockburn, George Cockburn, horse hirer, George Young, son of William Young, James Cathie and James Hadden were exempted from military service because they paid 'scot and lot' (a parochial assessment of the poor) and did not earn a daily wage.

30th March

The Council agreed to give the Company of Scotland, trading in Africa and the Indies, £400 sterling, of which £100 would be paid by 1st June 1697. Alexander Edgar would represent the Burgh, and the Clerk drew up a warrant to this effect.

1st June

A receipt arrived from Mr Paterson and Robert Blackwood, Edinburgh merchants, of the Scots Africa Company, for £100 paid by the Burgh of Haddington, representing the first instalment of £400 due, whereby the Burgh was included in the Capital Fund Book of the Company. The receipt was placed in the Charter Chest.

Andrew Gray, Treasurer, was instructed to pay John Hunter in Petercraig £8, with 40s. in his hands, totalling £10, for persuading someone to be soldier in HM service.

1697

30th January

The Treasurer was instructed to pay Richard Cockburn, pedlar, £3 every year for providing Bibles for Magistrates in their Council seats.

16th February

The Lord Advocate's letter, which referred to the sale of oatmeal in the market by weight, was to be placed in the Common Book.

The Council ordered that all those living in the Mealmarket were to keep the streets clean, and to leave no muck middens either on the streets or on the stairs, but to dispose of them every week. Failure to do so would result in a fine of £5.

The Council ordered that the Peasmarket, which was held at the foot of the Tolbooth stair, was to be moved to a piece of waste ground at the west end of Thomas Hastie's house. All muck middens were to be removed. The Treasurer was told to see that all the streets were cleaned.

Patrick Ramsay, merchant, was still owed £68/4s., out of the original sum of £80/18s, being the price of five bibles bought for the use of the Magistrates. The Treasurer was instructed to pay.

17th March

Because gravestones in the Kirkyard, and the palings around the haughs, were broken, it was decided that, in future, any person found guilty of such vandalism would be scourged through the Burgh by the hangman, and then banished.

8th May

In relation to the exorbitant prices charged in the Burgh by horse hirers, it was decided that, in future, anyone hiring horses would be charge 16d per mile, for up to 12 miles covered on the first day, plus half a merk per day thereafter. If the horse was hired within a six mile radius, 20d per mile would be charged on the first day, and half of that for each day thereafter. All double hirers would be charged 2s. per mile; under penalty of a fine of double the cost of hire, plus any other punishment the Magistrates would think fit.

HM Privy Council Acts, drawn up against vagabonds, beggars etc., which had not been kept, plus the increasing numbers of such coming in from outside, had resulted in an Order that they would be arrested by the Burgh officials and detained in the Tolbooth for eight days on bread and water, and thereafter conveyed out of the Burgh. If they re-offended, they would be detained in prison for fifteen days, and then scourged.

15th June

Magistrates were forbidden to make any more burgesses without the Council's consent (except for Officers of the State and King's Commissioners), unless they paid for it themselves.

30th July

The Charter Chest was ordered to be searched for the Charter between the Abbot of Dunfermline and the Burgh, to establish what feu if any was due to him.

Because ribbon for burgess tickets was expensive, it was decided that, in future, only a piece of parchment and a seal would be given. The Great Seal would be affixed to Masters' tickets, and the small seal to servants' tickets.

1698

19th February

A letter from William McCall, former Provost, dated 3rd March 1687, was read out:

"I, William McCall, late Provost of Haddington, do hereby declare that John Eliot, Surgeon and Apothecary and Burgess of Haddington, for the kindness, love and favour that he has and bears to the town of Haddington and community thereof, where he has lived these many years, hath assigned for the use of the said Burgh, for buying a good Clock to bt set up in the Tolbooth, for the whole town, 800 merks, which he has deposited in my hands to be used as stated. Furthermore I am to show this to the Council, and get one Act of Council to buy the same. And when the Clock is set up, to get another Act of Councell, declaring that the Clock was bought by the said John Eliot for the use of the said community of Haddington. The Clock to have this inscription on it: "Ex dono Joannes Eliot, Chirurgie, Apothecarie, Hadinensis."

As witness my hand this 3rd day of March, 1687."

The Council instructed the Treasurer to pay Henry Cockburn, former Provost and now destitute, 30s. per week.

16th May

The Treasurer was instructed to buy clothes, shirt, cravat, hat, stockings and shoes for Henry Cockburn.

The Treasurer was instructed to repair the North Port at the Tolbooth to a reasonable height, not as formerly.

Magistrates were to choose a house in the Burgh to be hospital for the poor.

4th June

Baileys Cockburn and Forrest, plus Alexander Edgar, former Provost, were to meet landowners from outside, to see if they could accommodate the poor and repair the Kirk. Meanwhile their own poor would be allowed to beg within the Burgh before a decision was taken about their upkeep. Tuesdays and Saturdays were allocated as begging days. The Clerk would give each of them a card bearing their name and the Burgh's seal.

27th June

William McCall was to be asked straightway for the money he was given by John Eliot to buy a Clock.

The Treasurer was instructed to build a little stone pend over the Milldam at the East Mill, with a little dyke to the east of the Mill.

4th September

Henceforth, no extraordinary expenses would be allowed to the Commissioner representing the Burgh at Conventions. Instead an allowance would be provided.

An account was allowed to Alexander Edgar for his Commissioner fee, for the General Convention held at Aberdeen the previous July, amounting to £164/4/8d. Also an account to Alexander Edgar for attending Parliament in July, August and September, amounting to £236/2s. The Treasurer was instructed to pay.

8th November

Robert Brown, Treasurer, was appointed to go to Edinburgh to pay the first instalment to the African Company, due on 1st Decembert, and to give bond for the second instalment due next Candlemas.

The Council declared that any beggars in the Burgh who kept house would pay rent not exceeding £6 p.a. under the proviso that, if they continued to beg, they would lose all benefits accruing from the rent.

1699

8th May

Millers had always previously taken the ringing (leftovers) of the Mills for themselves. It was agreed that, in future, this should be the prerogative of those who ground the mills.

The Treasurer was instructed to give 7s. to Robert Napier.

4th August

Charity payments of 7s. were reduced to 5s.per week, commencing the last Thursday in August. Those whom received less than 7s. would continue to be paid as before, except for the Widow Kerr, David Clark's children and Henry Cockburn. 12d. was added to George Henderson's weekly allowance.

1st November

The Treasurer's account for the year ending Martinmas, 1698, showed Expenditure to be £4328/13s. and Income to be £5665/ 8/4d. The Balance was £1336/15/0d. to go to the Treasurer.

14th December

Richard Mickle, Richard Cockburn, George Learmonth and Adam Coates were appointed as Collectors of Taxes for the Poor. The money collected would be handed over to George Pringle, who would distribute it to the poor. Quartering or poinding would be used against those who did not pay.

Thomas Forrest and George Stevenson were appointed as Constables, with one member of staff.

The School Day commenced at 6 a.m. in both summer and winter, but would be altered to a 9.a.m. start from Halloween to Candlemas.

1700

4th March

Non-burgesses, who imported coal, would pay 2d. per load to the Customs at the West Port.

19th March

As a result of the damage caused by a fire in Edinburgh, Alexander Edgar, Provost, and John Robertson, Bailey, were to represent the Burgh to see what could be done to assist in this time of need.

The Great Bell in the Tolbooth was to be removed and recast. It would be replaced, temporarily, by a smaller bell.

8th April

The Treasurer was instructed to buy clothes for a boy to attend the Commissioners at the forthcoming meeting of Parliament.

A letter was received from Edinburgh acknowledging the kind offer of assistance following the recent fire.

1701

8th May.

Alexander Edgar, Provost. Robin Gray and William Gray, Baileys. Andrew Gray, Dean of Guild. William Begbie, Treasurer. David Forrest, Richard Millar, Thomas Reid, Alexander Millar, James Robertson, John Anderson, John Jack, George Young, Charles Heriot, William Henderson, William Anderson, John Young – Councillors.

Pending the forthcoming meeting of Parliament, a petition was drafted and ordered to be presented there by Alexander Edgar as follows:

"To His Gracious Majesty, High Commissioner and Right Honourable Estates of Parliament, the humble petition and address of the Magistrates and Town Council of the Burgh of Haddington, in the name of the community thereof, that, after a long and expensive war, we expected to have enjoyed the blessing of a happily concluded peace by the re-establishment of our foreign trade, encouraging of our home manufacture, employing of the poor in the improvement of our native products, and the lessening of our public burdens. But instead thereof, to the unspeakable loss and ruin of the Nation, we find our trade abroad sensibly decayed, and our coin carried out by the importation of commodities from places where ours are prohibited, our woollen and other manufactures at home by the same means and the remissness of Magistrates in putting of the law in due execution, received not that encouragement which the interest of the country requires, whereby our poor are neither maintained or employed as they might otherwise be. And, more especially, our Company trading to Africa and the Indies meets with so much opposition from abroad, and gets so little support from home, that after so great a loss of men and expense of treasure, their settlement in Caledonia may now, too probably, a second time fall under the same unlucky circumstances as at first, if not prevented.

And albeit, the Commissioners of the Army by law, are obliged to keep magazines of corn and straw for the Dragoons, or else to pay the current rates of the country that corn and straw grows for the time yet these three years begone, so great and heavy have our burdens been, that when the said dragoons were marching through the Burgh and from Langton Parks, that the said Commissioners neither kept any magazine of corn and straw, or paid our people the current rate of the country. Therefore, our people were necessitated the said troops of Dragoons at the said Commissioner rates, which was only 5s. for each horse per night. As declarations, under the hands of several officers of the respective troops given to Our Commissioner, will testify.

Whereas our burgesses and inhabitants could not provide these Dragoons' horses a night's corn and straw under 16s., whereby our people lost 11s. per horse per night. And yet, after all these hardships which the nation groans under, numerous forcs are still kept on foot, while our much wealthier neighbours are disbanding, which occasions, in time of peace, heavy and unnecessary taxes. All which misfortunes and calamities, which of late have befallen us, we cannot but look upon as the effects of the displeasure of Almighty God, for the great immorality that everywhere abounds, amongst all ranks and degrees of men, and to the dishonour of God and Our Holy Religion, and debauching the spirit and corrupting the manners of the people.

May it therefore please Your Grace, and the Right Honourable Estates of Parliament, to take some effectual course for the curbing of vice, and putting into execution the many laudable laws for maintaining and employing the poor, that they might be useful and not burdensome to the Kingdom.

And for encouragement of our manufactures at home, and carrying out our trade abroad with advantage, and to lay on such impositions on the branches of our imports as may overbalance our exports, and particularly that of France, and to assist the Indian and African Companies right to their Colony of Caledonia, which has been, and is still unjustly called in question, and to give such support to it as may encourage the Adventurers to go on with an undertaking which, if vigorously pursued, may so much tend, in the future, to the wealth, honour and interest of the Nation. And to relieve Our Country of so great a number of forces every way so uneasy to the people. And, in lieu thereof, to fall upon such other methods for security of the peace and support of the Government, as may be more for the interest of the Kingdom and more consistent with the liberty of the subject, and to lay down courses how our people may be reimbursed by the Commissioners of the Army for providing corn and straw to the Dragoons. And to order the said Commissioners to pay the same at the current rates of the country."

Signed – Robert Gray, Bailey.

The Council ordered the following instructions to be signed by the Magistrates and recorded in the Council Books, then delivered by the Provost and Commissiner as follows:

1   To vote for taking some effectual course for the curing of vice, and putting into execution the many laudable laws for maintaining and employing the poor.

2   To vote for encouraging our manufactures at home, and carrying on our trade with advantage, that the impositions on our imports may overbalance the exports.

3   To vote for asserting the Indian and African Companies' right to their Colony of Caledonia.

4   To vote for reducing the Army.

5   To vote for falling upon methods for security of the peace, support of the Government and interest of the Kingdom, and liberty of the subject.

6   To vote for taking courses, how the people of Haddington may be reimbursed by the Commissioners of the Army for providing corn and straw to the Dragoons, marching to and from Langton Parks, at the said Commissioner's rates.

7   To vote against pensioners voting in Parliament.

8   To vote against bankrupts voting in Parliament.

To present the Town's address and petition to the Parliament.

Signed – Alexander Edgar, Provost. 2nd October 1701.

James Dodds, Bailey, was appointed the Bailey for Nungate.

Conclusion

Haddington, in 1702, was a vastly different place to what it was in 1549, when everything was laid waste and hardly a building was left standing. The task that faced the survivors of the siege was enormous, but their commitment hardly less so. Once again, as their ancestors had done on at least three occasions, Haddington had to be rebuilt, almost from scratch. The question arises as to why it was felt to be so important to rebuild on the same site. Why not start afresh at some less vulnerable spot, which did not lie directly in the invader's path ?

The probable answer lies between several possible explanations. On the one hand Haddington was 'home' – the only place they, the survivors, knew as home. Familiarity with the houses, the streets, the area, was important to them. Secondly, the thought of starting afresh, in pastures new, was a daunting one, full of unsuspected hazards and pitfalls. Thirdly, but essentially, they were of farming stock. Haddington lay at the centre of rich, fertile land. Their main skills lay in farming this land. Indeed, their very survival depended on it. Finally, and probably the most important reason of all, was their devotion to their Kirk. It represented their finest and proudest achievement, standing in all its majesty on the banks of the Tyne. It was among the largest churches in Scotland, bigger even than St. Giles Cathedral in Edinburgh, and their commitment to it was total. It was not called 'the Lamp of Lothian' for nothing. Their dismay at seeing it almost destroyed, so that only a mere shell remained, was complete. Their determination to restore it, as best they could, was equally complete. For no other reason, even if all other ventures failed, they would rebuild their beloved Kirk.

Rebuild they did. They adhered to the town's former triangular shape, which made it easier to re-allocate property and ground. They gave out plots of land, or 'rigs', to each householder so the seed could be quickly sown and crops, grown. Animals had to be bought and brought in from outside, so that it must have been a hand-to-mouth existence for some time. Hard work paid dividends, and Haddington became, once more, a market for all sorts of produce from the land. Flesh, Fish, Peas, Corn, Meal etc., all had their separate markets and all brought in customers and traders from outside as well as inside the town. So successful did they become that the interest from outside became a flood, with vagrants, pedlars, thieves, vagabonds and the rest of the mischief-makers, making a bee-line for a place where they smelt money. Of course they brought a host of problems with them, which caused the Council to spend a great deal of time in seeking answers. They never quite appeared to get on top of the problems, however, and they remained a prominent feature of Council reports through the ages.

Haddington prospered, and this prosperity brought trouble in its wake. As well as dealing with beggars etc., there was an increasing tendency for the Central Authority to interfere, drawn to the town by the reports of rich pickings in the offing. Taxes became an increasingly frequent dilemma which required some ingenious solutions on occasion. Sometimes there was no answer other than to submit, as at the time when the Privy Council nominated the entire future Haddington Burgh Council. Democracy was hard to achieve, although it must not be forgotten that, as a Royal Burgh, Haddington always had membership of the Convention of Estates, which effectively legislated on domestic matters in Scotland.

Substantial progress was definitely made in securing Haddington's place as a successful market town, but was not to continue indefinitely. King James VII provided a reign which offered stability, after generations of warfare. Thereafter, there were no Scottish kings in residence in Edinburgh, and events, once again, offered an uncertain future. But Haddington survived, and seemed to have secured prosperity. When disaster struck, it was as near total as possible. The Council committed a grievous blunder, and paid heavily for it. If only they had stuck to what they knew best, i.e. rural matters. They would probably seen the town become increasingly prosperous. They made a mistake in risking all in a bid for a handsome and quick return by delving into an area in which they had no experience. They invested £400 Sterling (nearly

£5,000 in Scottish currency) in the Company of Scotland which hoped to found a colony on the Darien peninsula in far-off Panama, a place of which they knew nothing. Coupled with a series of bad harvests the resultant catastrophe nearly bankrupted Haddington, as it did the other Burghs. At their wit's end, the Council appealed for help. A helping hand was sorely needed. It duly arrived, albeit from an unexpected source. The Act of Union, 1707, was destined to restore economic matters, at least, on a true course to safety.

Nevertheless, Haddington at the beginning of the eighteenth century certainly looked the part. Stately mansions, such as Haddington House, were springing up all over the town. Tree planting programmes, begun in the late 1600s, added to the spectacle. The streets were kept clean and free of farm animals such as pigs, hens and geese. A new Burgh had risen from the ashes. Mary of Guise would not have recognised the place.

Glossary

Of Old Scots Words Found in the Text

A

Alterages – revenues for an altar

B

Balk – beam; strip of unploughed land

Bangestrie – violence

Barbour – barber; surgeon

Beiting – supply; act of aiding

Blude wyte – an action for bloodshed

Branks – iron bridle and gag

Broddis – best quality grain

C

Caddis – cotton wool

Caill – cabbage

Calsay – causeway; highway

Catholog – list; catalogue

Ca'ves – to fall over; case; dungeon

Cess-end – stop; tax

Chapman – pedlar; merchant

Chipman – woodman

Cloave – that which separates bridgeheads in a mill

Cloussis – sluices

Conwocion – agreement; convention; treaty

Coquet – the Customs House Seal

Corslet – cuirass

Cowper – dealer

Creme – booth; stall; bundle

Cullon – to cool; colouring

D

Dagmaker – gun maker

Daill – a plank

Daumis – confused

Deir – bold; untamed; wild; daring

Demitting – resigning

Dempster – a court officer who pronounced sentence

Derth – highly priced

Dowblar – a flat, wooden plate

Dunschen – pushing

E

Elwands – yardsticks

Escheit – forfeit

Exortar – one appointed to provide religious exhortation

F

Fawdoun – folded

Fecarutit – fought

Fewar – feu holder

Flaggis – greenswards; lightning; snowflake

Flaik – a hurdle

Frathynefurt – from henceforth

G

Gaiting – departure; road; run off; distance; method

Galanzier – a woman who seeks male company

Garron – a small horse; a Galloway

Geor – yokel; a bumpkin

Gildrie – body of members in a Guild

Girnels – large chests for storing grain or salt

Gopleting – handful

Graith – equipment

Guthrie – guitars

Gyrchstingis – poles for making hoops

H

Haiffyn – possession

Handzemie – banner; standard; flag

Hauchis – haughs; flat land next to a river

Heritor – landowner; property owner

Hodie ad Octo – from today for eight days

Horning – to comply, under penalty of being put 'to the horn' i.e. outlawed

I

Incontinent – without delay

J

Jambes – wings; projections

Joggis – hinged; iron collar

Jowp – jacket; coat; bodice

K

Knaistchips – a small fee paid in cornmeal to the under-miller

Kylful – a small heap of hay

Kyll – a narrows; a strait

L

Landlowper – vagabond

Landwart –- country; outside; landwards

Lawcher – low person; laughing man

Leiche – a physician

Litster – a dyer

Lowandill – cattle disease

Lunseth – cattle lung disease

Lykwake – watch over a dead body

Lyppen – lepers

M
Mell – mix; meddle; fight; company
Missal bakoun – measled bacon
Mortcloth – a pall
Muller – frame; moulding

N
Naveship – shipping; navy

O
Olik – oil

P
Passments – braid
Poik – a bag
Pokis – a disease of sheep
Portioner – co-owner; proprietor of a small feu
Punsheon – daggers
Pykrys – pilferers

Q
Quarrew – quarry
Queills – wheels
Quhinzer – a small sword or dagger
Qu'montie – unto whom?

R
Ragnatouris – enemies
Rawchtoris – nails; reached; racked
Railling – jesting

Roungscait – gnawed; clipped; paved
Rung – heavy staff

S
Scab – layabout
Schaikills – servants
Schynis – shoes
Sett leased – cobblestones
Seyt – seen; tried
Shank – knitted; stocking; handle
Sithing – compensation; afterwards; although
Skaffitis – scaffolding
Slainge – damage
Sowpills – drunks
Stankis – stagnant pools
Starling garmod – sterling; genuine; dependable
Stoke – stock of a gun: thrust; sword; enclosed
Stoup – pot; pitcher; tankard
Stowpis – pillars; flagons
Swasch – swagger; drum
Swordslipper – cutler
Sybbois – spring onions
Sychtit – sighted; surveyed

T
Taffeteis – taffeta
Tak – lease
Tauche – tallow
Tenement – land held in tender; property

Tofallis – building next to a
　larger one
Toties Quoties – the whole
　without exception
Triars – reserve; Roman troops
　placed in the rear
Tulzie – brawl; quarrel

U
Ugstar – huckster
Umbeset – surrounded
Underdales – undermanager

V
Vobstar – weaver

W
Waif – worthless person
Wakers – wanderers
Wandis – badge of authority; rod
　of correction; fishing rod
Warklarmes – tools
Weddel – neutered ram
Weif – weave
Wittel – victuals; grain crop
Wodlayer – carpenter; madman

List of Names

Of Persons in the Text

A

Abernethy, William
Achilles, Constantine
Adair, John
Adamson, Alexander
Aikman, Cuthbert
Aikman, John
Aikman, Patrick
Aikman. Thomas
Aitcheson, Cuthbert
Aitcheson, John
Aitken, Alexander
Aitken, James
Alan, James
Alderston, Laird of
Alexander, Margaret
Allan, William
Allen, David
Allen, Janet
Allen, John
Allen, Mungo
Allen, Patrick
Anderson, Agnes
Anderson, David
Anderson, Farquhar
Anderson, James
Anderson, John
Anderson, Margaret
Anderson, Robert
Anderson, Thomas
Anderson, Walter
Anderson, William
Arbuthnot, Peter
Archer, John
Archer, William
Argyle
Argyll
Arnot, Sibilla
Arnot, William
Arran
Auchinleck, John
Auchterlonie, David
Ayton, Bessie
Ayton, George
Ayton, Gilbert
Ayton, James
Ayton, John
Ayton, Laird of
Ayton, Margaret
Ayton, Marjory
Ayton, Thomas
Ayton, Walter
Ayton, William

B

Bago, Adam
Bail, David
Bailey, John
Bailey, Robert
Bailey, Matthew
Bain, Andrew
Bain, George
Bain, John
Baird, Catherine
Baird, James
Baird, John
Bald, Archibald
Bald, James
Bald, John
Balfour, Harry
Balwearie, Laird of
Barn, Harry
Barnett, Alexander
Barns, Alexander
Barns, George
Barns, James
Barns, Janet
Barns, John
Barns, Laird of
Barns, Margaret
Barns, Thomas

Bartilmo, Thomas
Bartram, James
Bartram, John
Basuage
Bathgate, George
Bearford, Lady
Begbie, Adam
Begbie, James
Begbie, Patrick
Begbie, William
Benning, James
Bennett, James
Bertram, George
Beveridge, Colonel
Bickerton, Thomas
Bickerton, William
Black, Agnes
Black, James
Black, John
Black, William
Blackadder, Janet
Blackburn, Alexander
Blackburn, James
Blackburn, John
Blackburn, Thomas
Blackwood, Robert
Blain, John
Blair, Adam
Blair, Jean
Blair, John
Blake, William
Blans, Laird of
Blyth, George
Blythman, Thomas

Boag, George
Boig, William
Bold, Hugh
Bolton, James
Borthwick, Alexander
Borthwick, David
Borthwick, James
Borthwick, Thomas
Bothwell, Francis,
  Earl of
Bowe, Matthew
Bower, Bartholomew
Bower, John
Bowes, John
Bowie, James
Bowie, William
de Bouillon, Matthew
Braund, William
Broderston, Thomas
Browhouse, Andrew
Brown, Adam
Brown, Alan
Brown, Alison
Brown, Bernard
Brown, George
Brown, James
Brown, John
Brown, Magdalene
Brown, Nicol
Brown, Patrick
Brown Robert
Brown, William
Brownhill, George
Brownhill, Robert

Brownlie, Patrick
Bruce, Howe
Bruce, Robert
Bryson, Thomas
Buchan, John
Buchan, Margaret
Buchan, Colonel
Buchanan, John
Buchanan, Margaret
Buchanstown, Laird
  of
Buncles, Janet
Burke, Captain
Burke, Stene
Burley, Lord
Burn, Harry
Burn, Patrick
Burn, William
Burnett, Alexander
Burnett, James
Burnhill, George
Burns, Harry
Burrell, Harry
Burrell, John
Burrell, William
Burrows, William
Burt, Laurence
Busby, John
Butler, George
Byres, Andrew
Byres, Bartholomew
Byres, Robert

C

Cabell, Hector
Calderwood, James
Caldoun, George
Caldoun, James
Callender, John
Campbell, George
Campbell, Hector
Campbell, Henry
Campbell, John
Campbell, Patrick
Campbell, Peter
Campbell, William
Carkettle, George
Carkettle, John
Carmichael, James
Carmichael,
  Nathaniel
Carmichael, Robert
Carnie, Marion
Carr, John
Carraill, Richard
Carrick, Alison
Cathie, James
Cay, David
Chalmers, John
Chalmers, Patrick
Chaplin, Christine
Chaplin, David
Chaplin, George
Chaplin, Richard
Chaplin, Robert
Chapman, Henry
Chapman, Hugh

Charters, Gawain
Chisholm, James
Christin, William
Clairgis, Thomas
Clare, John
Claverhouse
Clark, David
Clark, Nicol
Clavie, John
Clerk, John
Clerkington, Laird of
Coach, Adam
Cochran, John
Cockburn, Adam
Cockburn, Alexander
Cockburn, Alan
Cockburn, Alison
Cockburn,
  Bartholomew
Cockburn,
  Christopher
Cockburn, Cuthbert
Cockburn, Daniel
Cockburn, David
Cockburn, Ellen
Cockburn, George
Cockburn, Henry
Cockburn, James
Cockburn, John
Cockburn, Laird of
Cockburn, Laurence
Cockburn, Margaret
Cockburn, Marion
Cockburn, Mark

Cockburn, Patrick
Cockburn, Robert,
Cockburn, Thomas
Cockburn, William
Cockpen, Laird of
Collielaw, Margaret
Colville, Samuel
Congilton, James
Congilton, Janet
Congilton, John
Congilton, Laird of
Congilton, Margaret
Congilton, Patrick
Congilton, Richard
Congilton, William
Constance, David
Cook, Alexander
Cook, James
Cook, Patrick
Coreatill, John
Cothill, Patrick
Coupland, John
Coustane, David
Couston, James
Coutts, Thomas
Cowan, Catherine
Cowan, John
Cowden, John
Cowper, James
Craig, George
Craig, Laird of
Craik, James
Craik, Patrick
Cranston, William

Craw, David
Crawford, John
Creyton, Matthew
Cromwell
Cuby, Alexander
Cumming, Thomas
Cunningham,
    Alexander
Cunningham,
    Colonel
Cunningham, Robert
Currie, James

D
Dalgleish, Alexander
Dalgleish, James
Dalyell
Dalton, Daniel
Dalziel, David
Dalziel, John
Dalziel, Lt. General
Darling, Andrew
Darling, Isobel
Darnley, Earl of
Darrow, Janet
Dawson, James
Dawson, Patrick
Day, David
Denholm, James
Devine, Thomas
Dick, George
Dickson, Christian
Dickson, Edward
Dickson, Isobel

Dickson, Thomas
Dickinson, Thomas
Dodds, James
Don, Alexander
Donaldson, Elizabeth
Dormant, Robert
Douglas, Colonel
Douglas, David
Douglas, Gillis
Douglas, James
Douglas, John
Douglas, Isobel
Douglas, Margaret
Douglas, Patrick
Douglas, Richard
Douglas, William
Drummond, James
Drummond, John
Dudgeon, William
Dumbarton, Francis
Dunbar, George
Dunbar, Patrick
Duncan, John
Duncanson, Robert
Dundas, James
Dunfermline, Abbot of
Dunlop, Helen
Dunlop, Nicol
Dunn, William

E
Edgar, Alexander
Edinbrugh, Bishop of
Edington, Gilbert

Edington, James
Eglins, Ralph
Elibank, Patrick
Eliot, William
Elliott, John
Elphinstone, Laird of
Erskine, James
Eveling, John

F
Fairfax
Fairlie, James
Fairlie, Patrick
Fender, Thomas
Fenton, Isobel
Fenwick, George
Ferguson, George
Fleck, Friar
Fleming, John
Fleming, Patrick
Fletcher, John
Forbes, Janet
Ford, George
Forrest, Alexander
Forrest, David
Forrest, George
Forrest, James
Forrest, John
Forrest, Marion
Forrest, Michael
Forrest, Robert
Forrester, Andrew
Forton, Laird of
Fowler, John

Fraser, George
Fuller, Ludovic
Fuller, William

G

Gall, James
Galloway, Crystal
Galloway, George
Gardner, Alexander
Geddes, George
Geddes, Henrietta
Geddes, Mungo
Geddes, Thomas
George, Rev, Arch-
  bishop of St.
  Andrews
Getgood, Laurence
Getgood, Patrick
Gibson, Alexander
Gibson, Philip
Gibson, William
Gillies, Mungo
Gilzean, John
Gladstone, Mark
Gladstone, William
Glen, David
Glendinnon, John
Gollan, George
Gorden, Patrick
Gorden, Robert
Gosford, Laird of
Gowans, George
Graham, John
Grant, Isobel

Gray, Andrew
Gray, Barbara
Gray, Elspeth
Gray, George
Gray, James
Gray, John
Gray, Katherine
Gray, Robert
Gray, Walter
Grier, George
Guise, Mary of
Gulland, Archibald
Guthrie, George
Guthrie, James
Guthrie, John
Guthrie, Thomas

H

Hadden, Archibald
Hadden, Robin
Haddington, John,
  Earl of
Haddon, John
Haig, William
Halbertson, Thomas
Haliburton, Jane
Hall, Walter
Hallans, William
Hamill, Robert
Hamilton, Duke of
Hardie, William
Harrot, Catherine
Hart, John
Hastie, John

Hastie, Thomas
Hastings, Colonel
Hathaway, James
Hathaway, Janet
Hathaway, William
Haustman, John
Hay, Andrew
Hay, James
Hay, John
Hay, Thomas
Hay, William
Henderson, Alexander
Henderson, George
Henderson, Gilbert
Henderson, Helen
Henderson, John
Henderson, Thomas
Henderson, William
Henryson, Alexander
Henryson, Edward
Henryson, John
Henryson, Robert
Hepburn, Adam
Hepburn, Edward
Hepburn, George
Hepburn, Henry
Hepburn, John
Hepburn, Merion
Hepburn, Mungo
Hepburn, Patrick
Hepburn, Rachel
Hepburn, William
Heriot, Charles
Heriot, James

Heriot, John
Heriot, Robert
Hermiston, John
Heron, Margaret
Hewitt, Peter
Hislop, James
Hogg, Alexander
Hogg, James
Hogg, John
Hogg, Patrick
Hogg, Robert
Hogg, Thomas
Hoip, Thomas
Hoip, Robert
Holden, James
Home, Andrew
Home, John
Home, William
Horn, James
Horsbrugh, William
Howden, Adam
Howieson, Alexander
Howieson, David
Howieson, Grissell
Hume, Alexander
Hume, James
Hume, John
Hume, Patrick
Hunter, George
Hunter, James
Hunter, John
Hutton, John

I

Innes, James
Innes, Maurice

J

Jack, Alexander
Jack, John
Jack, William
Jackson, Janet
Jacobson, Charles
Jaffray, Alexander
James I
James II
Jameson, Edward
Jameson, Gavin
Jamieson, David
Jardine, James
Johnston, George
Johnston, John
Johnston, William

K

Kay, John
Kay, Robert
Kello, Bartholomew
Kello, Beatrice
Kelly, George
Kemp, Isobel
Kemp, John
Kennedy, Herbert
Kennedy, Hugh
Kennedy, William
Kerr, James
Kerr, John

Kerr, Nicholas
Kerr, Patrick
Kerr, Robert
Kerr, Thomas
Kerr, Walter
King, Alexander
Kirk, William
Kirkwood, James
Knight, Alexander
Knox, John
Knox, William
Kyle, Archibald
Kyle, David
Kymew, Patrick

L

Lamb, Christine
Lamb, William
Lander, John
Langlands, William
Lauder, James
Lauder, John
Lauder, Robert
Lauder, William
Lauderdale, John,
  Viscount
Lawrie, James
Lawson, David
Lawson, Henry
Lawson, James
Lawson, Robert
Learmont, Alexander
Learmont, George
Learmont, Robert

Legg, Robert, Captain
Lennox, Charles,
  Duke of
Leslie
Lessells, John
Lewis, James
Liddell, Bessie
Liddell, George
Liddell, William
Lilley, William
Lindsay, Lord
Lindsay, Marion
Lindsay, Robert
Lister, James
Lister, Robert
Lister, William
Livingston, Major-
  General
Livingston, Robert
Lockhart, James
Logan, Jane
Longformacus, aka
  Robert Sinclair
Lothian, Lord
Low, Barthel
Lowrie, James
Lucinyeis, Capitane
Lumsden, Charles
Lyall, Patrick
Lyle, John
Lyle, Paul
Lymm, John

M
Mackay, Hugh
Maclaren, George
Maclennan, William
Main, Alan
Main, Andrew
Main, Beatrix
Main, William
Maislet, Beatrix
Maislet, James
Maislet, Thomas
Maitland
Maitland, Alexander
Maitland, Charles
Maitland, Peter
Maitland, Richard
Maitland, Robert
Makmain, John
Makonell, George
Malloch, Andrew
Mann, John
Manuel, John
Manylaws, John
Marr, James
Marshall, Nicol
Martin, Patrick
Martin, William
Maria, Henrietta
Mary, Queen of Scots
Mathie, Gavin
Mathieson, Hugh
Mauchline, James
Mauchline, Thomas

Mayne, Alison
Mayne, Andrew
Mayne, Bessie
Mayne, John
Mayne, William
McCall, John
McCall, William
Maclain, Alistair
McConnell, Robert
McConquell, Walter
McCulloch, Adam
McCulloch, David
McGall, John
McKenzie, Colin
Melfort
Melrose, Thomas, Earl
  of
Mercer, John
Middleton, Earl of
Mildison, Elizabeth
Millar, Adam
Millar, Alexander
Millar, Richard
Millar, Robert
Millar, Thomas
Miller, George
Miller, Thomas
Mitchell, James
Mitchell, Margaret
Mitchell, Nicol
Moffatt, John
Monck, George,
  General

Moncur, Thomas
Montalembert,
    Comte d'Esse
Montrose
Moody, James
Moore, William
Morrison, Janet
Morton, Earl of
Mow, Isobel
Mudie, Henry
Murdo, Robert
Murdoch, R
Murgon, John
Murray, Gideon
Murton, John
Mylne, John

N
Napier, Robert
Naysmith, Robert
Neill. Margaret
Neilsen, John
Neilsen, Thomas
Nelson, John
Nemo, Thomas
Nesbit, George
Nesbit, Hanry
Nesbit, Robert
Nesbit, William
Nicolson, Elizabeth
Niddrie, Laird of
Nisbet, James
Nisbet, John
Nisbet, William

Nunraw, Laird of

O
Ogill, David
Ogilvie, Alexander
Oliphant, James
Oliphant, Robert
Orange, William
    Henry, Prince of
Orkney, David
Oswald, John
Outtersyde, James

P
Painston, Andrew
Panton, James
Panton, Robert
Paterson, Ellen
Paterson, George
Paterson, James
Paterson, John
Paterson, Josiah
Paterson, Robert
Paterson, Thomas
Paton, Thomas
Patterson, Andrew
Patterson, John
Patterson, Thomas
Peris, William
Perth, Earl of
Pitcairn, Doctor
Pollock, John
Ponton, Thomas
Porteous, George

Porteous, Marion
Pressmennan, Lord
Preston, George
Primrose, Archibald
Pringle, George
Provan, John
Punton, Thomas
Purves, John
Purves, William
Pynago, Simon

Q
Queensberry, Marquis
    of
Quentin, Adam
Quentin, Alison
Quentin Hester
Quentin, John
Quentin William

R
Rae, Thomas
Raeburn, James
Rammache, John
Ramsay, Alexander
Ramsay, James
Ramsay, John
Ramsay, Lord, of Barns
Ramsay, Patrick
Ramsay, Thomas
Ramsay, William
Rankin, Henry
Rantoun, Alexander
Ray, William

Redpath, Alison
Redpath, Marion
Redpath, Patrick
Redpath, Robert
Redpath, William
Reid, Alexander
Reid, James
Reid, John
Reid, Thomas
Reid, William
Richardson, George
Richardson, James
Richardson, John
Richardson, Helen
Richardson, Katherine
Richardson, Margaret
Richardson, Stene
Richardson, Thomas
Richardson, William
Robertson, Alexander
Robertson, George
Robertson, James
Robertson, John
Robertson, Robert
Robertson, William
Robinson, Maurice
Robson, James
Robson, John
Robson, William
Romananco, John
Romanes, Archibald
Romanes, John
Ross, Master
Ross, William

Rothes, Earl of
Roxburgh, Earl of
Russell, Janet
Rutherford, Andrew
Rye, William

S

Saddler, John
Sampson, John
Samuels, John
Saunders, Colonel
Sawers, Simon
Scott, George
Scowgill, Archibald
Scowgill, Patrick
Scowgill, Richard
Scraven, William
Scrimgeour, Lord
Seton, Alexander
Seton, Elizabeth
Seton, George
Seton, James
Seton, John
Seton, Hannibal
Seton, Thomas
Seton, Sir Walter
Seton, Sir William
Sharp, Janet
Sharp, John
Shaw, James
Shaw, John
Shaw, Robert
Sheil, Janet
Sheil, John

Sherwood, James
Shortswood, R
Sibbald, John
Sibbotson, John
Simpson, Alexander
Simpson, Cuthbert
Simpson, George
Simpson, John
Simpson, Robert
Sinclair, George
Sinclair, John
Sinclair, Robert
Sinclair, William
Skaithevy, Robert
Skein, William
Skeoch, David
Skirving, Robert
Slake, George
Smith, James
Smith, Robert
Smyth, Andrew
Smyth, James
Smyth, John
Smyth, Robert
Smyth, Thomas
Somervell, James
Somervell, Thomas
Somerville, Thomas
Spavin, James
Speir, Alexander
Spence, Isobel
Spence, James
Spottiswood, George
Spottiswood, James

Spottiswood, Richard
Spottiswood, Thomas
Sprot, George
Sprot, Richard
Stercovins
Steven, Thomas
Stevens, John
Stevenson, James
Stevenson, John
Stevenson, Thomas
Stewart, Agnes
Stewart, George
Stewart, Hercule
Stewart, James
Stewart, John
Stoddart, Cuthbert
Stoddart, William
Storey, James
Storey, John
Storey, Patrick
Straughan, Robert
Straughan, William
Strong, Alexander
Struthers, William
Summer, John
Swinton, Nicholas
Swinton, William
Swyton, John
Sydie, John
Sydserf, Archibald
Sydserf, John
Sydserf, Thomas

T

Taes, John
Tait, Janet
Tait, James
Tait, John
Tait, Patrick
Tait, William
Tarbolton, Lord
Thin, John
Thirlestane, Lord
Thomson, Alexander
Thomson, Bernard
Thomson, George
Thomson, Helen
Thomson, Henry
Thomson, James
Thomson, John
Thomson, Margaret
Thomson, Mungo
Thomson, Patrick
Thomson, Robert
Thomson, Thomas
Thomson, William
Thyne, John
Tod, Hugh
Tod, Richard
Todd, George
Toderick, David
Toderick, John
Trent, Archibald
Trotter, John
Trotter, Marjorie
Trotter, Robert
Turnbull, Alexander

Turnbull John
Turnbull, Henry
Tweed, James
Tweed, Margaret
Tweeddale, Earl of
Tweedie, Bernard
Tweedie, James
Tweedie, John
Tweedie Robert
Tweedie, William
Tweedy, James

U

Urquhart, Robert

V

Vache, Thomas
Vallance, John
Vallance, Patrick
Vallance, Richard
Vallance, William
Vaughan, John
Veitch, Adam
Veitch, Christine
Veitch, David
Veitch, James
Veitch, John
Veitch, Thomas
Veitch, Walter
Vincent, John
Vow, John

W

Wache, Adam

List of Names

Waite, John
Walderston, William
Walker, David
Walker, Robert
Walker, William
Wallace, Alexander
Wallace, George
Wallace, James
Wallace, Patrick
Warrender, John
Warrender, Thomas
Waterston, Robert
Waterston, Thomas
Waterston, William
Watherston, John
Watson, James
Watson, John
Watson, Robert
Watson, William
Wauchop, William
Wauchton, Laird of
Wauss, Abraham
Wauss, Thomas
Weddell, William
Weir, Archibald
Weir, James
Weir, Nathaniel
Wemyss, James
Wemyss, William
White, Andrew
White, James
White, Henry
White, Robert
Whiteford, John

Whitehead, Thomas
Wilkie, David
Wilkie, James
Wilkie, John
Wilson, Adam
Wilson, Alexander
Wilson, Bessie
Wilson, David
Wilson, Elizabeth
Wilson, George
Wilson, John
Wilson, Lucas
Wilson, Margaret
Wilson, Martin
Wilson, Richard
Wilson, Robert
Wilson, Thomas
Wilson, William
Winrame, Robert
Winrames, James
Winton, Earl of
Wishart, George
Witherington,
  Ephraim
Witherington, Lord
  William
Wolf, Robert
Wood, David
Wood, George
Wood, John
Wood, Patrick
Wood, Robert
Wood, William
Wright, George

Wylie, Patrick

Y
Yeaman, George
Yeaman, Isobel
Yeaman, John
Yester, Lord
Youll, Alexander
Young, Alexander
Young, Andrew
Young, David
Young, George
Young, Helen
Young, Janet
Young, John
Young, Patrick
Young, Robert
Young, William
Yowson, Carston
Yule, Alexander
Yule, Francis
Yule, John
Yule, Lawrence

List of Place Names

Found in the Text

A
Aberdeen
Aberlady
Africa
Anderson's Wynd
Arbroath
Ayr

B
Barney Loan
Beame
Beanmarket
Beanston Moor
Bearmarket
Beermarket
Berwick
Bolton
Borthwick
Bothans
Bothwell Bridge
Boulogne
Brookhill
Broughty Castle
Broxmouth Quarry
Burntisland
Butts

C
Cambuskenneth
Canongate
Carfrae
Carraill
Causeway
Chastedoup
Chatelherault
Cherrytree Haugh
Clartiburn
Clerkington
Clothmarket
Clothesmarket
Cockenzie
Coldingham
Colston
Constantinople
Cornmarket
Cousland
Cranshaw
Crossgate
Cromdale
Culross

D
Danzig
Darien
Dirleton
Dogcanflat
Douglas
Duddingston
Dumbarton
Dumfries
Dunbar
Dunfermline
Dunkeld
Dunkirk
Duns

E
East Mill
East Port
Edinburgh
Edrom
Elybank
Elphinstone
England
Eyemouth

F
Fast Castle
Fife
Fishmarket
Flanders
Fleshmarket
Forth
France
Friars Gate
Friars Kirk
Friars Wall
Fruitmarket

G
Gibraltar
Giffordgate
Gimmer Mills
Gladsmiur
Glasgow
Glassingall
Gullane

H
Hamilton
Hangman's Acres
Hardgate
Hawick
Hell's Hole
Herdmanflat
Heuch Head
Highfield
High Gate
High Street
Holland
Holyrood House
Hugeton Rig
Humbie

I
Innerwick
Inveresk
Ireland
Ironmarket

J
Jedburgh

K
Kelso
Killiecrankie

Kinghorn
King's St.
Kirk Mill
Kirkcaldy
Knox
Kokillmyln
Kylesmuir

L
Lambert Moor
Lanark
Lauder
Lauder Castle
Leith
Letham
Letham Burn
Lethington
Linlithgow
Linton
London
Lothburn
Lothian
Lydgate

M
Magdalen Chapel
Market Cross
Mealmarket
Merse
Mill Burn
Morham
Musselburgh
Mylne's Burn

N
Nisbet Lane
North Berwick

Northrig
Nungate

O
Oatmarket
Oat Mill
Ormiston
Over Liberton

P
Pans
Peachdales
Peasmarket
Peebles
Pencaitland
Pendrich
Pentland Hills
Perth
Pittenweem
Plant Market
Poland
Poldrate
Powbait Moor
Preston

R
Rathobyres
Rullion Green

S
Saltmarket
Saltoun
Samuelston
Sands
Selkirk
Shoemarket
Sidegate

Smeddyrow
South Port
Spittalrig
St Andrews
St Johnstone
St Katherine's
St Lawrence's
St Martin's
St Mary's Kirk
St Ninian's
St Towbart's
Stinton
Stirling
Strumpet St.
Sybbo

T
Teviot dale
Thorntonloch
Tolbooth
Trabroun
Tranent
Tron
Tweeddale
Two Mile Cross
Tyne
Tyninghame

W
West Gate
West Mill
West Wall
Westminster
Whittinghame